D0725595

SECOND EDITION

THE 110 BIGGEST MISTAKES JOB HUNTERS MAKE

(And How To Avoid Them)

By Richard L. Hermann & Linda P. Sutherland

Edited by Jeanette J. Sobajian

Published by Federal Reports Inc.
1010 Vermont Avenue, NW, Suite 408
Washington, DC 20005

▸ Cover design by Sherrie Good

TABLE OF CONTENTS

CHAPTER THREE: Mistakes On Key Resume Decisions

CHAPTER FOUR: Resume Style And Format Mistakes

CHAPTER FIVE: Substantive Resume Mistakes

CHAPTER SIX: Special Application Form Mistakes

CHAPTER SEVEN: Cover Letter Mistakes

CHAPTER EIGHT: Job Search Management Mistakes

CHAPTER NINE: Interview Mistakes

INTRODUCTION

There are thousands of books on the subject of job hunting. They range from those that offer practical advice on how to put together a resume to those that are psychological or "motivational" in tone (but don't offer much in the way of concrete insights).

However, not one of this vast collection of job hunting manuals tells you much of anything about what **NOT** to do. We think that is a serious deficiency... hence, this book. Our 14 years of experience counseling thousands of job seekers made us realize that, by knowing what job hunting techniques to avoid, and more important, **WHY** you should avoid them, will give you a much clearer picture of how to manage a job search to a successful conclusion.

This book describes the mistakes made by many job hunters and how to avoid them. It also gives you the **reasons why you should avoid these mistakes** and provides guidelines on how to land the kind of position and career you are seeking rather than just a job.

The vital importance of intelligent job search management to your life and your future cannot be overstated. Therefore, we have included as much solid and practical information as possible within the limited length of this book.

How do we know, you might ask, what the biggest mistakes are that job hunters make? We have been involved in the personnel field for many years in virtually every capacity:

- as job seekers;
- as employers who have had to hire numerous people for many different positions;
- as the editors of several national employment publications and the authors of others;
- as owners of a career counseling firm;
- as owners of an executive/legal search firm;
- as professional reviewers and critics of resumes and job application forms; and
- as formal and informal advisors to thousands of job seekers.

What we hope to share with you in this book is the distillation of our experience in the job hunting arena. We have tried to present the biggest mistakes job hunters make in a logical order that parallels the typical employment search itself. Chapters One through Seven cover the kinds of common mistakes job hunters make in the earliest, most important stages of the job hunting process: planning the job search and preparing the necessary documents--resumes, special application forms, and cover letters--central to "getting noticed." These chapters come first for a good reason: they are the most important ones in the book. Consequently, they have been accorded the most space. If you can avoid the mistakes cited in these seven chapters, you will be much farther along in a successful job search than most of your competition. The remaining chapters focus on mistakes associated with subsequent stages of job hunting, all the way through to making the decision about which job offer to accept.

How to Use This Book

There are several ways in which this book can help you. Certainly, you can read it all the way through and later draw on it for job hunting ideas. We hope you will do that at least once. You can also use it as a checklist, examining your own job hunting techniques and efforts against each common mistake. Finally, you can use it as a framework both to organize and plot your job search and to help you make informed choices at the many decision points you will encounter along the way.

This book will help you avoid many of the traps associated with job hunting. In the process, we hope it will help you learn not only about the job market, about tried and true job hunting techniques, but also about the *practical application of common sense.*

Job hunting should be viewed as a business. In a business, you sell a product or service. In a job search, you sell **yourself.** Your job search, therefore, merits the exact same treatment, concern, and respect you would accord your own business: good planning, good research, good management, smart marketing, and intelligent budgeting. If you think of the job search in business terms, you will already be far ahead of your rivals.

Job hunting, pared down to its essence, is about three things:

> • Getting noticed.
> • Beating the competition.
> • Closing the deal.

Virtually all of the major mistakes identified and discussed in these pages deal with one of these three essential facets of job hunting. In the 14 years since we founded our company, it has been our experience that most job seekers are either totally unaware of, or often lose sight of, these essentials.

Before you begin actively looking for a new job, you need some time to contemplate the job market. Ideally, you should spend some hours, days, or even weeks assessing yourself, your strengths, weaknesses, and interests, your financial situation, your employment needs, and what the economic future may hold for your current and prospective employers. In addition, you will want to weigh the impact of a job change on your family and colleagues. Finally, you may wish to sketch a rough job hunting plan for yourself in order to establish a frame of reference and a few objectives.

If you are looking for your first permanent job, you probably have the leisure time to devote to this kind of contemplative exercise. You may also have time to think before you begin job hunting if you are considering changing jobs and are not under any severe time pressure. Unfortunately, you may have to curtail your thinking time if you have been given notice of an imminent firing or lay-off. In that case, you will not be able to relax and plot your job hunting strategy in a leisurely fashion.

Career planning should be a continuous, ongoing exercise, regardless of your stage in life or current contentment with your job. Circumstances change rapidly and you never want to be caught unprepared.

✔ Mistake No. 1: Not Taking Job Hunting Seriously

This seems to be a statement of the obvious, but we lead off with it for two reasons:

• First, because making this mistake can taint the whole job search effort, affecting every phase of the hunt, causing it to fail miserably.
• Second, because job hunting is a serious undertaking and it is important to face that fact up front.

Job hunting is unpleasant because so much of the process involves **rejection**. No one likes to be rejected. To avoid that smashing blow to the ego, we tend to hold back--to tell ourselves it's only a casual job search or that the interview isn't really important.

Put yourself on notice that looking for a job **is** a serious business and should be treated as such from the outset. There is not an employer in the world who cannot perceive a **lack** of serious intent or interest, and will make hiring decisions accordingly.

✓ Mistake No. 2: Letting Everyone Know You Are Job Hunting

You have probably noticed that people love to talk about themselves. They simply cannot refrain from obsessively discussing the primary object of their affections. In most circumstances, that's fine. Concern for one's self and one's own future is the normal human condition.

Unfortunately, talking about yourself excessively while job hunting, or even when **considering** whether or not to look for a new job, can create big problems. Not everyone wants his current employer to know that he is looking for another job. The more people you confide in, the greater the risk that your plans will be revealed to someone you do **not** want to know about them...like your boss...or a workplace rival who might tell your boss. Since chances are overwhelming that your boss would not take kindly to your job search, a very uncomfortable situation could be created if the word got out. Instead of trying to dissuade you from seeking employment elsewhere, your boss may demand to know when you are leaving so your replacement can be selected as soon as possible. Worse, you may be terminated on the spot.

True, it is difficult to conduct a thorough job search if you do not tell anyone about your intentions. And we do not mean to suggest that a job search should be a covert intelligence mission. **Just be careful about sharing confidential information**. Balance the benefits to be gained through networking (perhaps your contact knows a lot about the industry in which you want to look for work) against the risks of confiding in a **particular person** (he may be your boss's professional colleague or golfing buddy). If the benefits vastly outweigh the risks, go ahead and reveal your job search intentions. However, if your cost-benefit analysis is either inconclusive or comes down even marginally on the too-risky side, do not assume the risk. Find the information you need elsewhere.

Be equally cautious about conducting actual job hunting activities while at work where colleagues are notorious for having a sixth sense about what everyone else is **really** doing. After all, your employer is paying you to handle your current job, not to look for a new one. If you are permitted to use office equipment for limited personal use and you want to revise your resume, do so before or after work, or on your lunch break. Bring your own paper to print out copies. Do not leave the document stored on the computer unless you have a special (private) access code.

If you use the office copier, make sure to retrieve the original copy of your resume from the equipment. More than one employer (including us) has learned of an employee's job search through tell-tale evidence left carelessly around.

When you send out resumes, note in your cover letter that your current employer is not yet aware of your job search. Request discretion when calling you at work.

When you **place** calls concerning your job search, try to do so while on a break or during lunch--preferably **outside your office**. There is no faster way to alert fellow workers about your private plans then to place "confidential" calls from the office.

So, **be careful**. Weigh the consequences before talking too much or acting indiscreetly.

✓ Mistake No. 3: Looking for a New Job Too Soon After Being Fired

Losing a job is similar to experiencing any other kind of loss: a divorce, a separation, even a death. A fired employee goes through many of the same stages of grief that others experience in comparable situations: shock, disbelief, anger, tears, guilt, and perhaps even a desire for revenge, en route to final acceptance.

Do not make the mistake of discussing your future with potential employers until you have come to grips with the fact that you have been fired, until your self-esteem has been restored to some semblance of equilibrium. If the experience is still too raw, too immediate, even a casual inquiry concerning why you left your last job may produce a stream of bitter invective--criticizing your former employer and colleagues. Even though you may well have been the innocent victim, your angry outburst will leave a highly negative impression. It is unlikely that any employer would want to hire such an obviously embittered soul.

Do not make the all-too-common, related mistake of thinking that prospective employers want a psycho-history of your last job experience. They couldn't care less about your subjective view of who said what to whom. What **will** be of interest to them, and what will linger in their minds after your interview, is your anger, your critical statements, and your defensive attitude. Does this sound like someone YOU would hire? Would you want an ex-employee or former colleague to talk about YOU in these terms?

3

Save your anger, bitter statements, and personal attacks directed at your former boss or colleagues for your close friends and relatives. They know you, they understand, they care...potential employers do not.

When being interviewed--and even when networking beyond your own inner circle--*you must present a positive, forward-looking attitude*. Prepare your version of the reasons why you left your last job carefully. You can expect questions about the circumstances of your departure. Such questions are considered routine and should elicit routine responses, such as:

- There was a budget cutback.
- Some operating divisions had to be eliminated.
- The company lost a major client/contract.
- The company was acquired in a merger.
- There were policy/personality conflicts.
- I'm seeking career advancement.
- I'm looking for a new challenge.

Of course, you must stick to the truth. Honesty is still the best policy, even in today's cynical world. Moreover, everything you say may be checked by the interviewer. But that does not mean that you are required to assume the role of unbiased, objective observer. No one expects you to do that. Every employer anticipates that you will put the best interpretation on an otherwise negative experience.

Do not consider being interviewed until you have really cooled off and developed an honest, defensible interpretation of your leave-taking. Successful interviews require confidence and self-control...and practice.

✓ Mistake No. 4: Writing a Mean and Nasty Letter of Resignation

Letters of resignation can be tricky. If you have to formally notify your employer that you are resigning, be careful about what you say in your letter of resignation.

Of course, there are **pleasant circumstances** for resigning...such as finding a new and better job, moving to another city, winning a zillion dollars in a lottery, or inheriting an island in the Caribbean...and letters announcing such good fortune do not require diplomacy.

More often, people find themselves writing a letter of resignation under **unpleasant circumstances**: if they're being forced out, if working conditions have become intolerable, or if they feel their boss or colleagues have left them no alternative. It is letters written in the heat of anger and disappointment that need care.

The most important thing to remember is that **your letter of resignation will remain in your personnel file long after you have left**. That letter will become the final chapter in your relationship with the company, so every time someone calls the company for a reference on you, or to inquire about your employment there, the file will be retrieved--and there will sit YOUR LETTER.

● The human resources personnel responding to the request for information may never even have met you, so their opinion of you will be shaped by YOUR LETTER. Without revealing the verbatim text of that letter, someone is apt to comment that there seems to have been something "unpleasant" about the reason for your departure. Since you will undoubtedly be presenting your credentials to a future employer as being a smooth, unblemished record of achievement, questions will soon arise.

● Your background may be checked someday for a security clearance, and suddenly the investigators uncover YOUR LETTER.

● You may be considered in the future for a government appointment or may run for public office, and a routine review of your professional background may produce YOUR LETTER.

Here is the point: We would all like to tell people we dislike, who have made our lives miserable, just what we think of them. One of the authors has a friend who spent six weeks crafting a scathing letter of resignation that criticized her boss, co-workers, and the company. By the time it was finished, it dripped with venom and sarcasm, ripping everyone's character, ethics, and morals to shreds.

Unfortunately, the letter became part of her employment record and has been resuscitated more than once in the past 15 years during routine checks of her past employment. **Instead of putting her former employer on the defensive, it has put her on the defensive.** She inadvertently put a weapon in the hands of her enemies that has been used against her ever since. She has told me many times how much she wished she had never written that letter, that a simple note commenting on "how much she had learned" while working there and that she "would never forget her colleagues" could have avoided a lot of grief.

So, if you write a letter of resignation, envision it being examined word-for-word, **out of context,** at some point in the future, by people who know neither you nor your former employer. Be diplomatic, be ambiguous, be succinct.

5

✔ Mistake No. 5: Plunging into the Job Hunt Without Planning

You wouldn't think for a moment of investing your hard-earned money in something without researching and weighing the pros and cons of the investment, would you? Of course not. You worked too hard to build up a little nest egg of surplus income, and you want to make sure it produces the maximum benefit.

So why is it that the same people who examine comparative interest rates, risk factors, price-earnings ratios, and growth possibilities before they put $1,000 in the **stock** market think nothing of jumping right into the **job** market without any preliminary investigation? After all, a job is an investment too, probably **the biggest one you'll ever make**. In all likelihood, it will ultimately mean tens or hundreds of thousands of dollars to you over a period of time.

In addition, work is where we spend most of our waking hours. Who would want to blunder into a job without thinking about the short-term and long-term consequences of that decision? Unfortunately, plenty of people do.

Most job seekers look for work casually and randomly. If they see something they **think** they might like, they apply for it. Don't you be the fool who rushes in and regrets later.

According to surveys, millions of Americans are unhappy with their jobs. Small wonder, when they were too lazy--physically or intellectually--to plan their job hunting and career strategies with care.

> *Don't start actively looking for a job, whether it is your first job,*
>
> *a job change, or a new career, until you have a clear idea about what you want.*

If you are an accountant who dreams about being a deep-sea fisherman, stop dreaming and start injecting a little reality into your planning process. Talk to fishermen. Read up on the profession. Try to develop a realistic picture of what it is like to be a fisherman. Don't quit your job on Friday and sign on with a crew out of Provincetown the next Monday. You may not like the 10-foot seas, lashing yourself to the mast to ride out a sudden North Atlantic squall, getting up at three in the morning standing boring watches, chipping paint, mending nets on Sunday, being inspected by the government to see if you've violated the endangered species laws, and getting into nasty confrontations with Japanese trawlers and Canadian fishing boats.

The time you invest up-front, learning all you can about the career you want to pursue, can pay handsome dividends--especially if what you learn makes you dead sure you don't want to have anything to do with that career.

If you want to start your own business or buy a franchise, see if you can **work part-time** (in the evening or on weekends) in a small business or franchise of the same kind. Owning a restaurant or travel agency can be very exciting, but before plunging into any new business, make sure you know as much as possible about it. What are the nuts-and-bolts of such a business? What is the typical work day like? What is the average profit margin for that kind of business? What are the bad points? The good points? What is the failure rate? What would such a commitment do to your leisure time?

If the nature of your goal or your current circumstances make working part-time impossible, perhaps you could **volunteer** your time and learn just as much--without having burned any bridges behind you.

Either way, you'll learn a great deal about the profession and your aptitude for it. Make no mistake, what you learn after hours or on the weekends could be a real eye-opener. What if you don't like getting up at dawn to make 3,000 varieties of doughnuts? What if you chafe under the managerial restrictions of a franchise? What if the profit-margins in the pizza business seem disproportionately slim? What if working in a hospital depresses you? What if you lack the patience and dedication that teaching requires? The time to discover these things is **before** you take the great leap, not after.

If you are deterred by what you find out, it will have been time well spent. Or, on the plus side, you may discover your niche and grow enthusiastic. The better prepared you are, the more you become familiar with the job demands, the greater your chance for success.

Another alternative is to take some **evening courses at a nearby college or university**. Such courses can introduce you to the practical as well as theoretical background of an occupation, can train you in a related field, or can sharpen your skills in your current field to enhance career advancement.

For someone who has been out of the workforce for a period of time, taking such courses is always a smart move. For example, there has been a technological revolution in the workplace in the past decade and anyone who is not familiar with current computer techniques has a problem.

If nothing else is possible, at least **talk** with people who do what you think you want to do. If you are totally uncertain about where you are going in life, go to

7

the library and read about different careers. For a reasonably small fee, you may even take aptitude tests that will tell you what you might be good at doing. Many reputable commercial firms offer such tests, as do high schools and colleges.

The point is, get off your duff and give this massive investment in your future the respect it deserves.

✓ Mistake No. 6: Making a Geographic Move Too Quickly

Many job hunters become so discouraged in their current location (with or without a job) that they want to pack up and move immediately to greener pastures. This usually means to a major urban center, to another part of the country (where it's sunny and warm), or abroad. Many people have done this more than once during their working careers, and it can be a valuable, enriching experience. Just make sure to do your homework before packing the car or buying the plane ticket.

Disaster stories we have heard over the years on this topic can be distilled into the following pieces of advice:

● *Have a job (or at least several solid job prospects) before you move.* Landing a new job can take three to six months, so why not spend most of that time at home where you know your expenses and can control them? Moving to a new city, finding a place to live (renting an apartment with a few months rent in advance as a security deposit), answering help wanted ads, and trying to establish professional contacts, **all with no money coming in,** can be very costly--and stressful.

● *Subscribe to a Sunday newspaper published in your target city.* Examine the help wanted and professional opportunity sections carefully. They will tell you a great deal about the state of the economy in that city (despite what you may have heard elsewhere), the kinds of jobs available, and the salary ranges being offered. Submit your application material to those you think appropriate and state clearly in a cover letter that you plan to move to that city as soon as possible and can go there for an interview at the employer's convenience. Follow up your application with a telephone call after a reasonable amount of time has passed (depending on the size of the organization) to determine the status of your application and to underline your interest in going there to be interviewed. The newspaper will also tell you a great deal about the cost of living in Greener Pasture, USA, particularly in its section dealing with classified ads for residential real estate.

• *Read the professional opportunity ads in the Sunday* <u>New York Times</u> *and the* <u>National Business Employment Weekly</u> *on a regular basis.* They advertise jobs in a variety of locations nationwide and abroad.

• *Several major U.S. companies now have toll-free 800 telephone numbers which have recorded information concerning current job openings.* Check the help-wanted ads in major Sunday newspapers and the <u>National Business Employment Weekly</u> to find the ones most appropriate for your needs.

• *If you are seeking a Federal job in another city or state,* subscribe to a publication like the <u>Federal Jobs Digest</u>, which contains information on thousands of current Federal job openings nationwide and abroad (see *Bibliography*).

• *If you are seeking a state or local government job, contact the appropriate civil service personnel office* and ask how you can learn about current vacancies. For your convenience, we have included a list of the central personnel offices at the state level in **Appendix B**.

• *Develop a long-distance network of professional contacts.* Your current business associates may have professional contacts in your target city. Determine who they are, the positions they hold, and contact them by phone or letter. Just like networking in your present location, these individuals may have a great deal of useful information concerning job openings--or may refer you to someone who does.

• *The professional associations to which you belong may have chapters in your target city.* If so, contact them, explain your plans, and ask for advice. Or, there may be related professional associations whose members are based solely in your target city that should be contacted--and joined.

• *You may live near a company which also has operations in your target city.* Contact the human resources office or a professional colleague in the company's office in your current location to discuss company job opportunities in your target city.

• *Find out if any of the companies for which you might like to work issue vacancy announcement bulletins.* If so, call them, explain your situation, and try to get on the mailing list to receive such bulletins on a regular basis. Offer to send the issuing office a stamped, self-addressed envelope to facilitate the transaction.

• *The career planning and placement offices of many colleges and universities issue job bulletins* (and offer career counseling) for their alumni. These bulletins contain information about job openings in the city (and state) in which the school is located...many of which have not been formally advertised. Most of these jobs are either entry or mid-level. Even if you did not graduate from a school located in or near your target city, you may still be able to subscribe to the school's bulletin. If that is not possible on a routine basis, contact the career planning and placement office of the school from which you **did** graduate and see if they have established a reciprocal relationship with the school in question. In many cases they **will** have such a relationship and you can obtain the bulletin (for a modest price) as a professional courtesy. Or, you will at least obtain permission to visit their career planning and placement office in person (when you are in town) to review their job opportunity notebooks.

 • *Take off some time and go to your target city to explore the situation first-hand.* Look at the downtown business area (is it thriving, full of well dressed shoppers and business people?); drive through the residential areas (are the homes and apartment buildings well maintained, without a lot of "for sale" signs?); if you have children, drive by and visit the schools (public? private?) and determine their yearly cost; ask about higher education facilities (are there four-year colleges, two-year colleges, professional schools?); look in the daily newspaper to discover cultural activities (museums, theaters, musical concerts) and sporting events. One easy way to discover a lot of this information is to go househunting with an experienced real estate agent, who should be a veritable fount of information on these topics. Real estate agents also tend to know a lot of professional people (current and former clients) and may be able to give you interesting job leads.

 • *If you are a licensed professional,* such as a doctor, dentist, lawyer, CPA, general contractor, engineer, and want to move to another state, make sure to determine the exact procedure for gaining licensure in that state, how much it costs, and how long it takes.

✓ Mistake No. 7: Jumping at a Job Abroad

There are many legitimate jobs abroad for Americans, mainly those offered by the U.S. Government, major U.S. multinational companies, international organizations, and academic institutions. Most of these positions require a specific technical or professional skill; many require possession of foreign language skills and multi-cultural experience. **No legitimate job abroad requires the applicant to pay a sum of money in advance to learn about the position or to apply.**

Unfortunately, thousands of eager Americans are ripped-off each year by bogus companies that require payment (sometimes amounting to hundreds of dollars) for information about jobs abroad. Don't be taken in by these scoundrels; they do not have jobs paying large, tax-free salaries with fringe benefits such as free transportation and housing...what they have is a scam. Certain international events, such as the rebuilding of Kuwait, seem to bring these characters out of the woodwork. Anytime you hear of some "fabulous opportunity" that sounds too good to be true, it usually is--and it **always** is if learning the details will cost you money.

There **are** legitimate sources of information about jobs abroad:

• *For U.S. Government jobs abroad,* either contact the Federal agency offering the kind of job you seek (such as the State Department, the Department of Defense, one of the armed services, or the Peace Corps) or subscribe to a publication such as the Federal Jobs Digest (see *Bibliography*).

• *For jobs abroad offered by major U.S. corporations or international organizations,* read major Sunday newspapers or the National Business Employment Weekly. Most jobs abroad in multinational U.S. corporations are filled from within that company, since they want to train their own executives for advancement within the corporate structure and want to give them international exposure. If they have to seek applicants from outside the company, they will advertise them in a major newspaper or use an executive search firm.

• *For academic jobs abroad,* read the London Times Sunday Education Supplement and the Chronicle of Higher Education (see *Bibliography*).

• *For information about general overseas jobs,* subscribe to a formal job publication, such as Overseas Employment Bulletin. (For information on this and related publications, see *Bibliography*.)

Further, when overseas jobs are offered by legitimate public or private organizations, they know how to handle all the bureaucratic red-tape and the cross-cultural situations involved. If you try to accomplish this on your own, you should consider the following:

• Do you have a work permit for that country? In most countries you will be unable to work without one. Check out the embassy of that country (or one of its consular offices) in the U.S. for full particulars.

• Do you speak the language of that country fluently?

• Do you have a technical skill or teaching credentials in demand in that country?

• Would practicing your profession in that country require licensing? In many cases, a prerequisite to licensure is possession of a degree in the discipline in question from a university in that country.

• Does your spouse intend to work there as well?

• Do you know the status of women in that country and how they are treated in the workplace?

• Will you be paid in foreign currency and are there restrictions on how much foreign currency can be taken out of the country?

• Do you know the general life style of the country--the cost of living, the school situation, the housing accommodations, the medical/healthcare system, the tax situation?

A job abroad can be a fabulous experience, but be careful. American embassies abroad have to deal daily with people who have been badly misinformed and/or have become stranded. So, check out all information and promises **VERY** thoroughly. Do not set out on your great adventure until you know what is waiting for you at the other end.

✓ Mistake No. 8: Failing to Recognize that Your Current Job May Be in Danger

---

You always should be prepared to look for a new position. This has never been more of a fundamental fact of employment life than at present, when the globalization of the economy and the rapidity with which change affects the marketplace make sudden disruptions of job security virtually inevitable.

Learn to recognize the warning signals that your job may be in jeopardy:

• *Pending legislation or regulations that may impact directly or indirectly on your industry.* As we write this, Congress is considering bank reform legislation that might permit banks to sell insurance and securities. If you are an insurance agent, you should be concerned about a major increase in competition from these potential new invaders of your turf. You should also be concerned that, having made a botch of their own industry (banking, about which they presumably knew something), your new competitors have the potential to ruin **your** industry, about which they know nothing. Any former Eastern Airlines employee can tell you all about the impact of deregulation on his or her economic present and future.

• *Your boss gets fired.* You cannot escape the taint of working for someone who is no longer loved or needed. If you were a loyal and selfless underling, you

12

may have sealed your own fate as well. One of the authors was once the deputy to an individual who sought every opportunity to dispute each little nitpicking issue with his own superiors. The author not only was unswervingly loyal to his immediate boss, but also became his close friend, a fact well known to the boss's increasingly exasperated supervisors. As soon as the boss was dismissed, the author's powers and freedom to operate his division were sharply curtailed. Eventually, the author was forced to seek employment elsewhere rather than eat a considerable daily dose of very humble pie.

• *Your workload drops.* If projects for which you were responsible are assigned to someone else (and you are not given an alternative responsibility), watch out. Or, if you are a lawyer used to billing 2,000 hours per year and suddenly you find yourself billing 1,200 hours, it's time to pack up and go while the getting is good.

• *Your firm loses a major client or a major contract.* There's no need to spell out your probable future if this happens. Inevitably, your company will have to cut staff. Even if you dodge the draconian bullet of immediate dismissal, it is clear that promotions will slow down; raises will be fewer, smaller, and slower; and work will no longer be quite as stimulating. Just ask anyone who works for a defense contractor now that the Cold War is presumably over.

• *Your industry slumps.* If your industry goes into a downturn, get your resume in shape and develop contacts fast. The tactic of "hunkering down and riding it out" may have worked well in the more stable, business cycle-oriented world of the recent past, but it is rarely advisable today. The rules of the game have changed forever.

• *Your industry is labor-intensive and companies begin to export jobs to low-wage countries.* If your company makes widgets and discovers that it can pay some Third World worker a tenth of what it pays you to do the same work, where do you think your job will go?

• *Your industry gets hit by intense foreign competition.* When a company is forced to re-think its product line as a result of foreign competition, jobs throughout the corporate structure will be re-evaluated. Changes needed to restructure the company could well mean the elimination of products or services, offices, plant sites, and personnel at all levels. The U.S. automobile industry and U.S. machine tool and electronics manufacturers can testify to the tremendous impact that foreign competition can have on corporate futures and job security.

• *Your organization imposes a hiring freeze.* This is never done unless the company is in dire straits. When imposed in the **private sector**, hiring freezes are a very serious affair. They are a first step in the inexorable cost-cutting process that often eventuates in "downsizing," a euphemism for putting long-time employees out on the street.

Hiring freezes are also a shop-worn device used *ad nauseam* by government agencies whenever politicians have allowed their budgets to get out of control and want to appeal to the voters by "running against the government" (of which they are part). Freezes are imposed in the **public sector** solely for public consumption, to make the taxpayers think their elected officials are actually doing something to alleviate the financial crisis. The point being that, while governments often announce hiring freezes, they are rarely precursors of actual personnel cuts due to the strength of civil service rules and regulations.

   • *Your organization becomes a takeover or acquisition candidate.* While the merger and acquisition binge of the 1980's has subsided, it has not ended altogether. Alert employees will do what is necessary to keep cognizant of their company's position in the market and potential attractiveness to would-be acquirers. Keep an ear to the ground and make it a point to stay current with the business news about your industry and company.
   If your company is taken over or merges with another firm, your job may be at risk. If you are an administrator, watch out. The new company is not Noah's Ark and will not need the services of two people for every type of position.

   • *Your company starts offering early retirement.* This a step often taken by companies facing desperate financial circumstances. If too few people choose to accept the early retirement option, the company may be forced to explore other avenues to achieve a reduction in personnel. So, get ready to move. You may be among those targeted next.

   • *Your company's balance sheet looks shaky.* For publicly traded companies, this is easy to monitor. Simply obtain a copy of the quarterly, semi-annual, or annual reports and/or read the business press. If your company is closely held, you need to do more, such as befriend someone in accounting. In small firms, business setbacks are impossible to hide.

   • *Your region suffers an economic downturn.* If this happens, analyze carefully whether your company is likely to be affected. For example: If you live in the Washington, D.C. area and the Federal Government starts slashing its budget, local businesses will suffer. If you live in Michigan and the car industry goes into a deep slump, your company is also apt to be affected. If you live in the Northwest and the forest products industry is hit by a recession, many aspects of local economies will feel the pinch.

▶ Going Down with the Ship ◀

What if you have already seen one or more of these warning signals alerting you to a bumpy corporate road ahead? Should you hang on until the bitter end, or should you act now and get out while the getting is good? There is no simple answer. Many people hang on to jobs in a troubled company or troubled industry for far too long and wind up going down with the ship.

The point is that you must remain in a state of constant vigilance. When you see danger signals, consider your options carefully. Never permit yourself to fall victim to the "it-can't-happen here" syndrome. It can and, if you have any inkling that it may, it probably will.

✔ Mistake No. 9: Mass Mailing Resumes: Failing to Identify Likely Employers

We have included this mistake in Chapter One although it is usually considered to be part of the active phase of job hunting. The reason for this is threefold:

- job hunters customarily hear about mass mailing resumes and do it at the beginning of their employment search;
- it seems universal--almost everyone does it; and
- it often winds up substituting for any **real** job hunting efforts.

You know how you read in the newspapers all the time about mass catastrophes in distant, overpopulated parts of the world? While not quite as dramatic, the typical job seeker also is in danger of becoming the victim of a disaster--a self-made disaster--when it comes to sending out resumes. Most people take the view that they are maximizing their chances for success if they flood the market with resumes.

The volume approach says that if you send out enough resumes, someone is sure to hire you. It resembles the telemarketing strategies popular among insurance agents, computer sales representatives, and sellers of securities. If you make enough "prospecting" calls, you will come up with some hot prospects. Don't believe it. While it may be true for the financial services industry and technology marketing firms, it has proven time-and-time again to be **one of the worst possible ways to look for a job.**

15

Where does this disastrous advice come from? Usually from some pretty credible sources. Oddly enough, some very respected educational institutions preach this methodology to their students and alumni. Which is, we suppose, why so many job hunters continue to use it...and then blame their own personal shortcomings for the lack of response from employers.

We have seen the volume approach used by thousands of job hunters and have rarely met anyone who used it successfully. It fails to work for a variety of reasons:

• Employers get literally thousands of unsolicited applications and most of them wind up in the trash basket.

• Employers get annoyed by this constant onslaught of impersonal resumes and cover letters, which are extremely easy to spot, and are almost always automatically rejected without an even casual examination.

• Employers perceive the volume approach as the lazy, unthinking person's way of job hunting. And who wants a lazy, unintelligent person working on the staff?

If you mass mail resumes, you set yourself up for a triple blow. First to your time and money. Then to your ego. Then to your future. Who needs it?

You can begin the planning stage of your job search anytime, including while you are still employed or in school. The sooner you begin this process and the more quality time you put into it, the more successful your job search will be.

Planning a successful job search involves many separate and related activities. Essentially, during this phase you will be mapping out a course to follow once you begin active job hunting. You will use this time to analyze yourself as well as prospective industries and employers. This is the time in which you should be gathering and evaluating information to assist you in conducting a successful and rational job search campaign. You will also be using this time to organize a management framework, including such items as a system of records that will be useful not only for your current job search, but also for future efforts.

✓ Mistake No. 10: Failing to Research Your Chosen Industry

Did you just sit right down, scribble out your resume, and send it out to potential employers in a currently "hot" industry? If the answer is yes, you are in trouble--especially if you are just starting out in your working career. Where do you think that industry will be in five, ten, or 20 years? Where do you think individual companies will be positioned within that industry? If you don't have any idea, you'd better pull back a little and do some strategic research.

How do you go about researching the industry in which you want to work? The starting point is your school or public library. Familiarize yourself with the wealth of data available in the library about the industry in which you are interested. The most valuable material can usually be found in the business and reference sections. In larger libraries, the business and reference librarians will personally help you with your search for material.

Two excellent U.S. Government compilations will serve as good starting points for your industry research efforts. U.S. Industrial Outlook examines the current status and future prospects for virtually all industries in the U.S. This publication is put together by Federal Government economists and industrial experts and will give you a good indication of where your particular industry is headed.

The U.S. Department of Labor's annual <u>Occupational Outlook Handbook</u> does essentially the same thing for a wide variety of occupations. It describes each occupation, tells you how many people work in the field, and predicts future growth rates. Using these two sources will give you a solid idea of how you might reasonably fare in a given industrial sector. The <u>Occupational Handbook</u> also provides the names and addresses of trade and professional association sources you may contact for further, more detailed information. The larger private associations usually have materials available to the public describing their industry or profession.

Since the U.S. Government also regulates or monitors most, if not all, industrial sectors, it can provide vast quantities of data on individual U.S. industries. Cabinet departments, Federal agencies, and independent regulatory commissions all publish studies and other data about the industries of concern to them. To begin your search for this kind of Government document, you should first look at the <u>U.S. Government Manual</u>, which contains a description of every department, agency, and commission. The <u>U.S. Government Manual</u> also gives you the address and telephone number of each listed organization, every one of which has a public affairs and/or publications division in the business of providing information about the agency and its programs to the public, most of it free.

The government agencies at all levels that are responsible for monitoring and/or regulating various industries and economic sectors can easily be identified by reference to an assortment of other readily available documents. For example, at the Federal level, you can resort to the <u>Code of Federal Regulations</u> (CFR), a 50-volume set published annually that contains all of the permanent regulations of the U.S. Government. A quick scan of the <u>CFR Index</u> will tell you all you need to know about which agencies are responsible for which industries. The <u>CFR</u> can be found in many public libraries and most college and law libraries. Comparable publications at the state level are also available.

The 100-plus committees and subcommittees of the U.S. Congress also have a continuing interest in various industries. Committee hearings, special studies, and proposed and recently enacted legislation aimed at specific industries can also be easily reviewed. You may learn something very important by reviewing such documents. Each committee has staff members responsible for handling public requests for documents. You can find the names, jurisdiction (i.e., the subjects the committee or subcommittee monitors), addresses, and telephone numbers of these bodies in the latest edition of the <u>Congressional Directory</u>. If you have trouble obtaining the documents you need for your job search, contact the Washington, D.C. or home district office(s) of your Congressman or Senators. They will be more than happy to help you obtain the materials you require. In Washington, D.C., you can write to:

Senator _____
U.S. Senate
Washington, D.C. 20510

Congressman _____
U.S. House of Representatives
Washington, D.C. 20515

Congress also has two research arms that produce a large number of reports, some of which may be useful. The **Congressional Research Service** (which is part of the Library of Congress) maintains a list of its reports and research projects. Ask your Congressman or one of your Senators for a copy of the list. Then, when you have reviewed it and identified reports of interest to you, ask your congressional representative to obtain them for you. **The Congressional Research Service will not respond directly to inquiries or requests from the general public; they must be made through a Member of Congress.**

In contrast, the **General Accounting Office** (GAO) is very responsive to requests from the general public. GAO is the auditing and investigative arm of Congress, and publishes hundreds of reports and analyses each year, many concerning private industry. Your library, if it is large enough, may maintain the GAO Index, a monthly compilation and abstract of GAO reports to Congress. When you have identified the ones you want, you may contact the following address and have them sent to you free of charge: U.S. General Accounting Office, P.O. Box 6015, Gaithersburg, MD 20877.

Some industries and professions, such as insurance and real estate, are regulated by the states, not by the Federal Government. States, especially the larger ones (in terms of population) also produce a wealth of study material about these industries. You can learn about what is available by contacting the state legislative representatives from your area.

Most medium-size and larger libraries also stock the Business Periodicals Index, an invaluable source of information about what is happening in various industries. Used in conjunction with the Reader's Guide to Periodical Literature, you will be able to identify magazine articles about your chosen industry. If you wish to "localize" your research, check the local newspaper microfiche files at the public library. There is generally an index that goes along with these files. In addition, many public libraries also maintain microfiche files for one or more "national" newspapers (e.g., The Wall Street Journal, The New York Times, The Washington Post) that are valuable sources of such information.

Reports compiled by companies in the securities business are also an excellent source. Organizations such as **Dun's, Standard and Poor's**, and **Value Line** follow the trends in many industries whose member companies are public corporations, meaning their stock is traded on one or more stock exchanges or "over-the-counter." While these reports are prepared for investors, they are quite useful to job hunters researching industries and employers.

We have included in the *Bibliography* a selection of basic reference sources that should be a good starting point for your own research. Many of these are quite expensive, and can be found in any major library. Others are more modestly priced and you may wish to purchase one or more for your private use.

✔ Mistake No. 11: Looking for the Wrong Kind of Job

Many people think working for the **government** or working for the **private sector** amounts to the same thing. Eager for a job, they assume that work in either sector will be essentially identical. However, there are differences between these two kinds of employers which can make one the **right** kind of a job environment for you, and one completely **wrong**.

By "government," we mean any job in the public sector, any job in a city, county, state, or Federal government office. These offices, and all salaries of employees, are funded through taxation or public debt (the sale of government securities to raise operating funds). Jobs in the public sector are usually protected through some kind of a civil service system and employees enjoy all the benefits (health, leave, retirement, etc.) which accompany such a system. When budgets are squeezed, programs may receive less funding (or may be cut) or taxes may simply be raised (or more debt instruments issued and sold) to cover the short-fall.

By "private sector," we mean a job in any business that falls within the private, entrepreneurial sector. These businesses traditionally sell a product or service and are funded through the profits made through such sales. Benefits vary widely and (except where employees are covered by a strong union contract) are usually at the discretion of the employer. When profits fall, jobs are in jeopardy.

The important thing for a job hunter to realize is that each of these sectors tends to value different skills and attitudes, as outlined in the following chart:

Public Sector	Private Sector
Employees in the public sector strive to follow rules and procedures. Sometimes the procedures seem to become an end in themselves.	Employees in the private sector must look at the bottom line. While rules and procedures are unavoidable, the end result--sales and profits--is what really counts.
Employees in the public sector are expected to follow orders and instructions without question.	Employees in the private sector are often expected to question established procedures in order to suggest a better, faster, cheaper way of doing the same thing.
Employees in the public sector can count on doing the same thing, at the same time, every day. Stability and predictability are prized.	Employees in the private sector must be flexible and must be prepared to respond to new ideas or a crisis. Innovation and the absence of predictability are prized.
Employees in the public sector find satisfaction in doing their assigned tasks.	Employees in the private sector perform assigned tasks but are always looking for a greater challenge.
Employees in the public sector customarily work at an average pace from 9:00 a.m. to 5:00 p.m. every day.	Employees in the private sector must be able to thrive in a roller coaster schedule of slow times, hectic times, and overtime.
Employees in the public sector value job security, job benefits, and a structured salary schedule.	Employees in the private sector like competing for the prize--greater responsibility, greater salary, greater risk.

Few people feel truly comfortable in both environments. **Many times the typical "complainers" in an office are those trapped in the wrong kind of work structure.** How many times have you wanted to turn to a co-worker and say "If you don't like all this overtime, why don't you go work for the government?" Or, "If you want to challenge these decisions all the time, why don't you go to work for a private company?"

21

There is no perfect job, but there are work environments in which you might feel more comfortable than others. It's important for job hunters to appreciate some of the basic differences between public and private employment to avoid falling into the old "round peg in a square hole syndrome." Think about the atmosphere in which **you** thrive--and go for it.

✓ Mistake No. 12: Looking for Opportunity in Adversity

Sometimes, the best opportunities are with companies or divisions facing disaster. Obviously, firms like these are prime candidates for a superstar who can help them turn their situations around. A lot of job hunting manuals emphasize approaching these companies and touting your problem-solving skills. That's a fine approach IF:

- you really possess these skills and they are proven;
- you will be in a position of key responsibility in the company
  in which you have some control over your destiny; and
- you plunge into the job mindful of the consequences if you fail.

Sure, there is opportunity in adversity, but in the majority of situations, it is the opportunity to fail. On balance, you will be much better off if you look for your opportunities in companies with a solid future.

✓ Mistake No. 13: Relying Exclusively on "Networking"

"Networking" remains a hot concept in job hunting manuals and seminars. It is not really anything new. Basically, it means cultivating your circle of acquaintances--social, recreational, and professional--in order to obtain either actual job leads or the names of contacts who may be well positioned to provide either the names of additional contacts or other job leads. *Networking is simply the modern repackaging of common sense.*

Unfortunately, the idea of networking has become so widely touted as a brilliant new revelation in the well-trodden employment field that it has led many job hunters astray. Its promoters seem to think that networking is the be-all and end-all of the job search. There is no doubt that **networking can be an extremely**

22

effective job hunting tool if used skillfully. The problem is that many job hunters lack either the contacts or the skills required, which take time, practice, self-confidence, initiative, and a degree of assertiveness.

Here are some suggestions that can help you network more effectively:

1. If you are going to "network" (and we do recommend it), do it intelligently. Don't rely on the cocktail party circuit or chance meetings with friends and acquaintances to get you a job. First, sit down with your address book and your Rolodex and make a list of the people who can **really** help, or who you think come into contact with people who can boost your chances of employment.

2. Distinguish between your intimate network of close friends to whom you can freely spill your guts, and your expanded network of more casual acquaintances and professional colleagues from whom you need job leads and, perhaps, introductions to future employers.

3. Don't restrict your networking activities to your present social and business circle. Exhume names from the past. They can be very effective if used properly. One area where such prospecting has paid valuable dividends for many people is among fellow alumni of the same colleges, universities, and graduate and professional schools. Obtain your school's current alumni directory and study it carefully for the names of people who can help you. Rarely does a fellow graduate turn down another alum of good old State (or Private U.). At a minimum, you ought to be able to cultivate some excellent information sources from among your alumni colleagues. If your school does not have an alumni directory, the best alternative approach is to contact the college or university career or placement office. The best ones keep tabs on their alumni's professional lives and may even have a ready-made network established which you can invoke. If your school's career office does not know where the alumni are, contact the fundraising office (now commonly called the "development" office). It is the fundraisers' **business** to know where alumni are located and they may be willing to help.

4. Expand your professional network of acquaintances by attending conferences, trade shows, professional association meetings, job fairs, lectures, or workshops. Since you want to meet professional colleagues in other companies, go to events they attend.

5. If you've never bothered to join professional associations and related organizations, now is your chance. You might be surprised at the information you can learn from their meetings and newsletters--many of which list positions available.

6. If you want to meet business leaders and other people active in your community, volunteer in a cultural or civic association.

7. Keep your close acquaintances and contacts posted on your progress. Tell them what you are doing at different stages of your effort, and solicit their advice from time-to-time. Not only may you be able to elicit a few good suggestions from them, you may also revive their interest in being helpful if you give them periodic up-dates.

8. Keep track of important suggestions and who made them. If Sam Successful at Worldwide Printing suggests that you go and talk with Mark Master at Nationwide Publishing, you will want to make the contact by invoking Sam Successful's name..."Mr. Master, Sam Successful at Worldwide Printing suggested that I call you concerning your expansion plans. He thought my experience in this field might be valuable to you in this effort. Perhaps we can meet, when it's convenient, to see if my background matches your needs."

However, don't rely exclusively on networking. For one thing, your network may quickly lose interest. For another, you will be missing out on a lot of information and opportunities if you do. Finally, effective networking can take a long time to produce results.

There are also signs that networking is losing its effectiveness because it has been oversold and, consequently, overused. Like the proliferation of junk mail, everybody is doing it, and the recipients are being overwhelmed. Use networking as **one** facet of your overall job hunting strategy, not as the only one.

✓ Mistake No. 14: Not Doing Informational Interviews

Rare is the job hunter whose job search planning includes informational interviewing. That's too bad. If you don't engage in this greatly underused practice, you are really missing out on a valuable and informative exercise.

Informational interviews are different from practice interviews. In an informational interview you are not practicing your interviewing techniques. Rather, you are the one doing the interviewing. You are picking the brains of an expert in your chosen field or industry, asking well-prepared, cogent questions about job prospects, industry issues, the nature of the work, the future of the field, etc. Talking to an insider can fill in a lot of the blanks about a prospective career, as well as point you in the right direction. Informational interviews can be major contributors to your job hunting strategy.

Since, if done properly, informational interviews can be valuable planning tools, you should try to schedule them at the beginning of your job search, preferably before you formally begin, so that you will be able to incorporate what you learn from them into your job search strategy.

You will be surprised at how many seemingly busy people, considered to be experts in a field or industry, will be kind enough to talk to you about your future. The fact that you consider them experts will be extremely flattering...which is always a good entree.

We are not suggesting that you burst in upon your informational interviewees unannounced. Contact prospective experts beforehand, explain the purpose of the meeting, and ask for an appointment.

Once at the meeting, it's up to you to establish the ground rules. Do not waste this valuable time by sitting through a vague over-view of an industry (you should already have such information before you set up the appointment). You need to explain the **kind** of functions/responsibilities you can perform and **at what level** you can perform these responsibilities. This explanation will allow your contact to focus specifically on information concerning **your kind of position** industry-wide.

If you have already identified companies where you might like to work, ask your contact if he or she knows anyone of influence in these companies. If so, make sure to get their names and, if possible, corporate titles. Ask if you can use your contact's name when calling these people. If your contact hesitates, you have not made a positive impression. The targets of informational interviewing have their own professional reputations to protect and will only allow you to use their names in networking if you've made a good impression on them during the interview.

If you're told you're not qualified for the kind of a position you seek, ask where you could go for appropriate training or experience. Ask for **specific** information: What courses should you take, and at what kind of school? What kind of job would give you the required experience? What kind of background would be reflected on the ideal resume for this kind of position? How do companies in this industry usually fill this kind of position?

If you show that you're eager and enthusiastic, and are willing to "pay your dues," experts may grow sympathetic and provide invaluable advice.

Whatever you do, do not ask the following kinds of questions:

"How did you get your job?"
"How much money do you make?"
"How did you get to be such an expert?"
"Where do you think you'll go from here?"

Informational interviewing is not investigative journalism. You are there seeking professional information and guidance on your own career path, hoping the expert will share some of the general knowledge he or she has gained over the years as well as some specific, current inside information which may be useful to you.

Of course, not all experts are created equal. Some will have the time...and inclination...to be helpful and forthcoming to a potential professional colleague. Others will be hesitant or even abrupt, guarding the information they themselves have worked so hard to attain. Your best strategy is to act confident and profession-al throughout. No matter what you might think of that person, you must strive to make a positive impression. Even if they're competitors, industry experts all tend to know each other and travel in the same professional circles. Word can travel quickly if you are judged "bush league," overly aggressive, or uninformed.

Make sure to follow-up the informational interview with a brief letter thanking that person for taking the time to meet with you, enclose a copy of your resume, and re-state your immediate career goal. If you think the meeting has gone well, conclude by noting that you would like to telephone him or her in a few weeks to see if any information of interest has come up during that intervening period of time. This kind of letter accomplishes several things:

- It shows you are polite and professional.
- It reiterates the kind of job opportunity you are seeking.
- It provides a record of your interest to which the contact can refer in case a piece of relevant information crops up.

A WORD OF WARNING

Do not use an informational interview as a ruse to ask for a job. This kind of tactical switch is offensive and counterproductive, effectively ruining whatever chances for contacts and information you may have had.

✓ Mistake No. 15: Not Exhausting All Sources of Job Vacancy Information

Newspaper help-wanted ads, networking, and informational interviews are not the only sources of job information. Depending on your field and interest, you can usually find a group of job publications and professional journals containing current job listings. These highly targeted information sources are overlooked by the vast majority of job seekers. Generally, for a relatively small amount of money, these publications can provide you with a large number of job opportunities in your field or area of interest. They do a lot of the spadework for you, uncovering job opportunities that would take you an enormous investment of time and effort to find.

We have included a representative sample of such publications in our *Bibliography*. These publications can be used as a starting point (or additional resource) for information on current job openings.

✓ Mistake No. 16: Relying Exclusively on One Job Hunting Method

Never rely on any single line of attack to find the job you want. All sources of information should be used simultaneously to increase your chances for success.

• Don't rely exclusively on friends or acquaintances for job leads.

• Don't assume informational interviews will automatically produce referrals.

• Don't assume that newspaper ads list all available jobs.

• Don't attend job fairs expecting a job offer on the spot.

• Don't just take a civil service examination or submit a government application form to a central personnel processing facility and assume you will be automatically referred for vacant jobs. Landing a good government job requires a lot of personal attention on your part.

27

- Don't limit your job search to one geographical area.

- Don't restrict your job hunt to positions in your current industry if your skills can be transferred to another industry.

- Don't send your resume to some job bank maintained by your professional organization and sit back waiting to be called.

- Don't just interview on campus if you are a graduating college student. The vast majority of employers don't hire this way.

In summary, make use of every available job information source you can discover. How many times have you heard that people just happened to be in the "right place at the right time" when they heard about their current jobs? Don't you believe it...being in that place at that time took a lot of effort. Chances are they were in a lot of places at many different points of time when not a single job lead surfaced. Those who are unhappy with their job hunting results tend to say someone else was just "lucky." Many times achievement is not the result of luck, but of perseverance and total effort.

✔ Mistake No. 17: Depending on Executive Search Firms

One automatic reaction to job hunting is often to submit a resume to, or even make an appointment for an interview with, an executive search firm (a.k.a. executive recruiter or headhunter). Many job hunters who elect this course of action do not understand how these firms operate. They mistakenly think that the search firm is out actively seeking to broker a position for them. Not only is that usually dead wrong, that misimpression also fosters an unfortunate complacency in the job hunter. After all, if a professional job finder is doing your work for you, what could you possibly add to the effort?

The reality of executive search is that only a small percentage (10-15%) of individuals are executive recruitment material, so the effort expended on the vast majority of applicants is usually nothing at all.

This erroneous view of executive recruiters does not usually result from a deliberate intention to cheat you or pull the wool over your eyes. It generally results from a misunderstanding concerning what such companies do.

Executive search firms do not look for **jobs for people**; they look for **people to fill jobs**. They are hired by companies which have vacancies, usually at the higher salary levels, and which need superb candidates to fill those vacancies. It is then the function of the search firm to go out and find such candidates. While, on rare occasions, they do find the ideal candidate among the unsolicited resumes submitted by people who walk in off the streets, most of the time executive search firms work to identify people who are currently working--and performing very well--and explore their interest in working for the client company. Ordinarily, these targeted candidates are quite happy in their current jobs and are not actively seeking new opportunities until approached.

This is not to say that you should not submit your resume to a search firm. Actually, you may as well go ahead and send it--as long as it will cost you only the price of photocopying and mailing it. But be forewarned that **you may never hear from the firm at all**. Chances are very slim that an executive search firm would find you to be the perfect match for one of their corporate or professional clients.

If you do consider yourself to be prime executive search material, make sure to contact **more than one firm** in order to get your resume the widest possible exposure. Although search firms in one geographical area may be competing to fill the same job, it is highly probable they will also be engaged in searches for **different** positions. Maximize your chances for success by using as many search firms as possible that meet your criteria for integrity and competence. Whatever you do, never give any executive search firm the exclusive right to find a position for you. That's tantamount to putting your future in someone else's hands.

Keep in mind that executive search firms do not target individuals **who want to be** executives; they target those **already established** as executives in their chosen fields. If you have just finished college or graduate school, and are about to embark on your first serious job search, do not even waste the stamp to submit your resume...**they're not searching for you.**

▶ Not Cross-Examining Executive Search Firms ◀

If you happen to be one of those rare individuals contacted by an executive recruiter, look before you leap. Naturally, your ego will be bursting with pride. After all, a third party sought you out and is trying to lure you away from your current job with promises of a better one. While flattering, this kind of thinking can be dangerous if it makes you act impetuously.

There are a few questions you should ask the search firm before you throw caution to the winds and "sign up" for whatever it is they say they have in store for you. These are questions almost no one ever asks, but which almost everyone (including the employer that hired the search firm) later regrets not broaching:

29

1. What are the search firm's credentials, that is, is it accredited by the Association of Executive Search Consultants (AESC)? Government regulation of executive recruiters is virtually non-existent. AESC is a loosely organized self-policing body with fairly strict membership requirements. It has been in existence since 1959 and serves as the unofficial accreditation agency for the industry. This is very important in the absence of state licensing boards. AESC has a strict code of ethics (called the Code of Ethics and Professional Practices) to which member firms must adhere.

The <u>Directory of Executive Recruiters</u>, which is updated annually (see *Bibliography*), lists 2,500 executive search firms and also indicates which ones are AESC members. This fine publication also lists the areas of specialty of search firms (some are "generalists" while others specialize in one or more industries or professional areas) and the minimum salary levels of the positions for which they will conduct searches. The <u>Directory</u> also cites the professional and trade associations to which listed companies belong, but do not let these many acronyms delude you into thinking that these affiliations mean anything in terms of establishing credibility. Read the plaques on the wall carefully.

2. How long has the search firm been in business? Executive recruiting is a business notorious for rapid turnover. An unusually large number of companies are always newcomers on the search scene. As a rule, you will be in better hands with a seasoned company.

3. How long has the firm been in the **executive recruiting business**? A lot of companies that began by doing other things later expanded into the executive recruiting business. Their reputation for excellence in other business areas may or may not translate into success in the field of executive recruiting.

4. How will the firm be compensated for this search? Unless the response to this question is "100 percent by the client organization for which we are conducting this search," run as fast as you can in the other direction! The applicant should pay nothing.

▶ Failing to Distinguish Search Firms from Employment Agencies ◀

Not knowing the difference between a search firm and an employment agency can be a disastrous mistake. Especially if you did not take the trouble to ask the specific questions listed in the preceding section.

Unlike executive recruiters, employment agencies are state-regulated in most jurisdictions. As a rule, they are paid by the employer, but only if a placement is made. Like search firms, the standard fee charged the company is quite high, usually running around 20-30 percent of the first year's salary.

However, there are many employment agencies **that charge the job hunter** something for their services. A number of states permit an up-front charge that may be quite high. Some fees are determined as a percentage of the first year's salary; other states do not regulate fees at all.

If you sign up with an employment agency, make certain that **everything** regarding your relationship is documented in writing and signed by an official of the agency.

In that signed agreement with the employment agency, make sure you examine **how the fee you paid is handled if it turns out that you do not like the job and quit.** Will the firm then find you another job at no charge? Will they provide you with a partial or pro-rated refund of the fee? Assume nothing. Employment agencies have attorneys who have drawn up these agreements and all common contingencies have been addressed in some way, usually tilted in favor of the agency.

The majority of employment agency work is done with applicants seeking white collar jobs in the lower salary ranges. Typing, shorthand, and word processing tests are a routine part of initial interviews at such agencies.

✓ Mistake No. 18: Not Looking for Positions Related to Your Field

The American system (if you can call our haphazard approach a "system") of preparing people for the job market is woefully deficient in many respects. Chief among these is that it tends to give job hunters, especially those that are ready to enter the job market, tunnel vision. Our obsession with credentials (sometimes, unfortunately, at the expense of any substantive basis) may be the root cause of this dismal development.

Most people receive very little career counseling at any stage of their educational development. We send young adults forth into the working world without giving them the basis for making sound decisions about their professional futures...despite considerable amount of information available on the subject.

A friend of the authors spent almost 20 years and tens of thousands of dollars obtaining a PhD in Architectural History, then in his late thirties began looking for an academic position in his specialty only to discover that there were only a handful of jobs in the U.S. teaching this subject--and they were filled! He was then forced to explore collateral careers in which his credentials would be an asset...an exercise which might have been undertaken years earlier (in a more relaxed atmosphere) with a career counselor.

Whatever the cause, most job hunters look for jobs that have the very same title as appears on their degree or certificate. Here's an example: You have just graduated from a paralegal program. On graduation day, you received a document certifying you as a trained paralegal. You are eager to plunge into the job market. After all, the paralegal profession is one of the fastest growing fields in the 1990's, according to the people who follow such trends.

What do you look for when you are a credentialed paralegal? Why, jobs with the title, "paralegal," of course! It never occurs to you to examine any other job titles. None of your academic advisors ever told you there were lots of other job titles you could fit into quite nicely with your paralegal background.

If you restrict yourself to only those jobs that are labeled "paralegal," you will be doing yourself an enormous disservice. Instead of attuning yourself to 100 percent of the available positions, you will only learn about 25-50 percent of the jobs for which you may be qualified. A few of the titles paralegals are eminently trained and qualified for include: Documents Examiner, Export Assistant, Insurance Benefits Claims Examiner, Disability Claims Specialist, Health Benefits Specialist, Retirement Claims Examiner, Equal Employment Officer, Contract Administrator, Procurement Analyst, Employee Relations Specialist, Legal Instruments Examiner, International Trade Specialist, Realty Specialist, Copyright Examiner, Workers' Compensation Claims Examiner, Tax Law Specialist, Estate Tax Examiner, Public Utilities Specialist, and Unemployment Compensation Claims Examiner.

We took all of these positions from either newspaper advertisements or published vacancy announcements issued by private and public sector organizations. All of them sought applicants with some legal background, but did not require a law degree or admission to the bar. Many of them stated in the fine print that they were seeking someone with a paralegal certificate or background. In short, each and every one of these positions would have been perfect for a paralegal. Sadly, it is likely that very few job hunting paralegals applied for these positions because the job title did not say paralegal. When they open up the newspaper, they head right for "P" for paralegal and look no further.

Paralegals are not in a particularly unique position. Every professional has a broad range of occupation-related job titles which job hunters should examine closely.

When you open up a newspaper and examine the help-wanted section, you must not only take the time to read the ads under your particular professional title, but also to read the fine print of **all of the other ads that sound as though they are looking for someone with your background**. Make a list of the categories under which you find related job titles and examine job openings falling under such categories on a regular basis. Only then will you be able to say with confidence that you have made an exhaustive search of this one particular source of job information.

Another good way to find job titles related to your occupation is to examine the annual Occupational Outlook Handbook published by the U.S. Department of Labor (see *Bibliography*). This publication groups related occupations, describes the nature of the work and training/education required for each, and provides the names and addresses of organizations to contact for further information. The Dictionary of Occupational Titles, also prepared by the U.S. Department of Labor, is included at the end of the Handbook.

You should use this approach when reading any employment bulletin or job list...**always read the fine print** to determine whether or not your background matches the job requirements. College degrees come in a few basic flavors; job titles (filled by individuals holding such degrees) come in a million flavors. Don't limit your job search through self-imposed restrictions.

✔ Mistake No. 19: Not Scanning ALL the Job Ads

If you are truly serious about getting a new job, you should examine ALL the help wanted ads in the Sunday newspaper, from A to Z. You may be surprised at what you find.

• For example: Companies which have just won new contracts or are starting up a new operation frequently mention that fact in an ad--as a justifiable point of pride and as a lure to attract qualified applicants. Such companies also usually hire from the top down. This means that if they're looking for computer programmers or computer specialists, they may soon be looking for other technical support staff with skills in that area. If they're hiring attorneys, they may soon be looking for paralegals. If they're hiring project engineers, they may soon be looking for project administrators. If they're looking for a chief accountant or Vice President-Finance, they may soon be looking for staff accountants.

When you submit your application, mention that it was prompted by the fact that the company **did** win the new contract or is starting up a new operation. Express your desire to be part of the new team and your enthusiasm for its success. What do you have to lose? This is another way alert people manage to be at the right place at the right time.

• Further, employers frequently put ads under unexpected employment categories. For example: If you are looking for a position as a manager or management trainee, the logical place to look is under the letter "M" where most such jobs are listed. However, many employers list such positions under the **industry** in which the job is being offered...i.e., under "hotel," "retail sales," "computer," "real estate," or "transportation." If you do not scan the entire help-wanted section, you would miss all these positions.

• Finally, employers with a number of jobs to advertise frequently do so in one composite ad--with a large-type headline, a heavy border, and usually the company logo. This composite ad can identify several positions for which the company is seeking applicants, many times in a variety of professional fields. It is not unusual to see an ad from a private company (or from a municipal or local government) in which the organization may be simultaneously looking for a chemical engineer, human resources specialist, financial analyst, and environmental specialist. The ad could be positioned **almost anywhere** in the help-wanted section. We have seen them under the category identifying the nature of the employer, under "E" for engineer (the first kind of job listed within the ad), under "M" for municipal, or under "P" for professional.

Most employers are **not experts** in how newspapers lay out their help-wanted sections. They call in (or send in) their ad and may not specify exactly where it is to be placed, or they may ask the paper's classified ad department to suggest where it should be placed, or they may request placement under a category that seems logical to them but may be unexpected to the average reader.

So, **scan the entire help-wanted section** before concluding that it contains nothing of interest to you.

► Applying for a Job for Which You Clearly Are Not Qualified ◄

Job notices, advertisements, and vacancy announcements generally contain some information on applicant qualifications. The better ones are usually broken down by education, general experience, and specialized experience. Frequently, some education may be substituted for certain experience requirements. You should be able to tell, in most instances, whether or not you qualify for the job. If after reading the job notice, you are still uncertain, you should contact the employer (if possible) and ask for clarification. If it is clear to you that you do **not** qualify at all for the position, don't waste your time or the employer's by applying for the job. Rather, identify other jobs for which you are qualified and spend your valuable time preparing topnotch applications for them.

Government agencies and many other large organizations publish detailed vacancy announcements describing their job openings. Time permitting, you should obtain a copy of the announcement which interests you before submitting an application. The full announcement usually contains detailed information about the responsibilities of the position and minimum educational/experience requirements.

There are additional steps you can take if you want to be even more exhaustive in your research about job qualifications. Many large employers have published specific standards for their positions. These are usually very detailed descriptions of the background requirements and qualifications deemed necessary to be considered for, and successful in, particular positions, and contain valuable information in addition to that found in a vacancy announcement.

In the Federal Government, for example, the <u>Office of Personnel Management Handbook X-118: Qualification Standards for Positions Under the General Schedule</u>, is a manual containing all of the qualification requirements for "white collar" positions. A parallel handbook (known as the <u>X-118-C</u>) covers trade and craft ("blue collar") jobs. These reference books are generally available at any Federal Job Information Center (see **Appendix A**), most Federal agency personnel offices, and many large libraries. Basically, they describe the education and training required for each grade level within each occupational field in the Federal Government. Private sector firms and state and local government agencies often maintain comparable handbooks that are available to the public. If you visit the human resources office of a private organization, you can ask to examine their handbook, if available. In addition, industry trade associations often have similar information compiled for their industry or member companies.

► Taking a Job Advertisement at Face Value ◄

It is customary for job hunting handbooks and seminar gurus to preach that you should not apply for jobs for which you are not qualified...a point we have just addressed in the preceding entry. As a broad principle, this is sound advice. Why should you waste your time when it seems apparent from the wording of the job ad that you haven't got a ghost of a chance at the position?

However, before passing up the job completely, ask yourself if you are **absolutely certain** you would be wasting your time? Sure, if you have an eighth grade education, why bother responding to an ad seeking a nuclear engineer? Or, if you can't type **at all**, why apply for a job that requires superior secretarial skills? These are clear cut examples of job requirements that exceed the applicant's skill and/or education. However, many times the gap between the stated job requirements and the applicant's background is not all that great.

For Example

An ad may ask for applicants with typing speed of 60 words per minute (wpm), and you can type 50 wpm. Would you apply?

OR

An ad may seek an editor with 3-4 years of related experience and you have two years. Would you apply?

OR

An ad may seek an accountant with a graduate degree which you lack. Would you apply?

WHY NOT?

Keep these facts in mind whenever you read a job ad or vacancy announcement:

• *Any ad is a "wish list" outlining the attributes of the ideal applicant.* The education and experience described are what the employer is hoping to find in the **perfect** candidate for the position. But this is not a perfect world and 99 times out of 100 the employer is compelled to accept something less than perfection.

• *Education may frequently be substituted for experience and vice versa.* For example: An employer seeking applicants with an undergraduate degree in business and four years of experience may well consider someone with an undergraduate degree in business, a year of graduate education, and two years of experience. Or, an employer seeking someone with a graduate degree in economics and two years of experience may consider someone with an undergraduate degree in economics and 3-4 years of experience. The variations are endless.

• *Ads are expensive so only a limited number of words can be used.* This means that all the various combinations of substitute qualifications cannot be spelled out. **Employers outline the ideal requirements and then wait to see who applies. If an** ad attracts truly inadequate candidates, the employer will re-word the ad and have it published again.

• *Every job involves hundreds of factors, of which only a few--the most obvious-- can be included in an ad.* You may well have some asset, not mentioned in the ad, that could automatically make you a serious contender for the job. Such an asset could be some volunteer experience, the type of word-processing equipment you know how to use, a summer job you may have held, or the **kind** of job experience you have had as opposed to the total number of years involved.

The bottom line is: if you see a job ad that interests you, for a position which you think you could handle, submit an application. What do you have to lose? A stamp and an envelope? Every employer dreams of a superhuman employee who can leap tall buildings in a single bound, but they will happily settle for one who takes the elevator.

✓ Mistake No. 20: Applying Carelessly in Response to Help Wanted Ads

A typical way to attack a Sunday newspaper full of help wanted ads is to take a stack of resumes, each accompanied by a general cover letter, and to submit a set to each ad that seems appropriate. This is not a good way to attract attention to your application. Of course, you may get lucky. By sheer chance, your resume may reflect **exactly** what the employer was hoping to find.

To increase the odds in your favor, you should **tailor your resume to make it reflect the fact that you have the kind of experience cited in the ad.** If this is not possible, you should **at least compose a cover letter which clearly indicates that you possess the required skills and experience, and ties your application to the listed position.** Standard cover letters can be spotted in a minute and make the applicant seem careless and not truly interested in the position. From the employer's point of view, it looks as though the applicant was throwing darts randomly at a job board...hoping somehow to score.

Although all job ads must be responded to as quickly as possible, if the ad seems cryptic or overly general ("small manufacturing company seeks mid-level manager..."), see if you can telephone the employer to request more information about the position. The human resources or personnel department can frequently provide additional facts that would help you target your application. Alternatively, you may be acquainted with someone in the organization who probably knows what the job involves. This kind of knowledge gives you an edge over other applicants. They will be throwing darts while you use a laser beam.

We know you groaned when you read this piece of advice. We know applying carefully for three or four positions may take as much time as applying carelessly for 50. But taking the time to target your application material to the position will pay off. Your application will stand out...and will have a better chance of being taken seriously.

✓ Mistake No. 21: Answering "Blind" Job Ads Without Assessing the Risks

You have all seen help wanted ads which do not identify the employer but simply ask applicants to respond to a post office box number or some other designation. **BE CAREFUL.** You must assess the risks presented before responding to such ads. We have known many people *who have responded (unknowingly) to their own organization* or one whose management was closely associated with their own. When this happens, their "confidential" job search was blown out of the water and they found themselves in troublesome situations.

One individual we know was actually called into the personnel office to explain his actions. "We didn't know you were looking for a new job...when are you leaving?"

Another person we know wanted to move to a different part of the country, thought he was safe applying to a "blind" ad in another state, and discovered--unhappily--that the ad was from a regional office of his own company.

The advice is to use caution. If you can think of even **one organization** that you would not want to know about your job search, answering a "blind" ad may not be a prudent course of action.

There are TWO exceptions to this:

1. If you are out of work, your job hunt should be without limitations. Even if the "blind" ad turned out to be from the company that just fired you, who cares. They'll just throw your application away. No harm has been done.

2. Sometimes employers don't go to the effort of getting a post office box, newspaper reply box, or other designation, but simply ask people to reply to the "Personnel Director" or similar title at the organization's real street address. This laziness on their part gives you a break, because with a little effort you can identify the company before deciding whether or not to respond. One way to do this is to go to the public library and ask to see the "criss-cross directory," which is typically organized by street address. Once you look up the street address, you may well have the name of the employer. Or, if it is a large office building, you may be able to determine (or discover) the identity of the employer. **Note:** Public libraries customarily maintain such directories only for their own local areas. For comparable information outside your local area, call the reference librarian at the public library serving the city for which you are seeking information.

✓ Mistake No. 22: Faxing Your Resume
Without Assessing the Risks

If an organization announces a job vacancy and gives applicants the option of faxing in their resumes, don't do it from your current place of employment (or from a commercial fax service outside your current place of employment) without assessing the risks.

If you are concerned about job search confidentiality, keep in mind that most fax machines at the receiving end are not located in the relative privacy of personnel or human resources offices but tend to be centrally located with almost unlimited access to anyone passing by. This means that your resume may be seen by a number of people who would not feel compelled to respect the confidentiality of your communication. "Hey, look at this. Harry Hotshot from Mega Manufacturing is applying for a job here!" By lunch time your resume and application would be common knowledge.

Further, if you fax a copy of your resume from your current office to a location beyond your immediate telephone area code, there will ultimately be a record of the date, time, and fax number to which it was sent on your own company's telephone bill. Many companies routinely allocate the cost of all long distance calls and faxes to individual departments or projects, so questions will soon arise.

If speed is that essential, submit your application package via one of the many efficient overnight delivery services. It will cost more, but you will have the advantage of submitting "hard copy" application material (some faxes tend to look blurry and unprofessional) and the confidentiality of your job search will remain protected.

✓ Mistake No. 23: Not Taking Advantage of Special Recruitment Opportunities

---

For 25 years, government policies have either mandated or encouraged certain special hiring programs designed to help people deemed disadvantaged to obtain employment. In addition to programs mandated by Federal or state law, many private sector organizations have independently developed their own recruitment programs that have the same objective: identifying and hiring people who have traditionally been at a disadvantage when it comes to competing for jobs.

A surprising number of job hunters who are eligible for such programs **know little or nothing about them** and, consequently, do not take advantage of them. Many such programs actually go out and actively seek applicants to take advantage of their benefits!

Programs such as these are in place all over the country and for many different population groups: racial and language minorities, women, older Americans, people of various national origins, veterans, and disabled persons.

The 40 million-plus Americans deemed "disabled" or "physically challenged" are perhaps the best example of a disadvantaged group that has not maximized its opportunities in this area. To demonstrate the extent to which these programs are not being utilized to the fullest, here are some startling figures: Disability experts estimate that approximately 50 percent of the college-educated disabled people of working age in the United States are unemployed! This is by far the highest unemployment rate in the country for any measurable group. Both public sector and private industry recruitment coordinators frequently state that they have to go out and actively **pursue** disabled workers and encourage them to apply for the jobs they have available.

The reason such programs go unnoticed is that they are not widely advertised. In order to find out about them, you, the job hunter, will have to do some investigative work on your own. If you think you might be eligible to take advantage of the enhanced employment opportunities offered by such programs, contact prospective employers and ask them how you may apply under their special recruitment procedures. You may be ignoring an outstanding opportunity if you don't.

► Not Applying for a Job Because You Have a Disability ◄

If you don't apply for a job you want because you have a disability, you're making a mistake. You know exactly what you can do and what you can't do. If you think you can handle the job, go for it.

Even if a company does not have a special recruitment program in place, most are fully aware of the goals of the recent, wide-ranging *Americans with Disabilities Act* (ADA) and are making serious efforts to comply.

The *Americans with Disabilities Act of 1990* prohibits private employers, state and local governments, employment agencies, and labor unions from discriminating against qualified individuals with disabilities in job application procedures, hiring, firing, advancement, compensation, job training, and other conditions and privileges of employment.

The *Act* provides that:

- Employers may not discriminate against an individual with a disability in hiring or promotion if the person is otherwise qualified for the job.

- Employers can ask about one's ability to perform a job, but cannot inquire if someone has a disability or subject a person to tests that tend to screen out people with disabilities.

- Employers will need to provide "reasonable accommodation" to individuals with disabilities. This includes steps such as job restructuring and modification of equipment.

- Employers do not need to provide accommodations that impose an "undue hardship" on business operations.

- All employers with 25 or more employees must comply, effective July 26, 1992.

- All employers with 15-24 employees must comply, effective July 26, 1994.

For more specific information about ADA requirements affecting *employment,* contact the:

41

```
U.S. Equal Employment Opportunity Commission
1801 L Street, NW
Washington, D.C. 20537
    Tel: 202/663-4900 or 1-800/669-EEOC (Voice)
    Tel: 202/800-3302 (TDD)
    Tel: 202/663-4494 (TDD for 202 Area Code)
```

We have also included in **Appendix C** a list of the offices at the state level that are responsible for handling civil rights and employment discrimination issues within their respective jurisdictions.

Many feel that this new Federal law opens employment doors that had been formally or informally closed against the disabled. It's now up to you to take advantage of the employment possibilities it offers.

✓ Mistake No. 24: Not Taking Advantage of Free (Or Cheap) Advice

If you have been fired or laid off by your company, the first free service you should use is any "outplacement" or job counseling program your company may have established. These may fall under the heading of "Employee Assistance Programs" in many organizations. Many people don't take advantage of these company programs, which is a mistake. They are free, they have been set up to assist individuals in your predicament, and the best ones can either set you off in the right direction or, perhaps, encourage you to look in an entirely new direction.

If you are a mid- or senior-level executive who has been laid off, and your company does **not** provide "outplacement" assistance in-house, you should try to have such assistance included in your severance package. Many well known outplacement and career counseling firms derive much of their revenue from companies **paying for counseling services on behalf of laid-off employees.** A common corporate practice is as follows: "If an employee doesn't ask for formal outplacement assistance, none is offered."

Job placement and counseling services have become a growth industry. There are a lot of commercial organizations that will gladly take your money in return for job hunting assistance. Most of these are respectable and will give you what you have paid for. Many of these are not as expensive as you might believe. Some even provide advice, assistance, and support (psychological and otherwise) free of charge, or as a benefit of membership in a particular organization.

The business sections of a growing number of newspapers now list career and job assistance seminars and conferences at least once a week. In addition, the Wall Street Journal's <u>National Business Employment Weekly</u> periodically lists a calendar of such events nationwide.

In many cities, churches and other community organizations sponsor job hunting, mid-career crisis, and other self-help meetings or groups. These kinds of meetings are not widely advertised but are frequently cited in local newspapers under "community activities."

It is a good idea to attend one or more of these functions, especially when you are planning your job hunting strategy. You are certain to come away with at least one good idea about how to look for a job that you may not have thought of on your own.

✓ Mistake No. 25: Getting Ripped Off

The job counseling industry has its share of scoundrels. **Make sure you know exactly how much a service is going to cost before signing anything.** Job hunting annals are filled with too many stories of individuals who have paid thousands of dollars to career counseling firms in return for practically nothing. Don't get ripped off. Unlike purchasing tangible commodities, purchasing a service can be more difficult to measure. When you buy $10 worth of peaches, you have a pretty concrete, specific idea about what you'll get in return for your money. When you spend $100 or $1000 for counseling, the value of the service rendered is in the eye of the beholder. If **you** think it's the pits, it **is** the pits. No tangible results can ever be guaranteed.

Before even considering spending big bucks on something that may be of little value to you, ask the firm for the names of at least three (presumably satisfied) clients. If the names are provided, contact them. If the names are not provided, make a fast exit.

Assuming the information from the satisfied clients is good news, then you must proceed with a careful examination of the services to be provided.

43

Even if the organization is an outplacement firm whose fees are paid by your employer, you should still check out the nature of the services offered and staff capabilities. Will you have an office of your own or someplace to share? Will office space be reserved for you or offered daily on a first-come, first-served basis? Is there secretarial support? Is there a telephone, fax, word processor, copier, postage-meter? Is there any in-house reference and research material? Are staff members trained counselors? Is counseling offered in group sessions or individually? How many hours of counseling will be provided? Will they offer guidance in the nuts-and-bolts areas of resume and other kinds of application preparation, job targeting, and interviewing skills? Will they provide only psychological support and hand-holding? What are the time limits involved?

Outplacement and other career counseling organizations frequently offer their services as a "package deal," so it is up to you to examine exactly what will be included in that package. As with so many other things in the marketplace, the caution is "buyer beware."

✓ Mistake No. 26: Overlooking Tax Deductions

Job hunting expenses are treated as deductible from your income for Federal and state income tax purposes under certain circumstances. You should familiarize yourself with the rules governing both the Federal and your own state deductions before you begin any job hunting activities. Most job hunters do not realize the significant tax advantages permitted under the law. Consequently, they do not maintain records of their job search expenses adequate to claim the deduction.

The most important deduction allowed, in terms of dollar amounts, is the Federal one. Although Federal tax laws seem to be in a constant state of flux, for years they have included special deductions relating to expenses incurred while job hunting. To take advantage of these deductions you must:

1. Keep careful records.
2. Obtain the relevant publications that outline permissible deductions directly from the Internal Revenue Service: call 1-800-829-3676 and request Publication 529-Miscellaneous Deductions and Publication 521-Moving Expenses.
3. Consult your tax preparer to verify your interpretation of these regulations and to ensure you're basing your actions on the most current information.

Generally speaking, you can claim job search expenses in your present occupation to the extent that such expenses exceed 2% of your adjusted gross income. For example: To quote directly from IRS Publication 529:

44

You may be able to deduct certain expenses you have in looking for a new job in your present occupation, even if you do not get a new job. You cannot deduct these expenses if you are looking for a job in a new occupation, even if you get the job.

If you are unemployed, the kind of work you did for your past employer is your occupation. If there is a substantial break between the time of your past job and your looking for a new one, you cannot deduct your expenses.

You cannot deduct your expenses if you are seeking employment for the first time, even if you get the job.

Employment agency fees. You can deduct employment agency fees you pay in looking for a new job in your present occupation. If, in a later year, your employer pays you back for employment agency fees, you must include the amount you receive in your gross income to the extent of your tax benefit in the earlier year (which is explained under **Recoveries** in <u>IRS Publication 525, Taxable and Nontaxable Income</u>). If your employer pays the fees directly to the employment agency and you were not responsible for them, you do not include them in your gross income.

Resume. You can deduct amounts you spend for typing, printing, and mailing copies of a resume to prospective employers if you spent the amounts in looking for a new job in your present occupation.

Travel and transportation expenses. If you travel to an area and, while there, you look for a new job in your present occupation and also engage in personal activities, travel expenses to and from this area may be deductible as a miscellaneous itemized deduction. To be deductible, the trip must be primarily to look for a new job...Even if the travel expenses to and from an area are not deductible, the expenses of looking for a new job in your present occupation, while in the area, are deductible.

Looking for a new job "*in your present occupation*" means that you must be seeking a position in your current professional field. If you are an engineer, you must be seeking a job as an engineer, not as a pharmacist. Expenses incurred while looking for your first job do not qualify.

You **cannot deduct** expenses you have for education if the education:

*is needed to meet the minimum educational requirements to qualify you in your work or business, or
*will lead to qualifying you in a new trade or business.

Moving expenses. Moving expenses are an itemized deduction, not subject to the 2% of adjusted gross income limit that applies to the categories of miscellaneous deductions outlined above.

IRS Publication 521 discusses the circumstances under which you can deduct a limited amount of expenses incurred when moving to a new home because you changed job locations or started a new job. To qualify, expenses must first meet a **distance** test and a **time test**.

> **Distance test. Your move will meet the distance test if your new main job location is at least 35 miles farther from your former home than your old main job location was...*
> **If you go to work full time for the first time, or go back to full-time work after a substantial period of part-time work or of un-employment, your place of work must be at least 35 miles from your former home to meet the distance test.*

Some of the basic elements of the **time test** are as follows:

> **Time test for employees. If you are an employee, you must work full time for at least 39 weeks during the first 12 months after you arrive in the general area of your new job location. You do not have to work for the same employer for the 39 weeks. However, you must work full time within the same general commuting area. You do not have to work 39 weeks in a row...*
> **Time test for self-employed persons. If you are self-employed, you must work full time for at least 39 weeks during the first 12 months AND for a total of at least 78 weeks during the first 24 months after you arrive in the area of your new job location. You do not have to be self-employed in the same trade or business for the 78 weeks.*
> **Joint return. If you are married and file a joint return and both you and your spouse work full time, either of you can satisfy the full-time work test. However you cannot combine the weeks your spouse worked with the weeks you worked to satisfy the test.*

If you are able to meet the time test and the distance test, you can deduct reasonable expenses of:

> **Moving your household goods and personal effects (including cer-tain storage expenses),*
> **Traveling to your new home,*
> **Househunting trips before you move,*
> **Living temporarily in the new area,*

*Selling your former home and buying a new one, and
*Settling an old lease and signing a new lease.

Clearly, the above material is just a basic outline of the elements involved. Whenever you're dealing with the IRS you know that there are tons of fine print, limitations, and exceptions, not all of which are clearly spelled out in the <u>Internal Revenue Code</u> or relevant IRS publication. Consequently, if you contemplate deducting significant job hunting expenses, seek professional advice and assistance.

However, it should also be clear that these job hunting and related moving expense deductions can amount to a big tax break and should not be overlooked. The point to remember is to keep careful records of all expenses and then discuss the extent to which they meet IRS tests with your tax consultant or advisor.

The moment you begin plotting your job search strategy, you should simultaneously begin thinking about your resume. Ideally these two tasks will go hand-in-hand. They are, after all, intimately related. What you learn during your self-analysis, information-gathering, and data evaluation efforts will all contribute to the preparation of a top-notch resume. The results of these labors will also point you in the right direction as to the kind of resume--or resumes--you should be using.

The two kinds of resumes most popular among both job hunters and employers are: (1) the "chronological" resume, which presents a chronological summary of your personal history; and (2) the "functional" resume, which highlights your functional skills. However, a third option which is now gaining popularity, is a hybrid--using a functional skills summary in conjunction with a brief chronological statement of work history. You may want to experiment with these different kinds of resumes in order to see which one suits you the best.

Many of the mistakes made in the preparation of resumes are equally applicable to the preparation of special application forms that an increasing number of employers require, or prefer, as a substitute for your resume. The mistakes that apply equally to both types of application documents, as well as other special application form problems unique to that genre, will be indicated in *CHAPTER SIX*: **Special Application Form Mistakes.**

✓ Mistake No. 27: Forgetting the Purpose of a Resume

Most people sit down to write a resume because they want to get a job or want to change jobs. Unfortunately, once they get into the actual construction of the document, they lose sight of the forest because of the trees.

The sole purposes of a resume are to introduce you to a potential employer and land you an interview. In other words, to attract attention, get you noticed, and kindle interest. A resume is not an autobiography, and should not document every detail of your existence since conception.

A resume must be an "impact" document. That is, it must have an impact on the reader, or it becomes just another worthless scrap of paper. To have the desired impact, it must include only information which will interest the reader. It must be sufficiently compelling to make an employer want to meet the person behind the paper.

If an employer reads in your resume the same thing he reads about every other applicant, you will become lost in the shuffle. So above all, remind yourself every time you work on your resume, and every time you re-read it, that you are striving for IMPACT.

A good example of this is the second version of John Power's resume, on page 66. Note how he achieved impact by peppering each job description with a list of his work place achievements, labeled as such, so that a prospective employer would certainly take note of them and be suitably impressed.

✔ Mistake No. 28: Starting Your Resume with the Word "Resume" at the Top

Begin your document with your name, address, and telephone number(s)...**not** with the word "Resume."

The reader will know when he or she opens your envelope that you have submitted a resume. There is probably no more blatantly obvious document in the world, other than a tax return. It is not necessary to identify what is manifestly apparent. Let the reader figure out that it's a resume. There is no need to insult his or her intelligence.

NOTE: Everything stated above also goes double for the terms "Curriculum Vitae" or just plain "Vitae." The pretension of these archaic terms is certain to offend many, if not most, reviewers (a possible exception might be the higher education community, where this kind of affected language may still be acceptable).

✔ Mistake No. 29: Not Understanding How An Employer Reads a Resume

Job hunters, particularly those who have been in the work force for a number of years, tend to treat resume preparation as a necessary evil. They do it reluctantly, almost by rote, customarily by following a rigid, uniform format--usually without giving a lot of thought to the implications of what they are doing or to whether the particular format is the right one for them. No one ever told them to draft their documentation with the **reader** in mind. The unfortunate result is often a wasted effort. They have written a resume that misses the point, that is too long, too wordy, filled with irrelevant and distracting information.

Most resumes are not read word-for-word; they are scanned.

As you put your resume together, ask yourself what kind of immediate impression it will make. Employers do not have time to read thoroughly all the resumes they receive. They have to find some short-cut to winnow out the ones they really want to examine with care. So, at the outset, they scan them. They do this in order to cull the few from the many. Of course, you want to be one of the select few.

The personnel directors of America's top corporations say again-and-again that *if you haven't presented the most important information about yourself in the top half of the first page of your resume, you can probably forget about getting the job.*

The "20-Second Rule"

The head of personnel management for one of the largest and most prestigious employers in the Washington, DC area told the authors that she allows 20 seconds in which to scan each resume she receives. If, in that brief time, she does not see anything that gets her attention, she rejects the resume.

So remember: The top half of page one of a resume is about all that busy human resources professionals and executives have time to scan. They lose interest if they don't see something that grabs their attention right away.

This means that your resume may never be read carefully unless it can survive the initial scanning process. **You have to get yourself noticed right away and right up front.** You must devise a marketing statement that will stimulate interest in a particular product...you.

✓ Mistake No. 30: Believing Everything the "Experts" Say About Resumes

---

There is probably more expert opinion available on how to prepare a resume than on any other subject related to job hunting. A lot of the advice is costly, but much more is free. During the course of your life, you have probably absorbed quite a number of resume do's and don't's. We are sure that, in many instances, you didn't even have to ask for it. It was eagerly offered by high school guidance counselors, college career placement officials, career counseling services, lots of books and manuals, and virtually all of your friends, acquaintances, and family members. Most of it was probably given to you without hesitation and with great confidence in its value.

In this mistake's pristine form, an individual goes into a guidance or place-ment office and is presented with exact instructions, often accompanied by several "canned" examples, concerning THE ONLY WAY TO WRITE A RESUME. Usually, that "only way" means a chronological resume, that is, listing work experience and education in reverse chronological order from top to bottom. This advice is often accompanied by rigid restrictions concerning:

- length: "Never exceed one page!"
- style: "One inch margins all around are a must!"
- format: "Always lead with work experience, followed by education!"
- section headings: "Experience," "education," "memberships," etc.
- typeface: "Use only prestige elite!"

While it would be wrong in all circumstances to follow each of these rules mindlessly, it is equally important to remember that each one of them contains a kernel of, if not truth, some pretty good advice.

- A resume should not be too long. Like Supreme Court Justice Potter Stewart's famous comment about pornography--"I can't define it, but I know it when I see it," proper resume length is ambiguous. One page is great, if that one page says everything you need to communicate to an employer. Two pages are generally acceptable. Beyond that....?

- One inch margins are the standard, but no one will measure your margins and reject you if they are too narrow. What you should be concerned about is the visual impact, not a precise measurement.

- Work experience generally comes first, but not always. The problem is that while a formula resume is fine for many people, it is far too rigid to accommo-date the needs of others. For example: A person with little or no work experience will not necessarily be well-served by a chronological resume. Neither will someone with a significant gap between jobs. Similarly, an individual who was unable to work for a period of time because of family demands or a personal problem, such as a disability or illness, may also be better off deviating from the standard formula. A person in this situation may need a functional resume or some other non-chronolog-ical mode of presenting resume information.

Here is an example of how following this positioning "rule" slavishly can ruin a job hunter's chances:

The "rule" (and we use the term very loosely) states that if you have been out of school and in the working world for a while, your experience should always precede your education on your resume. Briefly stated, the reason for this "rule" is that employers are much more interested in how a seasoned worker performed in past jobs than in that person's educational background. Consequently, they want to see work experience right up front, without wading through something they consider less relevant in order to find it.

Recently, one of our clients asked us to evaluate his resume. The most noticeable thing about his resume was that, despite 15 years in the work force, he had placed his education prominently at the beginning of the document. Only after a fairly exhaustive and detailed rendition of all of his schooling did he describe his work experience. Our gut reaction was to criticize him for this and advise him to transpose his education and experience presentations.

But our gut reaction was wrong. After reading his job descriptions carefully and considering them as a whole, we concluded that he had been quite correct in how he had chosen to format his resume. He was an incurable job-hopper, and in 15 years had been employed by no less than nine different employers. Worse, he had displayed a considerable disinterest in staying with one industry or one field of expertise for more than a few years at most. In summary, he demonstrated a most unstable and unimpressive work chronology, one that would send shivers up the spines of most employers. However, he had a saving grace: his educational background was one of the most impressive we had ever seen, and moreover, was completely inconsistent with his feverish work history. After graduating from Princeton University with honors, he had simultaneously obtained both a Harvard law degree and a master's degree in Public Administration from Harvard's Kennedy School of Government--truly outstanding academic achievements. And because his educational background was so impressive, we agreed with his choice of placing education at the top of his resume. Despite conventional wisdom, he had selected a resume strategy that worked best for him.

• There are no standard resume section headings. Rather, there are quite a few acceptable ones. For example: Successful job hunters have used all of the following to highlight their work backgrounds:

> EXPERIENCE
> WORK EXPERIENCE
> PROFESSIONAL EXPERIENCE
> PROFESSIONAL ACHIEVEMENTS
> PROFESSIONAL ACCOMPLISHMENTS
> SIGNIFICANT ACCOMPLISHMENTS

• There is a vast array of very nice typefaces available in a word processing environment. The "rule" about using prestige elite is a survivor of the time when resumes were largely prepared on typewriters. It is irrelevant today. Our only admonitions are: (1) select a "mainstream" typeface and type size; stay away from the bizarre; and (2) don't mix different typefaces in your resume. If you want to highlight or emphasize a phrase or set of phrases (i.e., EDUCATION, WORK EXPERIENCE) do so by using *italics* or **bold face** type...in the same basic typeface that is being used in the rest of your resume.

For some reason, job hunting and resume preparation evoke very strong (and wide ranging) opinions and emotions among both personnel professionals and the general public. But there are virtually limitless ways to construct a resume or go about a job search. **There are no uniformly "right" or "wrong" ways to do these things. There are only ways that work and ways that do not work.** We are all unique individuals and what is true for one of us is not necessarily true for another. As long as you avoid the mistakes cited in this book, you should feel free to select your own personal strategies.

When you receive solicited or unsolicited advice about how to put together your resume, take it with a grain of salt. Ask yourself whether it is really good advice for **you**. Do not consider recommendations as articles of faith, consider them to be general guidelines that are probably true for most people, but nothing more than that. Evaluate advice against your own unique circumstances. You may find that you are the exception to the rule.

✔ Mistake No. 31: Submitting an Out-of-Date Resume

If you are a seasoned member of the work force, do not merely exhume your prior resume from the file cabinet and update it. Instead, force yourself to *re-write it*. You can always improve on what you said about yourself in a previous incarnation. In the intervening years since you prepared your last resume, you have probably learned more, experienced more, and now *want* more. Further, the workplace is constantly changing: terminology changes, technology evolves, and you should re-write your resume to reflect these changes.

For example: Do not cite experience on specific kinds of office equipment that is now obsolete or several generations behind what is in current use. If you last looked for work in the late 1970's, you may have alluded on your resume to your adeptness with MAG card typewriters. Now, the few people who even remember this outdated technology probably remember it as positively prehistoric. Cite experience in general terms according to the nature or kind of equipment in question.

For another example, job titles and the positions they describe have changed during the past 20 or 25 years. In addition to technological changes, there have been changes in many aspects of organizational structure and function. *Make sure to describe job responsibilities from that period of time in terms understood today.*

So, do not "update" your resume by scribbling something in ink or pencil in the margins or attaching an update sheet to the original document...either technique can be disastrous to your employment prospects. Sloppy short-cuts aggravate employers, who will not take you seriously. They will believe you are either lazy, unconcerned about appearances, or that you don't even know the difference between a well prepared and poorly prepared document.

Whenever you look for a new position, take the time necessary to craft a new resume. You may certainly use your old resume as a reference point, but it should never substitute for the analysis required to produce a fresh document.

✓ Mistake No. 32: Using the Wrong Type of Resume

We have already outlined the differences between a chronological and a functional (or "skills") resume. Probably 95 percent of all job hunters use the traditional, chronological type of resume, where work experience is summarized in reverse chronological order, with the current or most recent job first, followed by prior positions. The example on the following page sets forth a "mainstream" individual--a middle American, middle age, middle class, middle manager--who has followed a rather orderly and conventional career progression.

The chronological approach works fine for most users. It is the preferred format of employers, all other things being equal. It is what the vast majority of resume reviewers **expect** to see when they open your envelope. Unfortunately, it is not the best approach for everyone who uses it.

John Power
123 Main Street
Smallville, Kansas 66101
(H) 913/555-4567
(O) 913/555-4321

EXPERIENCE

1987-Present   Management Analyst, Kansas Limited, Smallville, KS
Analyze production and distribution operations to increase productivity and improve efficiency. Advise senior management on findings and recommendations. Assisted in improvement of machine tool maintenance functions resulting in 15 percent reduction of downtime. Proposed new transportation quality control procedures that cut delivery time to major customer by average of two days per order. Awarded "Manager-of-the-Quarter" honors, resulting in 5 percent bonus.

1984-1987   Purchasing Officer, Topeka Edison, Topeka, KS
Responsible for all purchasing functions of Line Repair Unit of $2 billion municipal utility. Determined best available sources of all hardware requirements of unit. Examined source quality control and production capabilities. Negotiated purchase agreements. Monitored performance under contracts. Re-negotiated transformer contract resulting in $5 million savings to company. Identified and contracted with foreign wire splicing crimping tool manufacturer whose tools reduced line failure rate by 20 percent.

1980-1984   Inventory Control Specialist, Consolidated Equipment, Kansas City, MO
Responsible for assorted inventory functions, including correlating timely arrival of ordered items with business operational requirements; quarterly inventory audits; streamlining ordering procedures in order to reduce paperwork; and coordination of point-of-sale operations with computerization of warehouse procedures. Supervised extensive inventory computerization program and advised procurement officers with respect to hardware and software requirements.

1978-1980   Management Trainee, Consolidated Equipment, Kansas City, MO
Trained in all aspects of diversified firm's operations, including personnel, inventory, budgeting, purchasing, leasing, pricing, production, distribution, and accounting. Successfully completed all rotations in top 10 percent of recruiting class.

EDUCATION   B.A., Business Administration, 1978
Kansas State University

Honors and Activities
Dean's List--three semesters
Business Club Membership Director
Volunteer at Family Shelter

REFERENCES   Available upon request

If you are a job-hopper, for example, a chronological resume may not be for you. Here is what a summary of positions held could show:

1986-Present	Procurement Analyst, Defense Contractors, Inc.
1985-1986	Procurement Specialist, Standard Buyers, Ltd.
1984-1985	Contract Manager, Amalgamated Production Co.
1983-1984	Contract Administrator, State Purchasing Dept.
1982-1983	Contract Specialist, City Purchasing Div.
1981-1982	Cost-Price Analyst, Aimless Manufacturing Co.
1980-1981	Rate Specialist, Global Utilities
1979-1980	Management Trainee, United Screening, Inc.

Eight jobs in six years! How do you think a prospective employer will regard this kind of unstable job history? Skeptically, no doubt. For most job seekers, itemizing this hyperkinetic sequence would be the kiss of death to their career prospects.

There is another way for this job-hopper to put his best foot forward: to use a functional resume that emphasizes the skills and achievements acquired in the contract and procurement area. In other words, the resume could "lump" discrete jobs together and discuss them as one progression of increasing skills and responsibility. This person's functional resume might include the following:

CONTRACT MANAGEMENT: Managed and administered more than 50 major architectural and engineering contracts worth over $1,000,000; advised contractors on duties and liabilities under contract; represented public and private sector organizations in prompt-payment disputes and other difficulties arising under contract; interpreted contract clauses upon request by contractors and sub-contractors; and successfully resolved numerous contract disputes and claims.

PROCUREMENT: Coordinated purchasing of more than 1,000 items for prime contractors and subcontractors; analyzed procurement needs and procedures for a wide variety of products; and recommended and implemented more than 50 improvements to procurement procedures.

NEGOTIATING: Negotiated more than 75 subcontracts in many diverse areas including architecture and engineering, oil and gas, and ADP; mediated ratemaking disputes between public utilities and municipal customers; and recommended settlements that were adopted in 10 instances.

The second, functional version of this applicant's work history is an improvement over his chronological one if only because it camouflages his constant job-hopping. It avoids projecting a potentially negative impact by transforming the same material into a format that creates a more positive impact.

If you are a **career-hopper**, you face a more difficult problem. If you stayed with your very different jobs for any length of time, you may still be able to get away with using a chronological resume. However, if, like many career-hoppers, you have had some difficulty finding your niche in the working world, you may be both a career-hopper and a job-hopper, a combination that is tough to handle on any kind of resume.

Most employers shy away from the unconventional person. An applicant who has held jobs in a variety of different professions or fields...and for a variety of different employers...falls squarely within most employers' definition of unconventional. When resumes are reviewed, those of unconventional people are generally the first to find their way into the trash can. One way to suspend reality, hopefully until the interview stage (when, face-to-face with your prospective employer, you can explain your wanderlust), is for you to use a functional resume which presents the skills you have amassed or the achievements you have contributed at each station along the way, or both. Here you will be trying to sell **your performance and overall competence** rather than an in-depth expertise gleaned from years in the same profession.

Those who choose a purely functional format should be forewarned that many employers jump to the conclusion that the job applicant has something to hide. Many do not. They simply want to present their skills in the most positive way--in light of their own work history. For this reason, many who need the advantage of a functional skills presentation opt for *a hybrid version of the resume: the functional skills material followed by a brief chronological statement outlining work history.* This demonstrates to the reviewer that nothing is being hidden while maintaining the advantage of a summary of skills.

See for example (on the following page), a possible resume for Super Mom, a successful executive who dropped out of the workforce for a number of years while her children were young. Super Mom remained an active volunteer during these years, and acquired experience and skills valuable to future employers. This hybrid resume highlights both her professional career as well as her interesting volunteer experience. She has hidden nothing, but has shown her professional development and skills to their best advantage.

In fact, a version of the hybrid resume is becoming increasingly popular for many job applicants who basically prefer a traditional chronological format. What

Super Mom
1225 East 79th Street, #224
New York, NY 10024
Home: (212) 555-1234

SUMMARY OF QUALIFICATIONS

Over ten years of experience in advertising, marketing, public relations, and management, with a background in both the public and private sectors.

EXPERIENCE

Marketing

- Directed overall marketing strategy, sales, advertising, sales promotion, pricing, product development and public relations activities of a $100 million company.
- Developed detailed marketing strategy that contributed to 10 percent increase in corporate profits during the 1982-83 recession when average corporate profits fell by an average of 7 percent.
- Reduced product development time by 15 percent.

Program Management

- Vice Chair, Advisory Council on Instruction, New York County School District.
- Coordinated recommendations to School Board from six advisory committees.
- Directed special study recommending revision of mandatory education requirement from a ceiling of age 16 to completion of 12 years of post-kindergarten education; drafted legislative proposal which was approved for submission to New York State Senate and Assembly.
- Testified on education issues before New York City Board of Education.
- Participated in successful campaign advocating affirmative vote for $100 million school bond issue.
- Created and produced an anti-drug promotional campaign for New York County school system.
- Planned campaign directed at over 500,000 students.
- Drafted public service messages for internal and media distribution.
- Developed ideas for posters and obtained volunteer artists to prepare them.

Fundraising/Development

- Organized and supervised special gift campaign for Hudson University, which exceeded fundraising goal by $10 million in two years.
- Directed Parent-Teacher Association fundraising for two schools.
- Participated in numerous fundraising drives on behalf of Hudson University as well as nonprofit research organizations.

EMPLOYMENT HISTORY

1983-1985: Executive Vice President for Marketing, Smith Jones Co., New York, NY
1982-1983: Account Executive, Prestige Advertising Inc., New York, NY
1979-1982: Assistant to the Director, Worldwide Public Relations, New York, NY

HONORS AND AWARDS

- Education Volunteer of the Year, New York County School District, 1988
- Elected to District, Regional, and State Parent Teacher Association posts
- New York County Representative, Governor's Conference on Special Education, 1990

EDUCATION

- M.A., Public Affairs, Columbia University
- B.A., English, Hudson University

REFERENCES

Available upon request

they do is begin their resumes with a brief statement summarizing skills and experience, and then proceed with the basic chronology of work history. If well written, this kind of presentation can be extremely effective. In most instances it creates a more positive impression than leading off with a "career objective," which can be cliche ridden and frequently offensive.

For example: While Super Mom's opening statement succeeds in summarizing her experience in a succinct and positive manner, someone with the same kind of background could have begun with the following:

Career Objective: A senior-level position in a major advertising or public relations firm that would allow me to use my executive, managerial, and leadership skills as well as my energy and creativity.

This kind of "career objective" statement creates a negative impact. It is a classic type of over-reaching, aiming high while simultaneously trying to touch all bases. Most people would laugh at its vanity, take points off for poor judgment, and lose interest in the rest of the resume.

✓ Mistake No. 33: Writing Only One Resume

Most of us are lazy and always seek the easy way out. We want to prepare one resume and go with it.

However, don't allow your basic laziness to affect your career prospects. Remember, *a simple way to maximize your marketability is to prepare more than one resume.* In fact, in today's extremely competitive job market, having more than one resume is critical, virtually a must. The extra hour or so that it will take you to do a second, and perhaps even a third, resume will cost you little, but may gain you much. Here's how:

If you're like most people, you have probably done more than one thing in your life that you would like to put into your resume. As you will read later in this book, employers generally prefer short (ideally one-page) resumes and so you agonize about how to cram all the vital information about yourself onto a single side of a sheet of paper. This creates a kind of "general" resume in which you try to give a hint of all the diverse things you've done without emphasizing any one element of your past experience.

That's fine for most potential employers, but there are invariably instances where you will want to demonstrate, unequivocally, *the strong connection between one of your particular areas of expertise and the prospective employer's business needs*. That may be tough to do with a general resume.

For these special cases, you should consider a specialized, more focused, resume that will concentrate the employer's attention on how you can be of particular value to the company.

An accountant whose resume we were asked to review is a case in point. She got her CPA license and did a little of this and a little of that for a number of years. She did some financial accounting, some auditing of publishing companies, and worked for a trade association where her publications accounting experience came in handy, since she was assigned to keep track of deferred subscription income from the various periodicals the association published. She also did tax returns for, and provided business advice to, a restaurateur on the side.

In her cover letter to us, she wrote that, as a long shot, she wanted to work for one of the "Big Six" accounting firms in New York or, alternatively, for a medium-size firm in her native city. Her preliminary research turned up the names of local firms that handled the auditing of the largest restaurants in town, and Big Six firms in New York whose clients included major publishing houses.

She did not want to send her general resume to these companies. Consequently, she asked us for help. We examined her general resume and broke it down into its component parts. Then we helped her reconstruct two additional, specialized resumes. One emphasized her publishing expertise and the other emphasized her restaurant experience. She intended to send the publishing resume to the Big Six offices in New York and the restaurant resume to the medium sized firms locally. We also advised her to personalize the cover letters accompanying each resume in order to point out her specialized experience while also indicating that she was something of a generalist.

Several months later, she wrote that she had received offers from one Big Six firm and two local firms.

Many people with multifaceted skills or experiences put together only one general resume which is then submitted for each position or to each company that comes along. That is fine if all of those jobs or organizations are clones of one another...but that is rarely the case.

If you have more than one area of specialization or professional expertise, it may be difficult to put all of that into a summary document like a resume. You will be much better off writing two (or more) resumes, each of which emphasizes one specialty. Then, you will be able to decide which resume will serve you best with respect to each job or employer you are attempting to interest.

Another example could involve someone like Ms. Marvella Sharp (see next page). Ms. Sharp is an attorney with considerable and diverse experience in several, distinct legal areas: health law, energy law, and regulatory law. In her "generalist" resume she attempts (unsuccessfully, in our opinion), to be all things to all people. She tried to compress all of her multifaceted legal experience into one resume.

Marvella Sharp
4444 Connecticut Avenue, N.W.
Washington, DC 20008
Office: 202/555-5678
Home: 202/555-1212

PROFESSIONAL EXPERIENCE

1989 - Present **Associate, Smith, Jones & Brown**, Rockville, MD.
- Obtain approvals for clients in medical device regulatory proceedings before U.S. Food and Drug Administration.
- Secure Federal contracts and grants on behalf of client companies.
- Obtain private financing for client seeking to market anti-smoking apparatus.
- Advise clients on legal implications of proposed business actions.
- Prepare testimony for clients appearing before Congress, state legislatures, and administrative bodies.
- Draft proposed legislation and regulatory comments.
- Lobby U.S. Government agencies on behalf of client interests.

1987 - 1989 **Staff Attorney, U.S. House of Representatives Special Committee on Federally-Controlled Energy Resources**, Washington, DC.
- Planned and directed investigations of on-shore and off-shore oil and gas lease sales.
- Identified issues for Subcommittee consideration.
- Pinpointed and briefed prospective witnesses for public hearings.
- Advised Members and staff on energy laws, regulations, and court decisions.
- Supervised staff.

1980 - 1987 **Attorney-Advisor, Economic Regulatory Administration, U.S. Department of Energy,** Washington, DC.
- Recovered over $3 billion in illegal overcharges from energy companies under the price and allocation laws and regulations.
- Successfully recouped over $1.3 billion from a single energy company, the second-largest single recovery ever by the U.S. Government.
- Litigated more than 20 price and allocation cases before the Federal courts and Federal administrative entities.
- Drafted regulations and proposed legislation.

1981-1985 **Adjunct Professor, Federal City College of Law**, Washington, DC.
- Taught more than 500 law students.
- Instructed students in Contracts, Natural Resources Law, and Civil Procedure.

EDUCATION **J.D., Federal City College of Law**, Washington, DC, 1980.
- Dean's List
- Order of the Coif

B.A., University of Maryland, College Park, MD, 1977.
- Dean's List
- Class Rank: top 15 percent
- Member, University Swim Team
- Sports Editor, *The Diamondback* (University newspaper)

BAR ADMISSIONS District of Columbia
Maryland

REFERENCES Available upon request

Note that Ms. Sharp's generalist resume makes a valiant attempt to include everything significant she accomplished in her three full time positions since she graduated from law school. However, depending upon the types of positions for which she wishes to compete, she could submit a much stronger resume if she concentrated on "targeting" her areas of expertise.

This targeting would involve expanding the work experience blocks involved in each of her sub-specialties (health care law, energy law, and regulatory administrative law) and simultaneously compressing her experience in the remaining two areas. This would also give Ms. Sharp the opportunity to include an "achievements" section to accompany each targeted experience block. An example of expanded work experience blocks *targeted for her health law subspecialty* could read as follows:

PROFESSIONAL EXPERIENCE

1989 - Present   **Associate, Smith, Jones & Brown**, Rockville, MD.
- Represent client companies in medical device regulatory proceedings before the U.S. Food and Drug Administration (FDA).
- Serve as lead counsel in natural resources, biotechnology, health and medicare litigation.
- Counsel client firms on marketing plans, antitrust matters, and Federal and state regulatory approval and monitoring systems.
- Represent clients in regulatory compliance matters before state regulatory agencies in five states.
- Advise health care clients on legal implications of proposed business ventures.
- Prepare testimony for clients appearing before Congress, state legislatures, and Federal and state agencies and administrative bodies.
- Draft proposed health care legislation, amendments, and comments on proposed legislation and regulations affecting client companies.
- Lobby U.S. Government agencies on behalf of health care clients with respect to the following issues: orphan drug legislation, peer review, catastrophic health care legislation, and hospital cost ceilings.

ACHIEVEMENTS:
- Obtained approvals from FDA on behalf of clients in over 80 percent of medical device proceedings.
- Successfully pursued over $5 million in Federal contracts and grants on behalf of client health care companies.
- Secured $350,000 grant under Small Business Innovative Research grant program for biotechnology research company.
- Negotiated agreement with foreign universities to conduct research trials of client firm's medical products.
- Obtained substantial private financing for client seeking to market anti-smoking apparatus.

A careful reading of Ms. Sharp's generalist resume reveals that she could, if she wished, also prepare several other targeted resumes: litigation, for example, or lobbying/public affairs.

We hope it is apparent that a targeted resume is invariably a stronger document, much more impressive to future employers.

✓ Mistake No. 34: Using a Resume Preparation Service for the Wrong Reasons

---

If at all possible, do not engage a commercial resume preparation service to actually **write** your resume.

In the first place, writing your own resume can be a valuable experience. It will force you to focus on your past experience in order to distill out the facts most important to your future. As your career goals change, your retrospective analysis of positions held in the past may need revision as well. You are not the same person you were five years ago. When you initially described a job you held from 1980-1986, you may have just left it. Looking back, you may now see many skills then acquired or responsibilities assigned which you took for granted or overlooked. The passage of time gives us all a better perspective on past events, and maturity should give us the ability to synopsize that experience in a more cogent and effective way.

In the second place, no matter what your profession, you undoubtedly know more about what is important to explain about your experience and background than someone who is **not** familiar with that profession. A computer programmer would find it difficult to craft a strong resume for an architect, or an architect for a biologist. So, don't put an outsider, a professional writer of resumes, in charge of distilling and describing **your** professional qualifications.

In the third place, resume preparation services are businesses, which depend on volume to produce a profit, so their resumes all tend to look alike. They can't afford to personalize resumes for individual clients. The result is a "canned" resume that can be spotted immediately by most employers.

However, once you have down on paper exactly what you want to say in your resume, you can then turn to a commercial resume service for assistance (under your strict supervision) **in the graphic and stylistic presentation of the**

substantive resume material you have already drafted. Such a service can also arrange for the reproduction of multiple copies of your resume on high quality paper and can create professional-looking stationery (on matching paper) for you to use in your cover letters.

✔ Mistake No. 35: Not Using a Word Processor to Write Your Resume

---

Not everyone has access to a word processor. However, computers are becoming ubiquitous and, in all likelihood, you probably know someone who does have one. There will never be a more important reason to invoke this friendship than when it comes to preparing your resume.

• **Appearance.** A word processor attached to a letter-quality printer will give you a very nice-looking resume. It will look just like a good, clean typewritten resume. If you are fortunate enough to have access to a laser printer, you may be able to make your resume look as if it had been professionally typeset.

• **Flexibility.** The most important reason for doing your resume on a word processor is the flexibility this gives you. Not only does this technology make it easy to create two or three versions of your resume, it also allows you to make changes simply and inexpensively. If you have to change your address or phone number, or decide that something you experimented with on your resume is not working very well, a word-processed document is a lot easier to amend than one that had been typed or typeset.

Many resumes we see have been typeset by a professional typesetter. Twenty years ago a professionally typeset resume probably impressed a lot of prospective employers. No one is all that impressed anymore...especially since many people can't tell the difference between typesetting and laser printing. So, why waste your money? Typesetting alone (without any of the special composing or editing services that can go with it) will probably cost you at least $100. If you cannot get your resume word-processed, type it yourself.

However, typesetting can be useful in certain circumstances. If, after editing and winnowing, you cannot cut your resume down any further, and it is still much too long, a typeset resume may be the answer. Typesetting **can** accommodate more words in a given space, while retaining a neat, clean appearance. Of course, keep in mind that you can attain a typeset appearance by using a laser printer in conjunction with a word processing program with a multitude of type styles and font sizes.

CHAPTER FOUR: Resume Style And Format Mistakes

One group of resume mistakes that can eliminate you from further consideration deals with questions of style and format. These items include matters affecting not only the appearance of the document but also how well it is written.

It is always discouraging to see a highly qualified job applicant present his or her background in a careless, unimpressive way. First impressions are always important, and in job hunting the first conclusions about your competence are frequently drawn from the appearance and tone of your resume.

✓ Mistake No. 36: Not Paying Attention to Style

Resume writers seem to fall into one of two categories. Either they are obsessed with how their resumes look, as opposed to what they say, or they are totally wrapped up in the substance of their resumes and style goes out the window. Both extremes are to be avoided. A little attention to style can pay big dividends.

Ideally, your stylistic goal (but not at the expense of substance) should be to use:

- wide margins (easier on the reader's eyes);

- plenty of white space;

- bold headings, bullets, or indentations (to draw attention to your key points); and

- a conservative, mainstream typeface that is easy to read.

These are goals, remember, and not absolutes. If you have wrestled with the substance of your resume for a long time and have to sacrifice something, better to sacrifice a few centimeters of margin than some essential facts about yourself.

The resume example we discussed earlier, that of John Power (see p. 55), could be reorganized to demonstrate the use of these points. As you can see on the following page, this presentation is easier to read and visually separates the items included in the experience sections. It also allows his job achievements to be identified as such and to be set off by the same kind of bullets.

John Power

123 Main Street, Smallville, Kansas 66101   (H) 913/555-4567; (O) 913/555-4321

EXPERIENCE

1987-Present

Management Analyst, Kansas Limited, Smallville, KS
- Analyze production and distribution operations to increase productivity and improve efficiency.
- Advise senior management on findings and recommendations.
- Assist in implementing innovations that were approved.

Achievements:
- Recommended contracting-out of machine tool maintenance functions, resulting in 15 percent reduction of downtime.
- Proposed new transportation quality control procedures that cut delivery time to major customer by average of two days per order.
- Awarded "Manager-of-the-Quarter" honors, resulting in 5 percent bonus.

1984-1987

Purchasing Officer, Topeka Edison, Topeka, KS
- Responsible for all purchasing functions of Line Repair Unit of $2 billion municipal utility.
- Determined best available sources of all unit hardware requirements.
- Examined source quality control and production capabilities.
- Negotiated purchase agreements.
- Monitored performance under contracts.

Achievements:
- Re-negotiated transformer contract resulting in $5 million savings to company.
- Identified and contracted with foreign wire splicing crimping toolmaker whose tools reduced line failure rate by 20 percent.

1980-1984

Inventory Control Specialist, Consolidated Equipment, Kansas City, MO
Responsible for assorted inventory functions, including:
- correlating arrival of ordered items with business operational requirements;
- quarterly inventory audits;
- streamlining ordering procedures in order to reduce paperwork;
- coordinating point-of-sale operations with computerized warehouse procedures;
- supervising extensive inventory computerization program; and
- advising procurement officers as to hardware and software requirements.

Achievements:
- Reduced inventory costs by more than 15 percent.
- During job tenure, audit questions decreased by 25 percent.

1978-1980

Management Trainee, Consolidated Equipment, Kansas City, MO
- Trained in all aspects of diversified firm's operations, including personnel, inventory, purchasing, leasing, pricing, production, distribution, and accounting.
- Successfully completed all rotations in top 10 percent of recruiting class.

EDUCATION

B.A., Business Administration, 1982
Kansas State University

Honors and Activities

Dean's List--three semesters
Business Club Membership Director
Volunteer at Family Shelter

REFERENCES

Available upon request

▶ Being Overly Obsessed with Style ◀

This is the opposite extreme. Unless you are looking for a job in the graphics business, an advertising agency, or a field that puts a high premium on creativity and novelty, avoid fancy or unusual deviations from the norm, such as bizarre type styles, oversized or undersized paper, paper of unusual weight or color, unique formats, etc. These gimmicks will definitely get you noticed, but perhaps not in quite the way you had in mind. In all likelihood, the reader will call up all his buddies and they'll share a good laugh at your expense.

A conservative approach should also be used toward **all** type style/graphic embellishments, such as underlines, boldfaced words, italics, stars, bullets, varying sizes of type, etc. Used sparingly, these tools can make a point or emphasize an important facet of your resume. But an injudicious use of embellishments, especially a complex **mixture** of graphic embellishments, can be distracting...and may show you lack a sense of style.

✓ Mistake No. 37: Using the Wrong Paper

First impressions are very important. The kind and quality of paper you use for your resume is one of the first things an employer will notice. For the vast majority of positions, anything other than a white, off-white, or pale grey bond paper should be avoided. Exotic papers and colors are generally unacceptable. The only possible exception is if you are involved in a graphic arts or comparable profession and you want to impress prospective employers in the field with your color literacy and sense of style. However, even there, you have to be careful. It is almost always risky to venture beyond the mainstream.

Further, the paper should be high quality bond paper, the kind used for stationery not the kind routinely used in copiers. Nothing is more discouraging than to open an application and find a resume that has been reproduced on cheap copier paper. The impression given is that the candidate either did not care about making a good impression or didn't know any better.

✓ Mistake No. 38: Preparing a Resume that is Too Long

Although personnel professionals often say that there are two schools of thought about long versus short resumes, don't believe it. Just ask anyone responsible for reading a lot of resumes which one they prefer. What do you think the answer would be? A short resume wins every time, preferably condensed onto one page.

People who read resumes as part of their livelihood are busy people. More important, even if they are not really any more overworked than the rest of us, they *perceive* themselves to be unusually busy people, under constant pressure and harassment from higher-ups to get new employees processed and hired. If reviewing your resume takes twice as much of their time because it exceeds the anticipated single-page length, you'd better have MORE than twice as much of value to say about yourself. In 1988 when he was running for president, George Bush presented the highlights of his life in a one-page resume. If someone who had been a Congressman, businessman, U.S. Senate candidate, Republican National Chairman, U.N. Ambassador, envoy to China, CIA Director, and Vice President could do that, we bet that you could, too.

If that is not reason enough to keep down the length of your resume, here's another strong argument for it: It is much more challenging and demanding to have to condense your life experience into a short resume, without losing your distinctiveness, than to write a book about yourself. It will take you longer, but the end result will be a much higher quality product, because you will have had to be a particularly sharp writer and editor to say the important things about yourself in the limited space available.

If, after thoroughly analyzing your personal history, you decide you cannot possibly keep the length of your resume within manageable limits, remember what we said about word processing or typesetting. Both will enable you to pick up anywhere from 15-40% more data about yourself per page, depending on technical decisions concerning which type style, pitch, and spacing mode to use. This will allow even the handful of job hunters who must go over one page to give the appearance of a short resume.

There are at least two alternatives available to get around the dilemma of too much to say in too little space. The most effective ones we have found are:

1. *A summary sheet.* One way around the length problem is to prepare a one-page summary of your resume that serves as a kind of cover sheet for the longer

version. If you feel you must do this, make sure you put the most crucial data about yourself near the top of the summary sheet.

2. *A "transactional addendum."* If it is killing you to have to condense all the significant things you have done during your working years in order to cram them all into a resume, consider appending a one-page addendum, labeled as such, in which you leisurely summarize your most compelling job-related "transactions." The selections for the addendum should, of course, be limited to only those that show your work-related achievements in the best possible light. If you are aching to tell prospective employers that you negotiated a deal with suppliers that saved your company $100,000 per year, but can't find room in the body of your resume, this is a very effective place to do that. It also gives a clean and neat orderliness to the document and does not technically violate any presumptions about length, since it is not really a part of the resume itself.

In our earlier example concerning the resume Marvella Sharp, she could have shortened the presentation of her experience by extracting selected items for inclusion in an addendum. In this way, she would be able to enhance the readability of her basic resume (more white space, fewer words), yet impress the reader with the substance and quality of her accomplishments:

ADDENDUM

• As lead counsel, successfully recouped over $1.3 billion from a single energy company, the second-largest single recovery ever by the U.S. Government. This complex action resulted in a one-month trial in which the team that I led prevailed over a Fortune 50 defendant represented by a team of attorneys from the nation's largest law firms. I was responsible for developing trial strategy, coordinating exchanges of information between the investigative and enforcement staffs and agency counsel, as well as among four Federal departments and agencies.

• Planned and directed extensive investigations of on-shore and off-shore oil and gas lease sales, resulting in revelations of conflict-of-interest and inside information. Upon my recommendation, the House Special Committee established as its initial priority determining why the Government did not appear to be earning a fair share of oil and gas royalties from leases sold by the Department of the Interior to energy firms. An analysis of the implementation of royalty accounting regulations revealed many abuses costing the Government hundreds of millions of dollars per year in lost revenues.

• Developed computerized analysis of pricing data demonstrating substantial underpayments in Federal energy lease sales and presented findings to committee members and senior staff. On the basis of these findings, the Committee decided to consider and ultimately mark up landmark legislation establishing rigorous new bidding procedures for Government energy leases. The legislation was eventually enacted by the House of Representatives (a companion bill was enacted by the Senate and the House-Senate Conference Committee compromise was subsequently signed into law by the President).

✓ Mistake No. 39: Cramming Everything onto One Page

The admonition about avoiding an excessively long resume is beaten into job hunters so incessantly that, instead of editing their material, they do their utmost to **squeeze everything they can onto just one page.** Their resumes look like a solid block of black type, edge-to-edge, top-to-bottom. This treatment rarely looks presentable, so don't do it.

The dictionary defines the word "resume" as a "summing up." Resumes are supposed to be **succinct summaries of your credentials and qualifications;** not detailed, autobiographical, stream-of-consciousness renditions of personal minutiae. Remember:

- Resumes require choices.
- You have to decide which facts would be the most relevant and salient for a particular employer.
- Having done that, you must forge them into a hierarchy from the most important to the least important.

There are also some tricks of the trade you can employ to save space. For example:

• *Economize on personal pronouns.* Everyone reading your resume knows that **you** were the actor who performed all of the activities described. You do not have to pommel the reader with constant reminders, such as:

"I advised homeowners on the salability of their properties. I appraised properties new on the market. I negotiated listing agreements with sellers. I listed homes for sale on the multiple listing service. I placed advertising for listed homes in the newspapers. I showed homes for sale to prospective purchasers. I acted as an intermediary in negotiations between buyers and sellers. I drafted sales agreements satisfactory to both parties. I attended settlements in order to expedite the transactions and troubleshoot any last-minute problems."

I...I...I...I...I....The job hunter who put together this paragraph would lose nothing by eliminating all but the first "I" and substituting semi-colons for the periods:

70

"I advised homeowners on the salability of their properties; appraised properties new on the market; negotiated listing agreements with sellers; listed homes for sale on the multiple listing service; placed advertising...."

This small change is quite an improvement. In addition to being a crisper presentation, the second version is also less egotistical and, therefore, less offensive.

• *Avoid adjectives.* They take up space and are usually unnecessary and boring to read.

"I advised <u>current</u> homeowners on the <u>potential</u> salability of their <u>residential</u> properties."

The underlined words, all adjectives purportedly modifying the nouns that follow, add absolutely nothing to the sense of this sentence. They merely take up valuable space.

• *Try to avoid all dependent clauses.*

"*As a real estate agent*, I advised homeowners on the salability of their properties."

Presumably, you have already indicated that you worked as a real estate agent. There is no need to repeat it in your description. Dependent clauses are even worse offenders than adjectives. They consume scads of precious space that could be better used for another purpose--such as detailing job accomplishments.

• *Don't worry that your resume does not conform to the strict grammatical rules of expository writing.* You are not writing an essay or short story but a deliberately condensed summary of your background. Employers allow some leeway for necessary condensations and deviations from strict grammatical rules, particularly with respect to sentence fragments, such as:

> • edited a weekly newsletter sent to 900 employees
> • wrote press releases
> • assisted in preparing the company's annual report

In most industries, your writing style, even if central to the position for which you are applying, will not be judged on the basis of your resume. You will probably be asked to submit writing samples for that purpose. However, if your resume is **poorly** written in terms of grammar, punctuation, incorrect word usage, logical sequence, or ability to be succinct, you will not be given the opportunity to submit a writing sample.

71

✓ Mistake No. 40: Wasting Vital Resume Space

The effective use of space on a resume is crucial. The way you utilize space on your resume is often the difference between landing an interview for a job and getting passed over at the outset.

The reason is simple: If you waste space, you will need a longer resume. That means you will be forcing the person who reads your resume to sift through more material in search of that kernel of distinction that sets you apart from your competition. What makes you think the reader will stay with your resume until the "real you" is finally unearthed? In all likelihood, he or she probably will not. Hunting for nuggets of gold in the Yukon can be exciting; being forced to hunt through a resume for key items is tedious and annoying.

A sensible approach to space utilization on your resume can also save you from being a victim of the "20-Second Rule" we discussed earlier. Here are some key points to keep in mind when planning the format of your resume:

• **Don't use excessive margins.** Many resume writers think they cannot begin their resumes unless they are already one-third of the way down the page from the top. Margins of one inch at the top and bottom and on both sides are perfectly standard and acceptable. Job hunters often assume that resume information is different, somehow, and must be crammed into only one portion of a sheet of paper, such as the central core or the right half. There are no rules beyond common sense and graphic acceptability as to where the information should be placed. Don't make life more difficult by artificially restricting yourself to 50 percent of the space available. The two sample formats on the following pages illustrate the startling differences in the amount of information you can include in the same space by altering your format slightly.

• **Don't go overboard skipping spaces.** Resumes frequently contain much more "white" space than lines of information. This is totally unnecessary. It is possible to be both sparing in the number of spaces skipped and still produce a neat and presentable resume.

• **Don't ignore the space on the left-hand side of the page.** Too many job hunters work themselves into a real space fix by adopting a model resume obtained from a career placement office or some book on the subject. The majority of these samples use a layout something like the following section of a resume used to illustrate the point:

Numero Cruncher

333 Jumping Bean Way, Hamlet, IN 46202. (W) 317/555-0000; (H) 317/555-1212

PROFESSIONAL EXPERIENCE

1991-Present   **Comptroller, Smith and Jones, Ltd., Indianapolis, IN**
- Implement financial management policies, procedures, and internal controls for subsidiary of national corporation.
- Oversee audit resolution and correction of material weaknesses within subsidiary.
- Ensure management controls are adequate to prevent fraud, waste, and mismanagement.
- Advise Chief Financial Officer and program managers on financial management issues.
- Prepare financial statements.
- Supervise accounting staff.

1990-1991   **Comptroller, Hoosier University, Indianapolis, IN**
- Supervised and coordinated University accounting and financial reporting.
- Managed prompt collection of student accounts.
- Accounted for and reported on disbursement of Federal and state grants and contracts.
- Assisted in managing University budget.

Look at how much valuable space on the left side is completely wasted, probably close to one-third of the page.

When you are struggling with the dilemma of how to cram all the key data about yourself into a resume of manageable length, you cannot afford to do this. Sure, this format looks great. It's neat, orderly, and very easy on the eyes. But if it causes you to leave out, or defer revealing until later, important information about your work experience and achievements, it won't get you an interview or a job. Then you can take your artistic masterpiece home and hang it on your wall so that you can contemplate it while you are filling out your application for unemployment insurance.

Let's examine another way to present this same information using a different resume format, a format that takes full advantage of the side margins:

73

Numero Cruncher

333 Jumping Bean Way, Hamlet, IN 46202. (W) 317/555-0000; (H) 317/555-1212

PROFESSIONAL EXPERIENCE

1991-Present   Comptroller, Smith and Jones, Ltd., Indianapolis, IN
Responsible for implementing financial management policies, procedures, and internal controls for subsidiary of national corporation. Duties include overseeing audit resolution and correction of material weaknesses within subsidiary; ensuring management controls are adequate to prevent fraud, waste, and mismanagement; advising the Chief Financial Officer and program managers on financial management issues; preparing financial statements; and supervising accounting staff.

1990-1991   Comptroller, Hoosier University, Indianapolis, IN
Supervised and coordinated University accounting and financial reporting. Managed prompt collection of student accounts. Accounted for and reported on disbursement of Federal and state grants and contracts. Assisted in managing University budget.

This same portion of the experience section of the second resume is seven lines of text shorter than the experience section on the first resume yet it contains exactly the same information. This means the writer has seven "extra" lines to work with. He would either be able to expand the experience sections to aggregate the same number of lines, or he could include additional information elsewhere on his resume.

✓ Mistake No. 41: Putting the Least Significant Information About Yourself at the Top of Your Resume

Resume reviewers see a large number of applications. They tend to scan resumes very rapidly (remember the "20-Second Rule") and form instant conclusions about the caliber of an applicant. They want to see the key information about you right away. You have to grab their attention quickly. If you make them search for your winning attributes, the chances are they won't take the time to find them. Your finest qualities will go undiscovered. So, make certain that you put the most important information about yourself on the **top half of the first page of your resume**. That way, it is sure to be seen.

Think of your resume as a newspaper article. Journalistic style calls for a hierarchical approach to news writing. The first thing reporters are taught in journalism school is to structure articles so that the most important information leads off, followed by the second most important information, and so on. This makes it easy on both the busy reader, who may not have time to read the whole news report, and on the editor who has to be conscious of space limitations.

The key questions you have to ask yourself are: What is the most important information about me? What qualities--in terms of education or experience--are most likely to attract the attention of the employer? Which of my skills or abilities would be most valuable for the kind of position I seek?

There is no easy answer that applies to everyone, since you are unique, with your own personal history and life experiences. For most people, work experience will come first. However, there are several exceptions (see below) as well as a few guidelines you can use:

• **If you are in school or are a recent graduate,** such as our hypothetical Susan Smooth, on the following page, present your education first. Lacking "seasoning," Ms. Smooth must highlight her education rather than her work experience. Consequently, she has reversed the more customary order of presentation, placing her educational background before her work experience. Note that, unlike the other sample resumes, this one identifies references. This is an option that anyone, not only a new member of the work force, may select, given available space. Of course, it is much easier for a recent graduate without extensive work experience to find space to list references.

• **In contrast, if you are out of school and have been in the work force for more than one year,** put your work experience first.

• **If you have just received a graduate degree** but had to work at a variety of jobs while pursuing this degree, put your education first. For example: If you bounced around from small company to small company for a number of years while working toward an MBA from Stanford, your Stanford credentials should lead off the resume.

The choice of what to put first in a resume is, of course, is not merely between work experience and education. Depending upon your unique background, there may be other items that should be considered in your resume "positioning" strategy.

• **If you have been a job-hopper or career-hopper, or have been out of the workforce for an extended period of time,** put a summary of skills or qualifications first.

• **If you have been in the work force for ten or more years,** and have held a series of jobs during that time, put a summary of skills or qualifications first. Make sure it clarifies for the reader what job or career you are now seeking.

EDUCATION   B.A., Human Resources Management, 1992
                           University of Illinois
                           • Dean's List, five semesters
                           • Intercollegiate Field Hockey Team
                           • Gamma Gamma Gamma Sorority

PROFESSIONAL EXPERIENCE

Summer, 1991   **Personnel Intern, Windy City Communications Inc., Chicago, IL**
                           • Assisted in all aspects of multi-billion dollar corporation's human resources
                             function, including recruitment, equal employment opportunity, affirma-
                             tive action, staffing, promotions policy, job classification, compensation,
                             employee benefits, employee development, adverse actions, grievance
                             proceedings, and outplacement counseling.
                           • Contributed to special study on health care cost containment.

Summer, 1990   **Administrative Assistant, Superior Life Insurance Co., Champaign, IL**
                           • Coordinated claims document flow among several sections of corporate
                             headquarters monitoring division.
                           • Briefed claims supervisors on status of complex cases.

Summer, 1989   **Employee Development Specialist, Training & Performance Development
                           Unit, Illinois Department of Central Management Services, Springfield, IL**
                           • Assisted in evaluation of major state programs and policies designed to
                             strengthen management competency throughout the Illinois Civil Service.
                           • Participated in meetings with state agency career development committees
                             and other senior level executives.
                           • Contributed to study of various courses and job aids conducive to improving
                             management skills.

REFERENCES   Theresa Thorne, Ph.D., School of Business, University of Illinois,
                           Champaign, IL 61801. Tel: 217/555-1234

                           Prof. Steven Shark, School of Business, University of Illinois,
                           Champaign, IL 61801. Tel: 217/555-2345

                           Brinkley Stone, Director of Personnel, Windy City Communications Inc.,
                           Centennial Plaza, Chicago, IL 60606. Tel: 312/555-6789

Remember, these are merely guidelines and not hard and fast rules. There are an infinite number of exceptions, depending on your own background. For example:

If you won the Nobel Prize for Economics, don't put that after the fact that you graduated with a B.A. in Economics from Great Salt Lake University, or that you have been working for Amalgamated, Inc. in Loose Ridge, Montana, for the last five years.

If you have spent the better part of the last two decades meditating in Katmandu, Nepal, but are now ready to join the workforce, you may want to put a skills summary first. Similarly, if you are returning to work after several years out raising a family, a summary of skills or qualifications should lead off your resume. See the "Super Mom" resume example on page 58.

Two Final Thoughts on This Topic:

1. Evaluate all options and construct a sequence for your biographical information that will present **your** qualifications with the most impact.

2. Always keep in mind that one of the central purposes of a resume is to illustrate **how your past education and experience can contribute to the employer's current and future needs**. So, use a little common sense: place at the top of your resume the information that will favorably impress the employer in terms of the job to be filled.

✓ Mistake No. 42: Including a Photograph of Yourself with Your Resume

---

In the 1970's it became in vogue for job applicants to include photographs of themselves with their resumes. That's great if you are applying for a modeling job...or if you want to be a movie or TV star. But if you want to work as a Management Trainee for AT&T, an editor for a weekly magazine, or an engineer for a public utility, who cares?

Under certain circumstances your picture may help you get an interview...if you look like Robert Redford or Whitney Houston...but there are still a lot of people out there with irrational biases. In a time when most people are fighting against being evaluated on superficial, irrelevant criteria, do not give anyone the opportunity to disqualify you before you get out of the starting blocks. Your age, race, sex, national origin, etc., are not relevant in the employment screening process and should not be presented to the employer via a photo attached to your resume.

✓ Mistake No. 43: Ignoring the Name Game

Despite all the affirmative action programs and prohibitions against discrimination on the basis of any non-merit factor, some women seeking jobs in professional fields dominated by men still have problems. Most women feel they could prove their abilities on-the-job, but the first hurdle is getting hired. To get hired they have to reach the interview stage. To reach the interview stage they have to hope their paper credentials, their resumes, will survive the initial review process. To avoid elimination before the real job competition begins, some professional women do not use their full first names on their resumes but use initials instead. Rather than Marie Curie or Susan B. Anthony, they put M. Curie or S. B. Anthony. This strategy has worked, on occasion, for some women. It allows the preliminary reviewer to concentrate on the candidate's **credentials** rather than that individual's **sex**. The same advice would apply to men seeking employment in fields dominated by women, such as nursing.

If you are a man who has a sexually ambiguous first name, you might want to make sure any lingering bias toward men works in your favor by resolving that ambiguity immediately on your resume: Mr. Carol Throckmorton, Mr. Joyce Kilmer.

Applicants of either sex should avoid nicknames, even if you HATE your given name and everyone calls you "Buffy." Names such as "Buffy" and "Chip" don't sound professional, they sound adolescent and cute--like someone you'd hire to mow your lawn or baby sit.

✓ Mistake No. 44: Overusing Buzzwords in Your Resume

Once when we were doing a seminar on job hunting, a member of the audience came up during a break and asked our impression of his resume. Under work experience, he described the responsibilities of his last job in this way:

> Drafted DOD rules and regs on DOA, DON, USAF, and USMC's (& USCG in time-of-war) DOPMA and ROPMA staffing requirements and obligations in the event of a 50 U.S.C. 447, as amended (Act of 14 June 1947, ch. 6, §17(a)(1)(ii), 49 Stat. 1685) mobilization; liaised with HASC, SASC, DMDC, DMA, DNA, UUHS, JCS, and other DOD components, and with Unified and Specified Commands on pending legislation and regulatory proposals; advised ASD (ISA), PDASD (Antiterrorism), and DASD (RA) on personnel and national security law issues; and coordinated legislative development of legislative program for GC office.

Government employees and veterans do this a lot. Their excuse for using tons of organizational or occupational jargon (that is virtually unintelligible to anyone outside their work environment) is that they are so used to speaking in these terms that they have forgotten how everyone else communicates.

But they are not the only ones who arouse the ire of prospective employers in this way. Many other job applicants are also guilty of the same transgression.

What few people realize is that not everyone who will review their applications is an expert in their field or even has the remotest idea what all the acronyms and special buzzwords mean. In many large organizations in the public and private sectors, job applications are reviewed initially by personnel specialists whose training is in **personnel issues**, not in the substance of a specific profession. Then, the resumes of those who survive the first round may be submitted to a "rating panel" consisting of current employees who **may or may not be** members of the professional group in question. If they are not, they will have little or no understanding of the applicant's professional jargon and will treat the application accordingly.

While "insider talk" may be acceptable in the limited situation where you are submitting a resume for a position within your current organization and/or career field, it is *totally unacceptable* in any other circumstance. Individuals trying to move from one employment sector to another (for example, from the public sector to the private sector) and anyone else attempting a career transition, should be the ones most conscious of avoiding this mistake. Unfortunately, they are usually its worst offenders.

"Career transition" is a very broad concept covering many types of individual situations: movements among the private, public, and nonprofit sectors; moving from one type of career to another; or translating the skills acquired in one environment to another. All three of these transitional situations are represented in some way in the example below, that of a career soldier separating from the U.S. Army. As in the earlier example of someone returning to the work force, anyone switching careers should consider devising a summary of skills or qualifications in order to assist prospective employers determine how the candidate's background could contribute to the employer's organization.

Murphy York's resume, on the next page, demonstrates a way to recast work experience when undertaking a major career move. Note (1) the almost total absence of "insider" (in this case, military) jargon, and (2) the effort Sergeant York made to redefine his military experience in terms civilian employers could understand.

Make the effort to prepare a document that anyone can understand. Sure, it will probably take you more time, but it will be time well spent.

Murphy York

121 Magnolia Lane, Fayetteville, NC 28303. (W) 919/555-6543; (H) 919/555-9876

Skills Summary

Over 15 years of experience in management education and training, budgeting, recruiting, and administrative support. My background includes working both in a supervisory, leadership capacity and as part of a team charged with promoting professional development and improving performance and productivity.

Experience

1989-Present **Reserve Training Coordinator, Fort Bragg, NC**
- Identify U.S. Army Reserve training needs and priorities for over 12,000 reservists performing summer training at Fort Bragg.
- Develop successful short and long-term training strategies.
- Plan integrated budget and administrative support to satisfy various mobilization scenarios.
- Monitor changes to U.S. Army Training Management System and both military and civilian training literature.
- Directly responsible for mobilization training of units participating in Operations Desert Shield and Desert Storm.

1986-1989 **Senior Education & Training Specialist, U.S. Army Training Center, Fort Irwin, CA**
- Planned extensive exercises for battalion and brigade-size infantry units.
- Supervised preparation of complex hypothetical "war gaming" problems.
- Evaluated training plans and exercise proposals for diverse military units.

1982-1986 **Instructor, Army Institute for Professional Development, Fort Eustis, VA**
- Taught over 4,000 students in the Adjutant General Noncommissioned Officer Education System.
- Supervised lesson plan preparation by junior staff.
- Prepared selected instructor personnel to undertake teaching responsibilities.

1979-1982 **Education Center Assistant, U.S. Army, Furth, Germany**
- Recruited faculty for post-secondary education courses with affiliated U.S. colleges and universities in a wide variety of curriculum fields.
- Participated in planning semester course offerings for more than 5,000 soldiers and dependents.
- Drafted and disseminated promotional information about Education Center activities.

1976-1979 **Administrative Assistant, Office of the Adjutant General, The Pentagon, Washington, DC**
- Supported staff professionals in all phases of Army administration.
- Served as liaison with administrative personnel throughout Headquarters, U.S. Army.
- Drafted Army Regulations, office administrative directives, and instructional memoranda for distribution throughout the U.S. Army worldwide.

1972-1976 **Miscellaneous Assignments in Vietnam and the United States**

Education

B.A., Business Administration, Troy State University, Troy, AL
- Obtained degree in evenings, weekends, and during annual leaves.

Honors and Awards

- Army Commendation Medals
- Department of Defense Service Medal
- Combat Infantry Badge

References Available Upon Request

✓ Mistake No. 45: Failing to "Universalize" Your Experience

Job hunters invariably assume that job titles and responsibilities are uniform among employers. However, that is rarely true and such an assumption can often lead to an extended period of unemployment. Let's illustrate this point by an extreme example, that of a member of the armed forces seeking to make the transition to the civilian work force. If any part of your resume reads something along the following lines, you may be in serious job hunting trouble:

> **Specialist Fifth Class Squad Leader, ADM Team, HHC, 82d Engineer Battalion**
>
> Headed team of special weapons specialists tasked with maintenance, repair, and targeting of tactical nuclear devices; supervised team armored personnel carrier and other vehicles and was responsible for their readiness condition at all times; participated in border exercises designed to test team response time and weapons expertise under all conditions; rated outstanding on Skills Qualifying Test and all IG inspections; developed security access control procedures adopted by special weapons storage sites throughout NATO area.

Anyone reading this gobbledygook would scratch his or her head in befuddlement. What does it all mean? How could this person fit in with my company? I give up!

However, if the military job hunter had **translated his experience into terms comprehensible to the average employer**, he could have come up with something like this:

> **Branch Chief, U.S. Army**
>
> Served as first-line supervisor of six-person unit charged with sole responsibility for company assets worth $60 million; managed complex maintenance and repair functions for assets, including four vehicles; successfully completed all testing of branch readiness and was commended for branch productivity by superior officers; and developed vital industrial security procedures adopted by all similar branches throughout Europe.

This version has brought our job hunter squarely within the realm of the civilian world. He has adopted, where possible, terminology understood by virtually all employers and made them feel far more comfortable about his application. He has "universalized" his job title and skills, and as a result, is far more likely to get a job he wants than if he had gone ahead with the first version.

✓ Mistake No. 46: Sounding Pompous

This mistake, at first glance, appears related to Mistake No. 57, the one about lying or exaggerating on your resume. It is, in the sense that when you use grandiose words or a pompous way of expressing yourself, you are apt to do so in order to show that you are a highly educated person who usually talks that way. In that sense, you are bragging. You may also sound affected and risk ridicule.

This effect is particularly common among those who write a "career objective" statement at the beginning of their resumes. For example, one resume we received this year began with the following:

> **Career Objective:** A leadership position which would allow me to demonstrate my outstanding administrative and managerial skills, my energy and resourcefulness, and my determination to strive for success.

When you prepare a resume, simplify your language. **Try to imagine the impact each statement will have on the reader.** Pompous statements (like the example above) are always inappropriate, whatever your age or circumstance.

✓ Mistake No. 47: Inconsistent Grammar and Boring Verbs

Employers love to get together and trade "war stories" about the worst and most bizarre resumes they have ever encountered. Often, the point they are making involves inconsistencies in grammar or style. For example: The resume writer may use complete sentences to describe his current or most recent job and may then, inexplicably, switch to short phrases and clauses to describe his former jobs. What this tells the employer is that this individual is careless, one who could not even be bothered to check his work for internal consistency. If you are a sloppy writer/editor on your own resume, why should anyone assume you would improve when dealing with company documents?

Another example involves experienced workers and job hunters who short-cut the resume preparation process by exhuming their old documents and "piggy-backing" new information on the old form. What they usually end up with is a series of work experience blocks all expressed **in the present tense**, since when they prepared each prior resume, it **was** the present. This kind of laxity--and the ambiguity it produces--indicates that the applicant was too lazy or uncaring to craft a new, timely resume.

If you seek a position in which the ability to communicate effectively is important (and in today's world that is true of most jobs), you can forget it if you make this mistake. When you proofread your resume, check it carefully to detect any internal inconsistencies.

▶ Using the Wrong Tense ◀

A common error made by resume writers is the use of the wrong tense in describing work experience. Often, you see someone describe his **present** job responsibilities as follows:

> "I wrote position papers for the Mayor and advised him on the day-to-day supervision of his public affairs and press relations staff."

Similarly, resume writers frequently describe **past** jobs in this way:

> "I perform many administrative tasks for the firm. I also prepare reports on budget matters."

Use the present tense to describe your current job and the past tense to describe all past employment. If you confuse the present tense with the past tense, even a semi-alert reviewer of your resume would conclude that you are either careless or worse.

Corollary to the Proper Tense Rule: Don't change or mix tenses in the middle of your descriptions. If you are describing a job you no longer have, use only the past tense. If you are discussing the responsibilities of your current position, use only the present tense.

However, if you describe your accomplishments or include "accomplishments" sections on your resume, always use verbs in the past tense to describe those achievements--even those related to current employment. (See the version of John Power's resume on page 66 or the portion of Earnestine Eager's resume on page 96.)

If you are writing a functional resume, all of the kinds of experience and skills acquired are described in the past tense.

Four

► Using the Third Person ◄

Resumes are first-person documents, with the "I" either stated or understood. Writing about yourself in the third-person by using "he" or "she" always sounds incredibly affected and outrageous. You are not royalty and a resume is not a novel. It is a summary of **your** education and experience, not someone else's.

► Not Using Action Verbs ◄

Nothing is duller or more desensitizing than reading a resume replete with inactive verbs--or without any verbs at all. It is a sure way to get your resume buried at the bottom of the pile.

One way to lessen the chances of having your resume consigned to oblivion is to give it a little zip through the use of action verbs. The place to do this is in describing your work experience. Instead of saying you "did" this and that, spice up your resume by using verbs such as:

administered	edited	investigated	provided
analyzed	established	managed	published
automated	evaluated	negotiated	recommended
conducted	examined	obtained	repaired
coordinated	expanded	organized	researched
created	identified	operated	resolved
developed	implemented	participated	reviewed
devised	increased	persuaded	supervised
designed	installed	planned	streamlined
directed	instituted	prepared	trained
earned	introduced	produced	wrote

Instead of saying:

"I was responsible for the day-to-day operations of the Remodification Division of the company."

try:

"I managed and supervised the company's Remodification Division."

(See, in addition to a much snappier presentation, you have also saved some space!)

If you are having trouble finding the right verbs to use, go to a thesaurus. Most popular word processing software programs now have very extensive easy-to-use thesauruses.

▶ Using the Passive (Instead of the Active) Voice ◀

The passive voice is in disfavor for resumes and for most other writing as well. It is called passive because, when using it, the subject of the sentence is acted upon, as in: "His failure to write a good resume showed that enthusiasm was lacking in him."

The active voice is preferred in almost all circumstances; certainly when writing a resume. The active voice is so labeled because, when it is properly used, the subject of the sentence **does** something, i.e., "acts." The example above, rewritten in the active voice, sounds like this: "His failure to write a good resume showed that he lacked enthusiasm."

The active voice version of this sentence is quite an improvement over the passive voice version. It is more direct and forceful. The active voice is a stronger voice. Moreover, it usually takes fewer words to say something in the active voice. Being able to say something in fewer words is vital in a resume.

Before you finalize your draft resume, review it in terms of the voice you used and change all incidents of passive voice to active voice.

✓ Mistake No. 48: Failing to Proofread Your Resume

More than one unsuccessful job hunter can tell you that he did not get the job because of a small mistake on his resume. Personnel specialists who get to look at hundreds of resumes each month say that an enormous number of them contain some flaw--either a typographical error, a blatant error in grammar or usage, or an obviously unintended gap in the work or educational history.

Would you hire someone careless enough to send you a flawed resume? Probably not, since each employee is a reflection of you and your company.

The simplest thing in the world is to take a few minutes at the end of your resume preparation ordeal in order to check your work.

Here are the basic items you should check:

• **Spelling.** If you are not sure about the correct spelling of a word, look it up in the dictionary.

• **Grammar.** If you have trouble with grammatical rules and usage, ask someone--a knowledgeable friend, relative, classmate, or colleague--for help. If they offer conflicting opinions, change the sentence construction to avoid the problem altogether.

• **Dates.** Have you left any unintended gaps in your educational or work experience history? Have you created confusion due to overlapping dates? Be especially careful of discrepancies in dates involving when you went to different schools, held different jobs, won various awards, etc. Make certain these dates are consistent with each other.

• **Internal consistency.** Have you left any major gaps in your chronological record? Did you say one thing at the top of your resume and another at the end? Did you use capital letters to describe one position title, but not for another? Did you change styles in the middle of the document? Did you inadvertently change verb tenses? If you did any of these things, rereading your resume should uncover the oversight.

It is always a good idea to ask a friend or colleague to read your resume for obvious errors, ambiguity, or inconsistency. Remember, if you want that friend to be frank, don't get huffy and defensive about the points raised. If your resume raises questions in the mind of a friend or colleague, you can safely assume it will do the same in the mind of a total stranger.

✔ Mistake No. 49: Annotating Your Resume

Too many job hunters spend massive amounts of time and energy preparing crisp, concise, neat, and beautifully typewritten, word-processed, or typeset resumes, only to spoil the effect by using a pen or pencil to make annotations in the margins.

The typical person who makes this mistake undertakes a major initial effort to get his resume in shape, only to find several weeks or months later that some documented aspect of his life has changed and must be recorded on the resume. Wary of spending another chunk of time or money to revise his resume to reflect the updated information, he skimps a little and scribbles in the change by hand.

The effect on the reader is not pleasant. He forms an impression that the person who annotated the resume is (1) too lazy to invest what it takes, in time, effort, or money, to put together a neat document; (2) sloppy; (3) not seriously interested in the job; or (4) incapable of preparing documents properly. "Let's say we hire this guy," surmises the reviewer, "will he send out correspondence that looks like this? Will he send out company reports that look like this?" In the absence of any other information, the reviewer would have to assume the worst.

There are several ways to avoid this problem. The sensible thing to do is to produce a new, neat, professional-looking resume every time there is a change in your old one. If you have your resume professionally typeset, revising it may be expensive. Knowing that resume information will have to be updated in the near future is one good reason to avoid typesetting it. If you prepare your resume on a typewriter or a word processor, changing it later will be relatively easy.

No matter how well you have conquered questions of resume style and format, if the substantive information you present is flawed in some way you may be eliminated from serious consideration. Whether it is an inadvertent omission, misrepresentation, or the inclusion of irrelevant (and potentially harmful) information, substantive errors can be knock-out blows because they reflect qualities of judgment and character.

✓ Mistake No. 50: Not Providing Complete Identifying Information

We are occasionally asked to review resumes prepared by secret agents and superheroes. At any rate, we have to conclude that they practice these glamorous and exotic professions since they chose not to reveal their true identities in their resumes. We see resumes without the name of the job hunter, or lacking an address or telephone number. An inordinate number of these startling omissions have been found in otherwise impressive resumes.

An employer who receives a resume without complete identifying information will not waste much time reading and evaluating the mystery candidate who submitted it. What is the point, after all, if the applicant cannot be located to invite him or her for an interview or offer a position?

Make sure that you have identified yourself completely on your resume. That means your full name, your current mailing address, and complete telephone numbers (with area codes) where you can be reached at home and at work. Keep in mind that a future employer will try to reach you **during working hours**. It's your responsibility to make that possible.

If you are concerned about the confidentiality of your job search, and you do not have a private phone line at work, you can leave off a work number. Explain in a cover letter that you would prefer **not to be contacted at work**, since your current employer is unaware of your job search, but that messages can be left at your home number. If you choose this option, try to have a mature individual (or answering machine) prepared to handle calls during working hours at your home number. You cannot choose this option without a precise plan of action. Never provide a phone number that might remain unanswered because someone went out for the afternoon. When this has happened to us while reviewing resumes, we simply tossed the resume aside and rarely tried to phone that applicant again.

✔ Mistake No. 51: Cluttering Up Your Resume with Personal or Irrelevant Information

---

Personal data, such as your height, weight, age, marital status, number of children, disabilities, etc., are completely unnecessary on a resume. Moreover, including such information may do you more harm than good. What if your prospective employer hates children? What if you are a single mother raising ten children? What if you have been divorced three times? What if you weigh 400 lbs? What if you are under five feet tall? So what?

Each item of personal information raises questions about you, and permits the person reviewing your resume to find reasons to reject you. It does not matter in the least that the antidiscrimination laws are rife with pronouncements prohibiting employers from asking intrusive questions about your age, race, color, creed, national origin, disability, and even personal life, or from basing a decision not to hire you on these characteristics. In the real world, employers have prejudices. Whether legitimate or not, they play an enormously important role in life. People who play God every day, such as resume reviewers, tend to be more biased than others, for a variety of complex reasons. For one, they have to make snap judgments about people, and a few years of that kind of work makes them think their ability to size people up is unerring. If they (or their company) have had a bad experience with someone having one of these traits, their compulsion to classify people may lead them to conclude that everyone possessing the same characteristic will also be a loser or troublemaker.

If you freely volunteer information that places you squarely within the irrational bias of a reviewer, you can forget about the job. Since the initial reviewer is usually not the person who will be conducting the employment interview or making the hiring decision, why give this relatively low-level, first-line official the opportunity to reject you arbitrarily without giving the real decisionmaker a chance to get to know you?

Personal information is rarely relevant to the job for which you are applying. An employer can get a pretty accurate idea of your age from the dates of your education and experience. The rest is a potential mine field. Why invite problems? Forget it!

► Including Your Special Interests and Hobbies on Your Resume ◄

Like your personal data, a description of your hobbies and interests is usually a waste of space on your resume and, in some instances, a dangerous bit of information. So, why do so many job hunters drop in a few lines about mundane hobbies or recreational activities? After all, this is a serious employment search, not an appearance on a television game show.

In fact, most employers don't care about what you do with your evenings or on weekends. Provided, of course, that your activities do not interfere with or become a detriment to your performance on the job or a public embarrassment to your employer. The management of the New York Mets, for example, would not be pleased if their superstar pitcher roamed the country looking for arm-wrestling tournaments to enter on days he wasn't scheduled to pitch a baseball game.

Someone whose curse in life is being forced to read hundreds of resumes knows that virtually everyone puts down the same cliches under this category: reading, travel, theater, sports, jogging, "being with people," to name a few. Big deal. Hooray. Next resume, please.

We live in a conformist society made into a national village by television. It stands to reason that many of us have the same interests. Don't take up valuable resume space relating uninteresting and irrelevant facts about yourself.

Exception: If there is some unique activity that either (1) distinguishes you significantly from the competition, or (2) is directly related to and enhances your prospects of securing the job, then by all means include it on your resume.

For example: Are you a member or official of a professional organization? Have you taken the initiative to learn a craft or skill? Have you traveled or worked in foreign countries? Do you speak a foreign language? Have you ever managed a fundraising drive? Have you coached a Little League or other sports team? Are you a member of a musical group? Have you ever volunteered for a civic or municipal organization? Have you ever received an award or commendation for your volunteer activities?

Any of these characteristics would set you apart from the crowd. And anything that differentiates you **in a positive way** should be included on your resume. Make sure your prospective employer knows from reading your resume exactly what you have done that is special or unique.

A word of caution concerning religion and politics, which are both dangerous topics to include casually. If you want to work for the Archdiocese, then your church-related interests or volunteer work may be relevant. Or, if you want to work for your Senator or Congressman, then your volunteer activities on someone's political campaign might be in your favor. But, be careful. People come to blows over these topics, so don't use as "filler" something that's potentially dynamite.

✓ Mistake No. 52: Including a Career Objective on Your Resume

A few years ago it became popular to include some kind of career objective on a resume. In a field in which little has changed in a hundred years, so-called resume experts eagerly seized this "innovation" and suddenly the inclusion of a career objective in your resume, in fact at the very **top** of your resume, became a non-discretionary must. Many experts even alleged that a resume without a stated career objective would be automatically rejected.

After years of hoopla surrounding the career objective phenomenon, a few dissident voices arose and raised the uncomfortable question as to what purpose it served. No one could come up with a really defensible answer. After all, of what value is the information that you want a "rewarding career in which [you are] able to maximize [your] talents, background, and abilities." Who doesn't?

So, do not waste your precious time formulating an ultimate career objective. In a society that lives for the short term and in which the top executives of major corporations and government agencies stick around in their jobs for 18 months on average, don't feel obliged to broadcast to the world where you want to be in 25 years.

▶ Composing a Meaningless Career Objective ◀

We do recognize, however, that there are some cases where inclusion of a career objective at the beginning of a resume is not a bad idea. For example: If you have bounced around from one field to another, a prospective employer might be interested in knowing your *immediate* employment goal. A career objective on your resume might temper, somewhat, the overall impression that you are an individual lacking direction.

If you are one of those people who simply MUST include a career objective, then make sure you craft a real one, one that is clear and unambiguous, and not just a bunch of meaningless buzzwords strung together. Most career objectives that we have seen flunk this test. The following is quite representative:

> **Career Objective:** A challenging position in a dynamic company that will allow me to make a significant contribution to corporate goals.

91

What does this mean? Who would want a non-challenging job? Even if you do, you would not admit it on your resume. Who would want to work for a static, dull company? What is a significant contribution? Obviously, an objective like this one is a waste of time and space. It is amorphous drivel. A more effective statement might be:

> **Career Objective:** A sales management position that would allow me to combine my technical background in electrical engineering with my computer marketing experience in the U.S. and abroad.

A career objective should be a clear statement of the kind of position you are seeking **right now**, not the kind of position you hope to achieve by the end of the decade.

Be careful. Since the statement concerning your career objective typically appears at the top of your resume, it is the first item an employer examines. **If you have not taken the time to target your "objective" to reflect the exact nature of the job for which you are applying, most employers will immediately eliminate you from consideration.** Why interview someone looking for something not being offered? A safer approach would be to lead off with a summary of skills or qualifications, which allows the employer to make the connection between what you have to offer and what the company needs.

► Composing a Pushy Career Objective ◄

Any statement concerning your career objective should be expressed in modest terms. If you're in your 20's, an objective that sounds alarmingly like the job description of the company president will arouse ridicule. Don't be naive.

If you are in your 50's, and your work history shows that you could realistically hope to attain such a career objective (i.e., the top job in the company), then you would pose a very real threat to everyone you would replace or displace en route to your stated goal. If you're really **that** smart, you're too smart to make such a strategic error.

Now you can see why stating a long-term career objective can be so tricky-- and why the practice has fallen into disfavor.

✓ Mistake No. 53: Using "Canned" Job Descriptions in Your Resume

If you are not a student or very recent graduate, the meat of your resume will be the information you include about your present (if currently employed) and past jobs. This is the section of the document that will be studied the most carefully by a prospective employer. Yet despite the overwhelming importance of the job experience section, despite the fact that it is the turning point upon which most job offers depend, despite the enormous weight it is accorded by employers, many job seekers view it as a place in which to regurgitate their standard job descriptions. In fact, many job hunters who work for organizations that publish job descriptions use verbatim language from those job descriptions in their resumes.

If you are tempted to do this, don't!

Using a "canned" job description is a convenient substitute for thinking, but your resume is too important to be left to the person (or committee) who wrote a formal position description.

Formal position descriptions are also uniformly boring since they are written according to a rigid set of rules and formulas. The last thing you want to do is to make a prospective boss think you are boring.

Further, any employer or personnel specialist with any savvy at all can spot a canned job description a mile away, and will probably summarily reject any application relying on one. By sending canned language, you are telling the reviewing official that:

- you don't take the job hunting process very seriously;
- which means you probably won't take the job or the employer very seriously in the unlikely event you get hired; and
- you cut corners, always looking for the easy way out.

These are not traits an employer wants to see in a new employee.

There is an alternative. Take the time to think about what you do in your current job (and what you did in past positions) that is related to the position you are seeking, then draft, redraft, revise, hone, and fine-tune your work experiences until you are truly satisfied. Think before you start writing. Sweat the details. Make your job experiences interesting and attractive to the employer. Make the reader want to know more.

93

✓ Mistake No. 54: Forgetting to List Your Job Accomplishments on Your Resume

In describing their work experiences, almost all of your competitors for any job will limit their job descriptions to the duties and responsibilities they were **required** to perform in their present and past positions. The rare applicant who goes beyond a mere statement of job responsibilities is the one most likely to jump to the fast track. He is the one who will get his foot in the door. This is the astute job hunter you want to emulate.

How do you do this? What is the secret of writing a successful job description?

Simple. While the vast majority of job hunters are busy describing their job responsibilities, you are going to describe your **accomplishments** on the job, as well.

Highlighting your job accomplishments sets you apart from the crowd. It gets you noticed. If you fail to include legitimate job accomplishments, your resume will look just like everyone else's. Why, then, should an employer select you over all the other "look-alikes?" You have not given him any reason to pick you.

What qualifies as an accomplishment worthy of inclusion in a resume? Broadly speaking, almost anything that you had a hand in that improved something on the job or contributed to a successful result. For example: Let's say you went to work for Beauty and the Beast, Inc., a seller of health care and cosmetic products, and you noticed that the company dealt with customer complaints on an ad hoc basis. A customer would call or come in with a defective product and whoever happened to be around handled the complaint in the absence of any routine policy for coping with such problems. You noticed this deficiency and recommended the establishment of such a policy. Your recommendation was adopted. That was an obvious achievement.

In other words:

- Doing anything positive above and beyond the call of duty qualifies as an achievement.

- Being selected to handle a special responsibility, project, or presentation qualifies as an achievement.

- Doing anything better, faster, or at less cost qualifies as an achievement.

- Receiving any kind of award or commendation for a j⟨
  done is an achievement.

> *You should try to cite at least one accomplishment*
> *for each major work experience you include on your resume.*

If you have combed the deepest recesses of your memory and just cannot come up with any achievements, why not list one under your description of any volunteer work you may have performed?

OK, you're the rare person who has absolutely *no* reportable job accomplishments worthy of your resume. Did you *learn* anything on your job that might prove useful to a future employer? If you did, say so. Here's an example of how you might do this:

Earnestine Eager just completed all the requirements for her paralegal certificate. Now it's time to for her to prepare an application for a paralegal job with a government agency. But she is facing a real dilemma. Before attending paralegal school, she worked for several years in retail sales and before that as a clerk in an office. How in the world can she describe those experiences so that she can relate them to what a potential employer might be looking for in a paralegal? The section of her resume in which she describes her current and prior employment is illustrated on the following page.

Do you see what Ms. Eager has done? She has taken two fairly ordinary, non-professional jobs and described them in a way that emphasizes the daylights out of their legal aspects.

- She took the opportunity to alert her prospective employer that she served in positions in which familiarity with things legal was a vital component of the jobs.

- In addition, she wrote interesting descriptions filled with action verbs ("advise," "assist," "explain," "inform," "interpret," etc.,) that impart both confidence and a sense of responsibility.

- Finally and most important, she was astute enough to label her accomplishments as such in order to draw attention to them, and was able to be very creative in describing them. Note, for example, that she described her familiarity with several laws that her employer administered as being an accomplishment.

95

Salesperson, Entertainment City, 1990-Present
  Duties:
  - Advise and assist customers with purchasing decisions with respect to entertainment equipment and accessories;
  - process orders;
  - determine status of charge accounts;
  - explain purchase contracts and lease agreements to customers;
  - inform customers of legal consequences of non-compliance with such agreements;
  - instruct customers in activating warranties;
  - interpret for customers Truth-in-Lending and other consumer protection rights associated with store-financed sales of equipment;
  - advise buyers on product safety;
  - explain rights and obligations of both parties under store service agreements; and
  - participate in preparation of advertising copy for print and broadcast.

  Accomplishments:
  - Received regular promotions and salary increases based on annual reviews;
  - became knowledgeable about truth-in-advertising laws and regulations;
  - suggested changes to store returns policies based on interaction with hundreds of customers; and
  - instructed store employees on the new policies upon adoption of my recommendations.

Clerk, U.S. Department of Obfuscation, 1987-1990
  Duties:
  - Typed draft and final copies of agency issuances, correspondence, notices, and related documents from written material and voice recordings on electronic typewriters and word processors;
  - proofread material for spelling, punctuation, capitalization, and grammatical accuracy;
  - filed and retrieved office documents; and
  - developed and maintained tracking systems for office grants, contracts, and notices required by the Office of Federal Contract Compliance.

  Accomplishments:
  - Received "Outstanding" ratings on each annual performance appraisal and letter of commendation from agency head upon departure; and
  - became familiar with the laws and regulations administered by the office, including the Labor-Management Services Act, the Federal Budget & Impoundment Act, and the Federal Obfuscation Act of 1980, as amended.

Note: Do not (as some workers, particularly in bureaucratic environments do) list the ordinary accomplishment of your daily work as an achievement. Finishing assigned tasks "on time and to the satisfaction of your supervisor" is not an accomplishment. It is fulfilling a routine expectation of the responsibilities of your position.

So, avoid saying something like the following, which was drawn from a criminal investigator's resume that we were asked to evaluate:

ACCOMPLISHMENTS:
- Completed several investigations within the specified time frame.
- Interviewed and recorded the testimonies of numerous witnesses whose statements were vital.

Maybe these were, in fact, legitimate accomplishments. Unfortunately, they decidedly do not appear to be significant achievements or accomplishments out of the ordinary. Perhaps if investigations almost always ran well beyond their specified time frame, then the first "accomplishment" would be a true achievement. But a new employer cannot be expected to know that and will draw his or her conclusions accordingly. If these were real achievements, the author of the document should have explained why they were worthy of inclusion.

While pinpointing achievements is central to composing a successful resume, the items you cite must be credible and immediately understood by someone who may know little or nothing about the nature of your past jobs. They must be objective, quantifiable, verifiable. If something that may sound routine is, in fact, a notable accomplishment, explain the context in which it became so commendable. If you managed a fast food restaurant on the top of Mt. Everest, then simply getting to work on time **was** an accomplishment.

▶ Not Being Specific Enough about Your Achievements ◀

If you have one or more achievements you want to include, don't do as most job hunters do and allude to them almost as an afterthought. *Significant achievements deserve star billing.* Emphasize them by titles, numbers, names, hard facts, things that demonstrate their magnitude. Provide concrete evidence that will rarely be questioned. These devices will add credibility to your claim, and will rightly impress the reader. In short, *quantify your accomplishments.*

Let's look at the criminal investigator with the dubious achievements. If he says something like the following, he may yet survive the skeptical reader's scrutiny:

ACCOMPLISHMENTS:
- Completed 50 percent of my investigations within the specified time frame, more than double the average efficiency rate of 20 percent.
- Interviewed and recorded testimonies of over 200 key witnesses.

This is a significant improvement over his first attempt. He has given the reader hard numbers to think about. Quantifying accomplishments in this manner is always a good way to get yourself noticed.

✓ Mistake No. 55: Not Taking Credit for Your Part in a Group Effort

When job seekers rack their brains for substantive material to put in their resumes, they often overlook a very obvious point: **the contribution they might have made to the overall success of the organization or subordinate unit.** If your division or branch has realized, for example, a significant increase in sales during your tenure, one thing you can say is:

"Contributed to an X percent increase in sales."

Of course, make certain that you can defend your statement by demonstrating the link between your work and the positive results.

On another level, be certain to indicate your participation in a group effort at more mundane levels. For example: If you were one of 35 contributors to a new company policy, say so:

"Participated in the development of company policy to streamline widget manufacture and sales."

Most employees in large organizations these days work as members of a team. So, unless you cite your contribution to the efforts of the group, you will be out in the cold when you prepare your resume.

▶ Taking All the Credit for a Group Effort ◀

Surprisingly enough, many job seekers flip to the opposite side of this same coin and try to take all the credit for something that was, in fact, a team effort. Of course you want to look like a star, but avoid grandiose claims that invite skepticism if not outright disbelief. You may have singlehandedly designed a new ad campaign, but not a nuclear submarine. Always keep in mind that your claims will probably be verified by communicating with your past employer(s). Try to strike a balance between projecting yourself as the office "nebbish" and a nominee for a Nobel Prize.

✔ Mistake No. 56: Failing to Include Volunteer Activities in Your Resume

For some reason, resume writers think they are only permitted to include information about jobs for which they received financial compensation. Consequently, a great many who have had terrific volunteer experiences where they have handled major responsibilities and achieved great results leave out that immensely valuable and revealing information.

This is particularly true of homemakers who are seeking to enter the job market. Interestingly enough, they are precisely the type of people who have usually had the most rewarding and fulfilling volunteer experiences.

If you have had volunteer experiences, by all means **include them**, particularly if they are relevant to the job you are seeking. For example: If you are interested in a sales career, the fact that you have extensive experience in door-to-door and/or telephone fundraising would be very relevant and interesting to an employer. If you are looking for a job in management, put down that you have management experience in the PTA, Red Cross, United Way, or other kind of volunteer organization.

The employer will not care that you were an unpaid volunteer. The important thing is that you can show you have had some experience in a related function, and not the money you may have earned while acquiring that skill.

✔ Mistake No. 57: Lying on Your Resume

Naturally, you want everyone to see you in the most favorable light. There's nothing wrong with that. After all, no one wants to hire a loser. But the key is knowing **how** to present yourself as being a winner without breaching the dangerous line between truth and fiction. You must present yourself as being an outstanding person--and potentially valuable employee--without saying a single thing that cannot be verified.

According to a number of disturbing reports in the media, "resume fraud" is increasing rapidly. More and more job seekers are resorting to just plain lying on their resumes. Paralleling this increase in untruths is an increase in the type of information people are lying about. No longer are the typical exaggerations on a

99

resume just little white lies, such as a slight embellishment of job responsibilities. Increasingly, employers are running into major league lies, such as college degrees that were not earned and past positions that the applicant never held. People who lie on their resumes often inflate their accomplishments and talents as well. Such misrepresentations often come to light later; and, when discovered, can result in immediate dismissal, a damaged reputation, and subsequent difficulty in finding another job. One recent report on this subject in a trade journal quoted an expert in the field as saying that fully one-third of all resumes contained significant lies!

To combat the resume fraud epidemic, employers are frequently resorting to the use of background investigations to check the credentials claimed by prospective employees. In fact, a growth industry has emerged out of this epidemic of lying; companies have been established that do nothing but **verify the backgrounds of job applicants.** Industry figures indicate that the business of these firms has grown more than 100 percent in the past decade.

The wave of the future when it comes to verifying resume and application data may be what the U.S. Government is now doing to combat bogus academic degrees. The U.S. Office of Personnel Management (OPM), the Federal Government's central personnel agency, began in May 1986 to check names on a Federal Bureau of Investigation (FBI) list of individuals with fake degrees against the names in its own Security Investigations Index. If the names match, they are sent to the Personnel Security Officer and/or Inspector General of the agency in which the individual works for an investigation to see whether the degree claim involved material fraud. If fraud is discovered, severe measures could be taken against the defrauder. Government employers also have a list of degree-granting institutions identified by the FBI as bogus.

Most employers have been burned more than once by resume fraud and now take the time to confirm facts and dates. If you say you have an undergraduate degree from Yale, a law degree from Harvard, and published the seminal law review article in the <u>Baylor Law Journal</u> on "The Clinch River Dam versus the Furbish Lousewort: David, Goliath, and Environmental Law," it is highly likely your employer will contact Yale, Harvard, and Baylor to check you out.

So, be careful. Using a flattering adjective (i.e., efficient, dedicated) to describe your abilities is one thing. This kind of self-aggrandizement is easily recognized and accepted for what it is. Making false claims about your academic background or job history is quite another. Lying on a resume is a serious matter-- one that can affect not only your chances for a particular job, but also your whole career, especially if you are a member of one of the 500-plus licensed professions in the United States and the employer to whom you lied reports you to the licensing authorities. You may never work in your chosen field again.

✓ Mistake No. 58: Revealing Too Much About Yourself

One of the hardest lessons to learn in life is when to shut up. Naturally, when we have a chance to talk about our favorite subject--ourselves--we could go on forever. Do not do that in your resume.

Remember, the main purpose of a resume is to get you to the next stage of the hiring process, which is usually the interview. If there are things about you that you feel warrant an explanation, you will be in a much better position to explain them in an interview than in a resume or cover letter.

There are **two** major items that are best omitted from your application materials, if possible:

1. *The fact that you are now, or have been, physically or mentally disabled.* This should not be a relevant factor to an employer. Of course, that is true only if you live in an ideal world where attitudes can be legislated. Unfortunately, we do not. Despite the existence of Federal laws like the *Rehabilitation Act of 1973*, the *Age Discrimination in Employment Act*, and the recently enacted *Americans with Disabilities Act*, as well as hundreds of state laws and local ordinances addressing disability discrimination, these applicant characteristics play a major negative role in hiring decisions. Why put more obstacles in your path? As you well know if you happen to have a disability, it is extremely difficult to get a job. Proof of that is the estimated 50 percent unemployment rate among college-educated disabled persons.

Employers who have hired disabled persons have been uniformly impressed with their diligence, commitment, and performance on the job. These employees frequently perform better and are more productive than non-disabled workers. But, to get to that stage, you must get over the first hurdle--the resume. So, if it is at all possible to avoid doing so, don't mention your disability on your resume.

If it is a hidden disability, one that is not readily apparent when looking at or speaking with a person, it may never come up as an issue.

If it is an obvious disability that will be instantly noticed at the interview (such as being wheelchair-bound), it is advisable to alert the interviewer that you have a disability before you arrive for the interview. There are roundabout ways of doing this, such as calling ahead and saying: "I am in a wheelchair and would like to make sure your building is accessible." Having put the employer on notice, he or she will not be surprised at the interview and you both will be able to spend more time discussing the substance of the job and your qualifications rather than spending time overcoming the initial jolt to his or her expectations.

101

If you were out of the work force because of institutionalization due to your disability, you should draft a "functional" or "skills"-based resume that focuses on your skills rather than on a job chronology.

If you are disabled, you may wish to consider positions in government agencies at the Federal, state, and local levels. Most such entities have fairly well-developed affirmative action programs and actively recruit disabled persons.

2. *If you have a criminal record, omit it from your resume if possible.* Of course, if you served time in prison, most employers will want to know where you were during the period of time you were incarcerated. Once again, you may wish to consider writing a "skills"-type resume rather than a chronological one. Just make sure to avoid applying for any kind of a job where a background investigation or security clearance is required. Keep in mind that when a company has a defense or defense-related contract, employees at many levels need clearances...not only engineers or chemists, but secretaries, accountants, and production workers.

A number of employers, both public and private, require job applicants to fill out special application forms, many of which include questions about criminal records. However painful the truth may be, never lie on an application form. Some government employers have developed recruitment programs targeted specifically at rehabilitated offenders, and you may wish to focus your initial job hunt on these programs.

You can obtain detailed information about Federal special recruitment programs for disabled persons and for rehabilitated offenders from any Federal Job Information Center (see **Appendix A**) and from most Federal agency personnel offices. You will find them listed in your telephone book under "U.S. Government."

✔ Mistake No. 59: Mishandling Dates on Your Resume

Since resumes are fundamentally historic documents, they generally contain a lot of dates, the most common being graduation dates from schools and colleges (or the periods of attendance) or dates showing the duration of past employment.

At first glance, a date seems like a fairly innocuous tidbit of information. But beware, for the inclusion of dates can, under certain circumstances, be very detrimental to your job search.

A date can become your enemy if you are an older worker. Regardless of numerous Federal and state laws and regulations against age discrimination, not to mention a rapidly aging population, there are still a lot of stereotypes and negative attitudes that older job hunters must confront. The U.S., for all its lip-service to the contrary, is still a youth-oriented culture, and this is nowhere more evident than in the context of looking for a job. It is no myth that older job hunters have a more difficult time finding employment than their younger competitors. Consequently, when an older worker prepares a resume, he or she must proceed with that in mind. And that means taking care with the use of dates. Here are a few guidelines for managing the date problem if you are over 45 years of age:

► Mishandling Dates Related to Your Education ◄

Do not use dates in your education section. The dates you attended school, as well as your graduation dates, are irrelevant in a resume. You include education information for three purposes:

- *First*, to demonstrate that you meet the educational and credential qualifications for the job.

- *Second*, to indicate any special training you may have.

- *Third*, to show where you obtained your academic degrees, under the theory that graduation from a certain kind of college or a college in a certain geographical location will boost your chances for the job you seek.

When you attended school is not very important. Thus, instead of--

EDUCATION:
        1954-1956 University of Pennsylvania, M.B.A., 1956
        1950-1954 Temple University, B.S., Business, 1954

you should say--

EDUCATION:
        University of Pennsylvania, M.B.A.
        Temple University, B.S., Business

If you specify dates (as in the first example above), the first thought that will occur to the employer is that you are almost 60 years old. All other factors being equal, you may not be invited for an interview if it comes down to a decision between you and a younger person. **Remember, a resume is designed to get your foot in the door.** If you have raised a concern about your age, you probably will never get to the interview and never have the opportunity to demonstrate, face-to-face, your youthfulness, energy, and vigor.

If you do not specify dates (as in the second example above), age may not be an issue when the employer decides whom to interview.

▶ Mishandling Dates Related to Work Experience ◀

Be careful about dates in the work experience section of your resume. It is customary, when using a chronological resume, to include the dates of your employment in past jobs. Providing the dates of each and every position you have ever held will also alert the employer to your age. He is likely to assume that you pursued your education straight through without interruption and then joined the work force. He will be able to quickly calculate your approximate age and draw his conclusions accordingly.

There are several ways to cope with this problem:

1. *You could leave off dates of employment altogether.* If you do this, keep in mind that this technique is something of a break from resume tradition.

2. *You could provide employment information that dates back only 10-15-20 years.* The only job hunters who may have a problem with this are those who have worked for the same company since graduation, but even these individuals have an alternative. If you fall into this category, you could omit your entry-level job title and perhaps also your job title when you got your first promotion(s). Your work experience would begin with a position you held some years after entering the work force and would then proceed with the other job titles (and responsibilities) you subsequently held, showing your advancement through the company hierarchy. The underlying theory being that since resumes are supposed to be such concise documents, many seasoned workers simply do not have room to describe all of their past jobs.

3. *You could use a functional, or skills, resume instead of a chronological one.* However, to avoid the impression that you have something to hide, you will still have to identify the positions you held and the names of the organizations for which you worked (in reverse chronological order) after the presentation of your substantive skills. If this would be an extensive list (because of your age or because you held a long series of short-term jobs), you could determine a cut-off date and identify only those which went back a certain number of years (i.e., 10-15-20 years as in the point discussed above).

Another category of persons who may have a "date" problem are those who have experienced *periods of unemployment.* If you have been unemployed, you should attempt to avoid saying so on your resume, without, of course, resorting to a fabrication. There are several effective ways of doing this. Let's say you worked for Commercial Widget Co. from October, 1980 until January 1987, got laid off, and did not find your current job with Global Exports, Ltd. until December, 1988. Here are two ways of documenting this work experience on a chronological resume:

[Resume A]	[Resume B]
EXPERIENCE	**EXPERIENCE**
Dec 1988-Present Administrator, Global Exports, Ltd.	1988-Present Administrator, Global Exports, Ltd.
Oct 1980-Jan 1987 Manager, Commercial Widget Co.	1980-1987 Manager, Commercial Widget Co.

Resume A screams out to the reader that you were unemployed for almost two years. Resume B, a perfectly honest recording of your dates of employment, gives the appearance of virtually continuous work. It will raise far fewer questions about your work history than Resume A.

Individuals who have experienced long periods of unemployment could also use a functional resume to avoid some of the difficulties dates may cause in a chronological resume.

✓ Mistake No. 60: Mishandling Your Educational Background

This catch-all mistake covers a number of smaller ones that crop up frequently. They are:

• *Including your high school education when you are, at least, a college graduate.* If you have a baccalaureate (undergraduate) degree, such as a B.A. or a B.S., you do not need to chronicle your high school education. It becomes irrelevant once you have a college degree. It is even more pointless to include high school data if you have an advanced degree. All it does is take up valuable space that could be put to better use elsewhere.

• *Presenting your education in chronological order.* Employers like to read things in reverse chronological order. Your most recent schooling should come first, followed by your next most recent, etc. The only exception is if you went back to school for another undergraduate degree after earning an advanced degree. In that case, your advanced degree, although earned at an earlier time, should come first.

105

• *Overwhelming the reader with dates of attendance.* The only appropriate date (should you decide to include it) is the year in which you received your degree. Anything else is superfluous.

• *Including the location of your schools.* This is a judgment call. If you can do this without having to add extra lines, go ahead. If you run into a space problem, leave the location(s) out. But be consistent: don't include one school's geographic location because there is sufficient space on that line and then omit citing the location for the other(s).

• *Failing to include your field of study when relevant to your current career aspirations.* Including your college major as well as your graduate field of concentration may assist a prospective employer evaluate your qualifications. On the other hand, the world of commerce is full of art majors who wind up as successful industrialists. If the kind of job you currently seek is totally unrelated to your youthful dreams, simply include the name of the college/university attended, the kind of degree you obtained, and (should you decide to include it) the year of your graduation. The nature of your work experience since graduation should attest to your ability to handle the position for which you are applying.

• *Omitting honors, awards, and pertinent extracurricular activities.* These embellishments can play an important role in a hiring decision. If you were on the dean's list at some time, say so. If you won a prize for an essay contest, include it. If you were elected to a leadership position in the class or student body, or are a member of an honorary academic or honorary professional society, put that in as well. Leave out activities that are not related to your job search.

• *Citing membership in a college fraternity or sorority.* Including the fact that you were a member of an undergraduate fraternity or sorority is fine for a fairly recent college graduate, but loses relevance and becomes inappropriate with the passage of time...no matter how well known or prestigious the organization might be.

• *Including irrelevant additional training.* If you have taken continuing education courses or attended seminars designed to further your career, include them under education, **after** your list of degree-granting institutions. However, if you have taken more than just two or three such courses, and they are relevant to the position you are seeking, note in this section of your resume that a supplemental sheet listing them is attached to your resume. Do not include any such courses that are not in line with the position you seek.

• *Highlighting unexceptional educational achievements.* We are often sent resumes that tout average or even mediocre grade point averages or say something like "top 50% of graduating class." Calling attention to your "averageness" is not a strategy that will land you the job of your dreams. If you were an average or less-than-average student, you would be better advised to leave such information off your resume completely. Moreover, these days, with every employer cognizant of the 15-20 year old phenomenon of rampant grade inflation on college campuses nation-wide, you must exercise even more care on this score than ever. It is common knowledge that many schools hand out A's and B's as if they were a constitutional right. Many resume reviewers consider today's "B" average the equivalent of the old "Gentleman's C."

Our usual advice to people on this point is as follows:

• If you have an exceptional grade point average, say so. Exceptional is, as a general rule, a 3.5 or above on a 4.0 scale. That kind of number looks good regardless of grade inflation. Otherwise, keep mum.

• If you were in the top one-third of your class, say so, unless you went to a school not known for its academic distinction. Any lower class rank should not be mentioned. If you say "top 50%," everyone will assume you were right in the middle.

• If you received special honors or awards in anything academic, say so (see Susan Smooth's resume on p. 76). If your only claim to college fame was tearing down the goalposts after the upset homecoming victory over State U., forget it.

✓ Mistake No. 61: Omitting Professional Licenses

We see a large number of resumes from attorneys who never mention that they are members of the bar. Since bar examinations are very difficult and have a high failure rate, we (and any other reader) must assume that the applicant has not yet passed the examination and been admitted to practice law. When we point this out to our clients, they almost always say: "Oops, I forgot to include that in my resume." Without such information, the candidate would be eliminated from consideration for almost everything except law-related positions.

In addition to lawyers, there are over 500 other licensed professions in the U.S. Getting a job in any one of these fields usually requires that you be licensed. If you do not advise the employer that you are licensed, you will probably have to seek work elsewhere.

✔ Mistake No. 62: Leaving Out Other Awards and Publications

If you are the recipient of awards and honors unrelated to your work experiences or education, include them under a separate category entitled "AWARDS" or "HONORS." Kudos such as these say something impressive about you. You will want your prospective employers to be suitably impressed as well.

If you are a published author, whether fiction, non-fiction, books, articles, etc., include information about your publications in your resume, under a heading entitled "PUBLICATIONS." Evidence of such achievements tells the reader that experts think you write well and that you had something of value and/or originality to express. All of these qualities are a big plus under any circumstances--and certainly in a job search.

Note: When you list such publications, make sure to follow standard citation rules concerning underlines for book titles, quotation marks for articles, dates, and punctuation. If you're unsure about these generally accepted rules, check them out in a reference book such as <u>A Manual for Writers</u> by Kate L. Turabian, <u>The Chicago Manual of Style</u> prepared by the Editorial Staff of the University of Chicago Press, or <u>The Write Word III</u> compiled and edited by the Houghton Mifflin Company (see *Bibliography*). Improper citations for publications are so distracting they tend to undermine the achievement itself.

✔ Mistake No. 63: Mishandling References and Letters of Recommendation

Job hunters often treat references as afterthoughts, as trivial postscripts on which not much time or effort is wasted. This can be a fatal error. The trend among prospective employers faced with a blitz of eager candidates is to rely more and more on what references have to say. Not only do decisionmakers contact references more frequently than ever before, they also ask them tougher and more detailed questions about job applicants. What this means is that you have to pay more attention to the references you include on your employment applications.

Many job seekers provide the names of references without first asking the permission of the people whose names they have included. References who are unaware that they have been so honored may not turn out to have been the best choices for this important task. They may resent not being contacted for permission to include their names on your resume. This resentment may temper their enthusiasm for you when they are subsequently contacted.

The authors have often been victims of the following scenario: Someone calls us up and says: "Tom Terrific has applied for a position with our company and he gave your name as a reference. What can you tell me about him?"

This is not a comfortable situation. First, it takes us several minutes to collect ourselves and try to remember all of the key traits about Tom T. (other than his presumptuousness in selecting one of us as a reference without first asking our permission). Then, not knowing what he is really up to in the job market, we become somewhat reticent about saying too much, which may have the effect of jeopardizing his chances for the job.

What Tom should have done was to have asked permission to use us as references first. Then, to better prepare us for any inquiries by prospective employers, he should have sent us a current resume and discussed his job hunting objectives with us. If he already knew the names of one or more companies which were apt to call, he should have identified those companies and specified the nature of the position for which he was applying. In an ideal world, he would have also mentioned (by way of a reminder) the skills and experience which make him so eminently qualified for the position in question. This kind of preparation makes giving references easy, and **the best references come from those who have been best prepared.**

Special Note: Employers are become increasingly skittish when it comes to expounding upon the qualities, good and bad, of former employees. Cognizant of the growing popularity of both "workplace defamation" lawsuits, in which an ex-employee, for example, sues the former employer on the grounds that something said as a reference denied him a new employment opportunity, as well as even more innovative lawsuits in which the new employer sues the prior one for providing false information that had prompted the hiring of the employee, many employers have opted to give out only dates during which a person worked for the organization. Make sure you know company policy before listing someone as a reference.

If your former employer has a practice of **providing only dates of employment** for employees, make sure to indicate that fact immediately to your future employer. When someone calls and is told only "Yes, Tom Terrific worked here from January 1, 1989 to June 1, 1991" the assumption may be that bad news is being hidden for fear of a lawsuit. See if you can locate a co-worker or former supervisor who has left the company who can provide a good reference for you. The point is that you must think ahead and avoid the problem before it arises.

► Not Mentioning References on Your Resume ◄

One of the trends in the evolution of the art of resume-writing appears to be omitting any mention of references. This can prove to be a mistake, since it requires the employer to do more work when trying to contact people in order to verify your work history and discuss your employee potential.

Another popular way of handling the matter of references on a resume is to state, usually at the end of the document, "References available upon request." Such a statement is perfectly acceptable, especially if you have not yet alerted all concerned that you are in fact looking for a new job. However, if you have **exceptional** references, i.e., people with recognizable names or prestigious titles, it is usually an advantage to include them on your resume. They will act as attention-getters, which, as you know, is what resumes are all about.

If, however, your references are not superstars, and you have a space problem, use the brief statement quoted above. If you **do** have space on your resume, include your references by name, title, address, and (day-time) telephone number. Having this information up front may save the hiring officer time and will be appreciated.

► Keeping Your References Incommunicado ◄

Another common mistake concerning references is providing incomplete, incorrect, or obsolete addresses or telephone numbers. Amazingly, two of the most frequent resume (and job application form) mistakes we have encountered are the omission of ZIP codes on addresses and area codes for telephone numbers! Making your would-be employer look up ZIP codes and area codes is a very bad way to begin your relationship. In many instances, it is a sure-fire way to nip it in the bud. By leaving out such essential information, you are telling an employer that you are sloppy and inattentive to detail.

Someone we recently interviewed for a position with our company gave us the names, addresses, and telephone numbers of four references, whom we proceeded to call with the following results:

- The first name on the list had left the employer (whose phone number our job applicant had given us) two years before.
- The telephone number for the second reference had been disconnected.
- The third reference could not remember our candidate.
- The fourth name on the list never returned our calls.

Despite our failure to glean any information from her four references, we felt that the exercise had been well worth our time. We learned a great deal about our would-be employee, namely that she was obviously a very careless person, the kind we could not tolerate in our business.

If you include the names of people with whom you have not associated recently, make sure you have their **current** addresses and telephone numbers. An employer who is unable to contact a reference because you gave out an obsolete or incorrect address/telephone number will not be impressed.

✓ Mistake No. 64: Being a Victim of Bad References

We all have professional colleagues who would not give us good references. People who have been fired, or have left a job due to personality conflicts, have a particular problem in this area. Make sure to think the problem through before simply stating "references available on request" at the bottom of your resume. The danger is that many prospective employers won't wait for your list of references but will simply pick up the phone, call your former employer, and ask to speak with someone who worked with you, preferably your supervisor. This has happened to many, many people--almost always with disastrous results.

Knowing that several key people at your last job will give you mediocre, luke-warm, or less than positive references should make you cautious. You might consider including the name, title, address, and phone number of a former colleague who **would** give you a good reference, thereby making an end-run around your old enemies. This must be carefully orchestrated ahead of time. Discuss the situation with your friendly colleague, request that person's permission to include him or her as a reference, and outline the kind of position you will be seeking. In this way, there will be no surprises and you can be assured of a good reference.

If your departure was so acrimonious, and the organization was so small, that there is NO ONE there who would give you a fair reference, list someone from a former place of employment--someone with whom you have already discussed your situation as frankly and openly as is needed.

Further, if you held a position which allowed you professional access to highly regarded or executive colleagues in **other** organizations, it is always impressive to include such individuals as references--**after** gaining their permission.

You have to recognize that chances are great that the negative information will emerge, but you want it to emerge in a way that does **the least amount of**

damage to your future job prospects. If someone gives you a bad reference at the very beginning of your interview/discussion stage with a prospective employer, you are dead in the water. If you can control how the information is presented--by you, in person--then your version of the events may prevail.

Finally, if you have been let go through no fault of your own, due to economic recession, loss or completion of a contract, company restructuring or reorganization, it is still wise to consider the same tactic. It is always smart to make "good references" a part of your departure package. If possible, get them in writing. It is easy to think of severance pay and extension of health benefits when you've been let go, but also think about specific references. More than one person has been uncomfortably surprised when their former boss did not want to admit that people were being let go because of economic distress. Instead, the boss implied that the employee was released due to poor job performance. Do not let this happen to you.

If you want to doublecheck what your references have to say about you, either have a friend or colleague call (presenting himself/herself as a prospective employer), or use a service like <u>Reference Check</u>. This organization will contact your previous employers on your behalf and will send you a confidential, written report on the recommendation provided. For further information on <u>Reference Check</u>, contact: Taylor & Whitehouse Inc., 460 Thornridge Drive, Rochester, MI 48307. (Tel: 313/651-0286). Taylor & Whitehouse's fee for the first reference contacted is $45, and $39 for each reference thereafter.

✓ Mistake No. 65: Generalized Letters of Recommendation

A good letter of recommendation is always a factor in your favor, but a general letter of recommendation is never as good as a specific letter recommending you for a particular position.

Younger job applicants, or those with little employment experience, all tend to have general letters of recommendation--frequently from school professors, summer job employers, or from clerkships or internships. The typical general letter of recommendation begins: "To Whom It May Concern: During her work with us, Mary Marigold has proven to be efficient, eager to learn, highly organized, and a valuable asset to our department...etc., etc." This is fine, and it is certainly better to have such a letter than NOT to have one, especially since younger people tend to move around a lot and their academic or first job reference may be located on the opposite coast.

But more experienced job hunters, who tend to be a little older, sl___ at obtaining a letter of recommendation targeted at the specific job in question. What an employer really wants to see is a letter commending an individual **for the position being offered**, citing the individual's skill and experience as it relates directly to the responsibilities of that position. The only way to obtain such a targeted letter of recommendation is to fully inform the person whom you have asked to write it exactly what the score is. **Most job hunters provide letter-writers with a proposed draft of the kind of information to be included.** No, this is not being pushy--after all, you already know these people well enough to request such a letter and they are, undoubtedly, busy with their own professional concerns. Give them a break by making it easy to craft the letter quickly and to the point. Also provide each letter-writer with the exact name of the person, title, organization, and address to which the letter should be sent (with a copy to be sent to you, at your address, so you know the letter has been sent and can keep the copy for your own files).

✓ Mistake No. 66: Sending Unrequested Materials with Your Resume

---

Nothing annoys an employer more than someone who sends tons of additional material with a resume. It is not uncommon for employers (who have requested only a resume) to receive, in response to an announcement of a job vacancy:

- a cover letter
- a resume
- several letters of recommendation
- writing samples
- a copy of college transcripts
- copies of awards received
- official position descriptions of current and past jobs
- etc.

Often, the applicant compounds the annoyance by stapling all this junk together, thereby making it even more difficult for the reviewer to sort it all out and find the resume.

Further, many employers feel obligated to spend a dollar or more in postage to send all this extraneous material back to the applicant. They do not like to do that. It's annoying and time consuming.

We once received a resume to which the job seeker attached photocopies of more than 50 pages worth of the coats-of-arms of countless honorary societies to which he belonged.

The last thing you want to do as a job applicant is upset your prospective employer before he has even looked at your resume. How do you think engulfing him with all this irrelevant paper will affect his judgment of you?

RULE:

When you apply for a job,
submit only what the job announcement or advertisement asks for...
AND NOTHING MORE...
(with the possible exception of a cover letter).

If the employer likes your resume, and if you interview well, you may be asked at a later time to submit additional documents.

Many employers substitute their own special application form for the traditional resume. Other organizations require you to fill out such a form in addition to your resume--they want to see both. The trend in the hiring business seems to be in the direction of such special application forms.

Government agencies at all levels--Federal, state, local, and international-- are the biggest users of special application forms. Since there are over 50,000 governmental units in this country that have the authority to hire people, and since governments currently employ about 18,000,000 workers, it is an advantage to know how to fill out their forms correctly.

Many government entities (and a growing number of private sector employers) have adopted the special form approach used by the largest governmental employer of them all--the Federal Government. The U.S. Government employs approximately two million civilian workers and another million-plus military personnel. Consequently, in this book, we use the standard Federal employment application form (SF-171) as our discussion prototype of this breed of special forms.

Many of the resume mistakes already discussed apply equally to special application forms. However, there are some significant differences. Perhaps the most important one is that, whereas a resume is a relatively "free-form" document which gives you a lot of leeway (within reason) concerning its structure, this is not the case with special application forms. The bureaucrats who review these forms for completeness and accuracy when they are initially received are not favorably impressed with creativity. On the contrary, they often appear obsessively concerned with whether you have dotted all the i's and crossed all the t's. In other words, they want you to complete the forms in accordance with the instructions provided, without any deviations.

✓ Mistake No. 67: Not Following Special Application Form Instructions

Federal agency personnel specialists often say they have rarely seen an Application for Federal Employment (SF-171) that was filled out absolutely correctly. If you are one of the few exceptions, you will go a long way towards impressing Federal or other public hiring officials, as the case may be, and improving your chances of employment.

Always read the instructions through completely before beginning to work on any special application form. If there is something that you do not understand, contact a personnel specialist and ask for assistance in interpreting the instructions.

Fill out the form only when you are sure you understand the general instructions and any specific instructions for particular information blocks on the application form.

Once the form has been submitted, personnel specialists in the public sector are **not** obligated to communicate with you concerning any deficiencies. They determine whether an application should be moved forward through the process or set aside.

✓ Mistake No. 68: Equating Public Sector Application Forms with Resumes

---

Throughout the section on resumes in this book, we told you to keep your information short, concise, and to the point. Now that you have taken that advice to heart for resumes, you must set it to one side and focus on a different technique when it comes to other kinds of application forms.

Many job hunters used to the ways of private employers become so steeped in the lessons of **private** sector job hunting that they apply them wholeheartedly to the **public** sector as well. That is a big mistake.

In contrast to the private sector's heavy emphasis on short, quick-to-make-the-point resumes, **the public sector likes to see long, drawn-out application forms that go into exhaustive detail about every facet of your past employment.**

Most state and local government application forms are modeled on the Federal Government's application form, so we will take that as a starting point. The key section of the Federal form (and all of its lower-level counterparts) is the section asking you to describe your duties, responsibilities, and accomplishments in your current and past positions. While these government agencies do not tell you to exceed the space provided on the form for this information, they really want to see as much descriptive narrative material as possible. By doing so, you will be making the job of the evaluator easier--and you will be rewarded for it. This is in stark contrast to the ways of private industry, where a premium is put on brevity.

The reason government employers want to see a ton of information is because, when they review your application, they have in front of them **a checklist of specific background qualification requirements and job "ranking factors" against which your application is evaluated.** The former is part of phase one of the review process, and requires the evaluator to run your application through the various qualification requirements to see if you meet the predetermined minimum requirements for the particular occupation and grade level. The "ranking factors" then come into play in phase two, when you are rated against your competitors for the particular job in question.

This evaluation system, at all levels of government, is part of the general civil service routine. These systems, whose goal is to treat all job applicants with fairness and objectivity, use established occupational standards and requirements as yardsticks against which all job applicants are measured. If you are able to demonstrate in your application that you meet these minimum standards, you **will** be considered for the job--without regard to your age, race, sex, disability or any other irrelevant factor. The competition will then be among the minimally qualified to determine the **best** qualified in terms of the specific ranking factors assigned to the position being filled.

Thus, the easier you make it for the reviewers to find statements in your application that correspond to these various requirements and factors, the better you will fare.

✔ Mistake No. 69: Preparing and Submitting Application Forms Unaware of How the Hiring Process Works

---

Very few applicants for government jobs have the vaguest notion of how the government (be it Federal, state, or local) hiring process works. This is a shame, because knowledge of the process provides a tremendous advantage. Unfortunately, most public sector job applicants merely fill out the appropriate application forms and send them in.

You can give yourself a big boost toward winning a government job if you take the time to learn about the hiring process. Virtually all governmental jurisdictions have published material available describing their recruitment and hiring procedures. Obtain this information and study it carefully before plunging headlong into the government job hunt.

In addition, most government entities have written standards and guidelines that their personnel professionals use to evaluate job applications. The Federal Government, for example, publishes a handbook that contains the specific qualifications and requirements for each Federal job title at each grade level in which

117

people are hired for those titles. This book, <u>Office of Personnel Management Handbook X-118: Qualification Standards for Positions Under the General Schedule</u>, is available from most Federal personnel offices as well as larger public libraries. Comparable handbooks for state and (the larger) local governments are also available. You should read the material devoted to the job titles under which you are applying **before** preparing your application forms.

Finally, a number of governmental jurisdictions employ more than one recruiting technique. For example: The U.S. Government has a central Office of Personnel Management that maintains a list of eligible candidates who can be matched to the job needs of requesting agencies. At the same time, many positions are handled independently by individual Federal agencies. Candidates for these jobs apply directly to the hiring agency, bypassing the Office of Personnel Management. Similarly, many states have both civil service commissions that provide a matching service, plus state agencies that hire people directly.

If you understand these hiring procedures, you can enhance your chances for employment by taking advantage of both hiring methods.

✓ Mistake No. 70: Inadvertently Restricting Consideration of Your Application

---

Often, public sector job applicants unwittingly limit themselves by the way they answer certain questions on the government application form. For example, the Federal application form asks for the lowest pay or grade you will accept. If your aspirations exceed what you can realistically expect, given your background, education, and experience, you are doing yourself a disservice if you enter too high a level of pay or grade. Government agencies will consider you only for jobs at or above the pay or grade level you indicate. **You will not be considered for a position at any lower grade or pay**, despite how well-qualified you might be for a position that comes up at that lower level. Since getting a foot in the door is extremely important, opening up many job advancement opportunities that are currently closed to you as an "outsider," you are only hurting yourself if you aim unreasonably high at the outset. Many public employees get promoted fairly frequently. Keep that in mind when you answer questions concerning minimum acceptable salary or grade level.

Typical government application forms also ask questions about your flexibility, such as your willingness to travel, willingness to move to another geographic location, and whether you would consider a job involving less than a 40-hour week. **You should strive to demonstrate as much flexibility as possible.** If you do, you will receive the broadest possible consideration for employment. If you do not, you will only be considered for jobs within the limitations you indicate.

▶ Applying Outside Public Sector "Areas of Consideration" ◀

Many public sector vacancy announcements contain a category of information called the "Area of Consideration." As a general rule, the information listed under this category indicates who may apply for the position in question. A typical entry under Area of Consideration in a Federal Government announcement might say, for example, "Career and Career-Conditional employees of the Federal Government and persons eligible for Reinstatement," or, alternatively, "All Sources."

Make sure you apply only for positions for which the Area of Consideration indicates that you are eligible. If you are uncertain, contact a personnel specialist at the organization that issued the announcement to obtain a clarification.

Note: Sometimes a Federal Government vacancy announcement can give the impression that it **geographically** restricts the area of consideration, by stating something comparable to "applicants are sought from the Atlanta, GA, commuting area." This does not mean that if you live in Boston you cannot apply...it means the hiring agency or organization **will not pay your relocation costs** from Boston to Atlanta.

✓ Mistake No. 71: Assuming Private Sector Job Titles Match Public Ones

---

Federal, state, and local governments, like most large organizations, have their own, often unique, job titles. Moreover, they may very well define seemingly straightforward job titles quite differently from a private sector company. To illustrate, if you are a Legislative Analyst for a private corporation, you are probably spending the bulk of your time studying bills introduced in a legislative body which may affect your company. In the Federal Government, however, a Legislative Analyst spends considerable time responding to requests for information about agency activities from Members or Committees of Congress. Other deceptive or confusing job titles include executive secretary, management analyst, labor relations specialist, program manager, etc.

The best way to determine the government job titles which most closely correspond to your private sector job title and/or your qualifications is to obtain access to a copy of the government-in-question's official manual describing in detail its various occupational fields. For the U.S. Government, the publication is called the Handbook of Occupational Groups and Series. Contact a Federal Job Information Center or state or local agency recruitment or personnel office to find out where you may see their manuals.

✓ Mistake No. 72: Not Taking Advantage of Free Job Search Assistance Programs in the Public Sector

---

A great many job applicants qualify for free assistance with public sector job hunting. This benefit is provided by Federal, state, and local governments in order to help disadvantaged applicants (targeted through affirmative action and related hiring and recruitment programs) find their way through the complexities of the public sector hiring process. At the Federal level, for example, there are individuals designated as special employment coordinators for minorities, disabled persons, and veterans, among others. These coordinators are knowledgeable about all of the nuances of their respective recruitment programs and will often assist eligible applicants with all facets of the hiring process, including completing the application forms.

It is up to you, the applicant, to take the initiative in invoking and exploiting these government recruitment programs; governments in general do a poor job of advertising their existence. If you think you might qualify as a member of a special category of persons eligible for such a program, inquire **before** you begin to submit applications. There may be special forms for you to complete and forward with your application, or precise codes or "buzzwords" that should appear in specific sections of the general application form.

If you are currently either in college or are an alumnus/alumna, you may contact the college career placement office and ask to speak to the person knowledgeable about such public sector recruitment programs. Many colleges and universities have designated individuals and staff offices to handle the affairs of students and alumni who are disabled, veterans, or members of other targeted groups.

Cover letters have been traditionally considered an essential part of the job hunting process. Lately, however, the dogma that every resume must be accompanied by a cover letter seems to be weakening. The reason why the cover letter is going out of favor is probably because so many of them are so **poorly planned and drafted.** Job hunters universally consider them a necessary evil and so tend to prepare them as afterthoughts, dashing them off rather hastily when they see a position for which they want to apply. In short, they simply do not get the attention they deserve.

While cover letters are declining in importance, a new phenomenon appears to be growing in significance--the "market letter." According to recent surveys, approximately 15 percent of executive job hunters are employing market letters instead of cover letters and even instead of resumes. The market letter is essentially a direct mail advertisement touting the achievements of the job applicant, and is customarily addressed directly to an executive of the employing organization rather than to the personnel office or hiring manager. It is largely a device geared to gain immediate notice. In the discussion of the mistakes that follow, we address both cover letters and market letters.

✓ Mistake No. 73: Writing a Cover Letter Unnecessarily (Or, To Write or Not to Write a Cover Letter)

Conventional wisdom says you should **always** accompany a resume or job application form with a cover letter. However, the cover letter tradition must be evaluated according to each situation.

When a public or private sector organization asks you to submit **its own standard application form** instead of a resume, that is usually the only document it wants to see. Many job announcements from such organizations specifically state **they do not want to receive any other application material.** Submitting a cover letter in addition to the application material requested can create the impression that you are unable to follow instructions or have trouble understanding written material. In most instances, the personnel specialist assigned to open job applications will simply throw it away. Chances are slim it will reach the person who will make the ultimate hiring decision.

If you want to take the time to write a cover letter when applying for these kinds of jobs, then merely use it to cite the specific job vacancy announcement or advertisement to which you are responding. This may help the person who opens your envelope route your application properly and promptly.

There are two other reasons why you may wish to write a cover letter to one of these organizations:

1. *If your application contains some detrimental information.* While it is always best to leave negative information out of an employment application, that is not always possible. For example, the Federal Government's application form asks whether you have ever left a prior job because you were fired, quit after being told that you would be fired, or left by mutual agreement with your ex-employer because of specific problems. Answering "Yes" without explanation may damage your job prospects. If your reason for leaving a job can be explained in a favorable light, or if there were extenuating or mitigating circumstances, you could provide such an explanation in a cover letter if you cannot find a suitable place for it on the application form itself.

2. *If you are applying for a high-level position.* The typical job applicant for a senior level position is a seasoned veteran of the work force with a lot of experience and accomplishments, often too many to relate in the confines of a resume or application form. A cover letter is a good place to **complement** the information in the application. It is also likely that, for senior level positions, there is some "special handling" mechanism in place. In the U.S. Government, for example, such applications are normally handled by a separate personnel office or team set up within each agency solely for this purpose. Since these specialists normally handle far fewer applications than the regular personnel offices, they tend to handle submissions with greater care.

When using a resume to apply for a private sector position, it is still customary to submit a cover letter. This is particularly true when responding to an employment ad in the newspaper. Special application forms (in the public or private sector) usually have a space in which to indicate the job title and/or vacancy announcement number for which you are applying. On the other hand, large private sector employers may place half a dozen employment ads in the newspaper each week...all of which request resumes from job applicants; if you do not specify the exact job title for which you are applying, your resume may not be handled appropriately. These are busy people--give them a break, and give yourself a break. Let them know what you want.

✔ Mistake No. 74: Submitting A Cover Letter that Looks Unprofessional

If you submit a cover letter, it must look professional. Why do some people spend $500 to $1,000 on a resume and then submit it with a tacky looking cover letter, perhaps even handwritten on a torn piece of notebook paper? As its name indicates, a "cover" letter is on TOP of a resume, so it is the first thing the prospective employer sees. It creates an immediate impression.

That first impression should be one of competence and professionalism. The paper must be a good quality bond paper of a standard size. It should be typewritten and in standard office correspondence format--including your name, home address, and phone number at the top. Most people use (or have made up for this purpose) personalized stationery with all this information pre-printed at the top. You must then type in the date, the name and address of the person to whom the letter is being sent, a salutation, two or three paragraphs of narrative, good margins, a standard closing (e.g., "Sincerely"), and an original signature.

It should go without saying that the letter must contain no grammatical or spelling errors. As employers, when we see a careless mistake in a cover letter we reject the application without even looking at the resume.

▶ Exceeding One Page in Length ◀

Unlike a resume, where there is no absolute consensus as to length (one page is preferred, as we discussed earlier), there is general agreement among professionals in the field **that cover letters should not exceed one page in length**. Their sole function is to highlight your relevant skills and experience so your resume will be noticed and read. And you decidedly do not need more than one page to accomplish that. Anything longer will likely get tossed, unread, into the wastebasket, often with your resume attached.

A market letter, on the other hand, incorporates resume-type information along with cover letter information into a single, targeted application document. Since the market letter is constructed to stand alone, its length is determined by the amount of narrative information included...but **does not usually exceed two pages**.

✔ Mistake No. 75: Using a Uniform Cover Letter for Every Employer

Using a standard, "one-size-fits-all" cover letter that you send to every prospective employer is generally a waste of time and paper. A uniform cover letter is easy to spot and discourages the reader from taking you seriously. You will be broadcasting the fact that you are mass-mailing resumes out to the world at large, which indicates that you know very little about the employer and are not particularly interested in the organization.

If you do not take the time to target your resume to a specific job opening, you should definitely **target your cover letter**. A well crafted, personalized cover letter can focus attention on your application and increase your chances for surviving the initial cut.

✔ Mistake No. 76: Coming on Like Gangbusters

Dear Employer:

Hi! My name is John (Go-Get-'Em) Doe and I can turn around your business! If you hire me, I assure you that you will get the services of a highly effective, efficient, loyal, and conscientious employee. And cheap!

I have enclosed my resume for your prompt and attentive consideration. Let me know when we can get together to discuss this great mutual opportunity.

I look forward to hearing from you forthwith.

With great sincerity,

John G.G.E. Doe

John G. G. E. Doe

P.S. Remember to act fast. I am in great demand.

This is an almost verbatim copy of a cover letter accompanying a resume an employer-friend received. What do you think he did with it? If you guessed that he saved it for our future book on the biggest mistakes job hunters make, you were correct. The real reason he saved it was because it is a classic--simultaneously offensive and ridiculous. The vast majority of employers (who do not have friends who are writing books about job hunting) would simply throw such bombastic junk away.

No one likes a know-it-all, even if the ideas presented in the application or advanced by the candidate at the job interview contain some merit. So, avoid giving the impression that you've got all the answers. Even if you think you know how to run the employer's organization better than its present management, don't say so.

Remember, there are positive, constructive ways to present suggestions or new ideas without dumping all over the status quo. Tone means a lot. Most employers are receptive to better ways of doing things, and if presented properly--and non-threateningly--these suggestions can prove to be very beneficial to the innovative job seeker.

✓ Mistake No. 77: Giving Away Ideas

Eager job hunters sometimes offer detailed, substantive suggestions concerning the employer's products or operations. Before presenting **your ideas** to an employer, be wary of the following points:

1. Make sure you are thoroughly grounded in the employer's operations, performance, and activities that you are seeking to improve. Otherwise, you will make a complete fool of yourself.

2. Some employers ask job applicants to submit narrative statements addressing a specific problem currently confronting the employer's organization. This is sometimes a tactic designed to obtain suggestions and ideas--without compensation--from a wide range of highly qualified "consultants" who think they are competing for a real job.

3. If your idea is truly innovative, think twice before offering it for free to someone with whom you do not yet have a professional relationship. Idea thieves abound today, and the world is full of "if only" stories told in late night corner bars by folks whose great notions have been pillaged. If your idea warrants legal protection (e.g., patent, copyright, trademark registration), make sure you have taken the necessary steps to protect it before you propose it to a prospective employer.

✔ Mistake No. 78: Writing a Dull Introduction

"I am writing in response to your advertisement in the Sunday <u>Blather</u> for a Sales Representative."

Zzzzzzzzzzzzzz. Wake us when it's over. This form of opening, or something very similar, is all too common when it comes to cover letters. Although acceptable, it will hardly grab anyone's attention. While you certainly want to let the organization know the position (or kind of position) for which you are applying, your opening statement should be designed to make the reader *sit up and take notice.* You want to interest the employer immediately. There are several effective ways to do this:

1. *Begin with one of your work achievements.* "While employed at Magnum Amalgamated, I increased sales in my division by an average of 50 percent annually. I would like the opportunity to do the same for your firm." This is not bad. Everyone wants to increase sales. And here is someone with a track record in the area. A hiring manager would have to be interested in this applicant.

2. *Start with a recent salient issue affecting the employer.* "Your article about the machine tool industry and foreign competition in <u>Tools Are Us</u> magazine stimulated my interest in working for your company." Here is a job applicant who actually read an article about the company and appears to have been so impressed that he is writing the author. Everyone is flattered to think someone out there is reading his work. Feedback from articles like this is a rare commodity, and what little there is can be very effective. The applicant has not only established a common ground for further discussion, but has demonstrated a rare interest in this narrow field.

3. *Refer to a mutual acquaintance in the introduction.* "Ms. Iris Indigo, Executive Vice President of Ink, Inc. suggested that I contact you concerning a position with your company." If the reader (1) knows who Ms. Indigo is and (2) respects her, you might be tendered an interview, if only as a favor to Ms. Indigo. But be careful if you use this technique. Develop as much information as possible about the relationship between your reference and the reader (maybe Ms. Indigo was only introduced to him once at a cocktail party) and the regard in which he or she is held. This is difficult to do, but vital if this method is to bear fruit. If someone in your network offers you the use of his or her name with respect to a particular company official, interrogate your reference as politely as you can about their relationship.

✓ Mistake No. 79: Repeating Your Resume in Your Cover Letter

Having exhausted all of their creative energies during the resume preparation ordeal, job hunters often feel there is nothing left to say in a cover letter. So, the best they can do is repeat the information in the resume. If the resume items are terrific, that approach is not immediately a disaster. It probably will get the resume read by someone who is intrigued by the litany of achievements itemized in the cover letter. The disaster occurs when the hiring official realizes that the resume and the cover letter are essentially the same, and that he has not really learned any more about the candidate from the resume. In fact, in many instances the cover letter even **restates verbatim** the language used in the resume! *Make sure you say something different about yourself in your cover letter.* Or, at a minimum, if you absolutely must reiterate your resume data, say it in a different way.

Exception: An exception to this would be a market letter that is sent alone, without a resume. Such a letter would not be sent in response to an advertised vacancy, but in an attempt to tap into the "hidden" job market of unannounced, unadvertised job openings. In a classic, stand-alone market letter you must include enough information about your experience and background (i.e., selected resume information presented in a narrative format) to attract the interest of the employer. Its purpose is to impress the employer enough to elicit a request for further information or to invite you for an interview. Try not to exceed two concisely written pages.

✓ Mistake No. 80: Talking About Goals and Objectives in a Cover Letter

A cover letter (or a market letter) is no place for ruminations about your philosophy of life. Leave out discussions of your career goals and objectives. Cover letters and market letters should contain "hard" detailed data about you, not "soft" abstract information. You do not want to lull your reader to sleep with a treatise about what you want out of the job or life. The reader wants to know what you can do for the company, not what the company can do for you.

✓ Mistake No. 81: Claiming to Be a Superstar in a Cover Letter

Most cover letters transmitting job applications to our office concentrate on self-promotion. It is almost as though the applicants were writing letters of recommendation on their own behalf. Not only is this inappropriate, but such letters are tiresome to read because we have no independent basis for an objective judgment of the claims asserted. Just because the applicant professes to be a "superstar with numbers," "great with people," "superb when it comes to answering the telephone," "highly organized," etc., there is no reason to believe it.

So, avoid abstract self-promotion in your cover letter. Let someone else gush about your virtues. Objective corroboration of the information provided on your resume is traditionally supplied by references.

Remember, egotistical claims of superstardom generally evoke laughter. Truly outstanding people never praise themselves in this way.

What a cover letter can do is **summarize the skills and experience which are particularly relevant to the position for which you are applying.** For example: You may have acquired a number of skills--all of which may be highly important to your candidacy for the current job--while holding **different** jobs. On your resume such skills were itemized separately, in conjunction with the individual positions with which they were associated. In your cover letter, you can aggregate these skills to **summarize** the extent to which your background qualifies you for the position.

- *For example*: You can state that you have "developed expertise in a broad range of computer software, including Aaa, Bbb, Ccc, Ddd, and Eee."
- *Or*, that your work experience has given you "the opportunity to handle a variety of complex financial transactions, including Xxx, Yyy, and Zzz."
- *Or*, that your sales experience with three manufacturing companies has allowed you to become "knowledgeable in many facets of sales operations at small, medium, and large-sized companies."
- *Or*, that your "contract administration experience with the Federal Government as well as with the private sector" has provided you with "first-hand knowledge of the legal and administrative requirements of many different types of contracts, such as Pppp, Qqqq, Rrrr, Ssss, Tttt, and Vvvv."

This kind of restatement, emphasizing your possession of the knowledge and skills required, creates a powerful cover letter. It becomes an **"executive summary"** of what you have to offer, which is just what the employer needs to know.

✓ Mistake No. 82: Failing to Quantify Your Accomplishments in Your Cover Letter (When Possible)

You may remember our advice to quantify your accomplishments in your resume. This advice is even more important for your cover letter or market letter. The best kinds of objective indicators of your skills and achievements are hard numbers. If you want to emphasize your skills, accomplishments, job functions, knowledge, etc., in your letter, try to describe them in precise, finite terms instead of vague, intangible ones. Employers are interested in, and impressed by, **measurable** demonstrations of your worth.

How do you get from a vague accomplishment or skill to a hard number? By counting. Take each one of your accomplishments, skills, etc., and quantify it. Were you a secretary who typed correspondence for a small office? Fine, say you "processed 1,500" (or whatever number is appropriate) "error-free letters to customers per year." In addition to the number of times you performed a function, you can also measure your performance by being attuned to profit, sales, number of customers serviced, number of calls handled, number of employees supervised, number of meetings/conferences arranged, number of articles written, dollar amount of budgets you administered, amount of money saved, company growth rate during your tenure, and much more.

A cover letter (or market letter) provides an opportunity to be concrete about your claims. Give the reader a reason to be impressed.

✓ Mistake No. 83: Failing to Respond to Requests for Salary History or Salary Requirements

Many job announcements issued by private sector employers ask applicants to provide information concerning their recent salary history and/or salary requirements. The best place to provide this information is at the end of your cover letter.

Salary history is usually requested to make sure your earnings history is in line with the salary being offered. If you're currently earning $25,000 per year, an employer would not be enthusiastic about giving you a great leap forward to $50,000. If your last salary was $60,000 per year, most employers would be skeptical about your interest in a job paying $30,000.

On salary history, only include data from your last few professional positions. The dollar amounts can be rounded off; employers need only a close approximation, not figures calculated down to the last penny. Remember to state "plus benefits" and/or "plus bonus," which for many positions can amount to thousands of dollars. Quantify this extra amount, if possible. Total compensation can sometimes move you into serious competition for a job otherwise out of reach. Keep in mind that your statements are easy to verify by contacting your current and/or former employers.

• If you work solely on commission, **you** will be asked to provide verification--usually accomplished through volunteered copies of income tax returns.

• If you're working part-time, let the employer know what your salary would be on an annualized basis.

• If you're currently working as a consultant, cite the hourly rate you're receiving. Let the employer calculate how that figure would compare to the salary being offered.

On salary requirements, state a salary range whose lowest figure is slightly higher than what you're currently earning (making sure to add in whatever compensation in benefits and/or bonus that you can quantify). For example, if your total compensation is currently $28,000 per year, state that your expectations are in the range of $30,000-$35,000. If your total compensation is currently $58,000 per year, state that your expectations are in the range of $60,000-$65,000.

If the employer does not request salary history but **only your salary requirements,** state a salary range that you think is realistic--in terms of your background, the kind of position being offered, and the nature of the employer. You may have to do a little research to make an educated guess about the salary range the employer has in mind. The level of compensation for the same kind of position would vary dramatically between a Fortune 500 corporation and a non-profit corporation, or between New York City and Peoria.

Many applicants ignore requests for current and/or anticipated compensation for reasons of confidentiality, lethargy, or for fear of leaving money on the table. **However, you always jeopardize your chances for serious consideration when you do not provide information that has been specifically requested.** As employers, the first people we call for interviews are always those who submit the application material we specified. The others we deem non-responsive and are left out of the competition if the first group interviewed includes a suitable candidate.

✓ Mistake No. 84: Sending a Letter to the Wrong Person or the Wrong Address

Job applicants who send letters to corporate executives whose names have been gleaned from a trade or association directory can make a big mistake. Executives move around a lot and it is quite common for a directory to be as much as 25 percent inaccurate only six months after publication.

Verify the current title and address of the executive by placing a telephone call to the company and confirming the information in the directory. This will save you a lot of wasted effort and, perhaps, from unnecessary rejection. Executives are not impressed by letters addressed to a former rival who may have been fired, ousted, or forced to retire from the company.

✓ Mistake No. 85: Failing to State Your Next Step

At the conclusion of your cover letter or market letter, make sure to state how you intend to follow up this communication. While it is perfectly proper to say that you are "looking forward to hearing" from the employer, it boxes you into a corner. It leaves the initiative in someone else's hands. A better tactic would be to indicate that **you** will be contacting the employer in about a week to discuss employment opportunities at the company--or to discuss the particular job in which you are interested (whichever is appropriate).

Part of your recordkeeping responsibility then involves keeping track of these timetables and following up within the specified time frame.

Once you have completed all of your job search planning and document preparation, you are ready to embark on a more active phase of job hunting. While you may be the exception, and might be able to land your next job (or first job) in a very short amount of time, for most people the process usually takes three to six months.

During that time, you will submit a number of resumes and application forms, go to interviews, weigh job offers, etc. These activities must be managed properly to achieve your goal: landing the best available job. Unfortunately, most job seekers don't think in terms of self-management, and do not go about job hunting in an organized fashion.

Our contention is that if you have already invested the massive amount of time involved in plotting a carefully crafted job hunting strategy and designing superior resumes and application forms, this is no time to abandon good job hunting habits. As with any business that transitions from the start-up to the operational stage, good management is vital to success.

✓ Mistake No. 86: Being Impatient

We live in an impatient world. Nobody wants to wait for things to happen according to their own speed. Everyone is always in a hurry. There is no relief in sight. If anything, the pace of life is accelerating.

Unfortunately, speed is not a hallmark of the job hunting process. Hiring procedures take time; and the larger the organization, or the more important the vacant position is, the longer it takes. All bureaucracies are characterized by layer upon layer of individuals who may participate in decisionmaking. Short of a national or corporate emergency, these decisions can rarely be rushed. It may well take six to eight weeks (or even longer) to reach the **interview** stage.

Job hunters must acknowledge and accept this time factor from the outset. This is one of the classic reasons why it is easier to look for a new job while still employed at your last job. If you choose (or are forced) to leave your current job before finding a new one, be prepared for a period between paychecks that may last for many months.

▶ Being Negative (And Impatient) ◀

Here is a scenario of the job hunting process when impatience is compounded by a negative attitude.

● *Stage One: Let's get this bad scene over with.* For reasons too complex and psychologically based to delve into here, most job hunters view the job search as a supremely unpleasant experience. Hence, they naturally want to have as little to do with it as possible. They come into the process with a bad attitude, and watch it fester and get worse.

● *Stage Two: Let's speed this up.* Spurred on by their "friends" who are constantly telling them how dismal it is to look for a job, they accelerate the process as much as possible and cut corners at every opportunity. For the Bad Attitudes, the quick and dirty route is the only one.

● *Stage Three: Take the first job offer.* They sit down one Sunday at halftime of the TV football game and scribble out a resume, circulate it, and take the first job they're offered.

● *Stage Four: The job's a bummer--just like the last one.* Every bad work experience (and there are many for these characters) only confirms how unpleasant the whole job hunting scene is. Unable to break out of this vicious cycle, they then wind up back at Stage One...forced to look for yet another job.

We know it's difficult, but you must TRY to adopt a positive approach to the job hunt. Take the time to rise to the challenge. No one wants to hire someone with a negative, cynical attitude.

✓ Mistake No. 87: Taking Your Time About Applying

When asked why he dropped an easy fly ball during a critical World Series game, Yankee great Yogi Berra replied: "I nonchalanted it." Don't fritter away your chance to grab the rare ideal employment opportunity by doing the same thing.

> **Recently, one of our clients called us and painfully related the following story:**
>
> He was applying for a six-figure position as the Director of Development (fundraising) for a major university. His qualifications matched the "ideal candidate" job description perfectly. He had had a prior rewarding business relationship with the university, loved the locale, had an outstanding background, and would have thrived in the position. Only one problem. He mailed in his application via regular first-class mail and heard nothing for weeks. When he called to inquire, he was informed that: (1) the position had been filled, and (2) the university had never received his application. Our client was devastated.

When you see a job advertised for which you want to apply, the most prudent course of action is to **apply as soon as possible**. In the absence of an application deadline, it is understood that the position is "open until filled." That means the job may be filled tomorrow--or it may not be filled for an extended period of time. Or, it may never be filled because the applications received were so off-target that the employer felt forced to re-write the position description and issue a revised ad in order to solicit applications from a whole new group of applicants.

Since many classified ads elicit a large number of responses, some applicants feel that waiting a week or two before submitting an application would mean their resumes will receive more careful attention. The theory is that applications which arrive en masse in immediate response to an ad are not examined as carefully as those which arrive later, one at a time. While this theory sounds logical, and would work well under certain circumstances, there are several points to consider before choosing this course of action:

1. The employer could receive the impression that you're not really interested in the position. After all, those who were **really** interested applied promptly and are already calling to check on the interview schedule.

2. If the employer assumes you **are** just as interested as those who applied promptly, then he or she must also assume that you are disorganized, inefficient, and perhaps a little careless.

3. All employers like to make hiring decisions as quickly as possible. After all, they have work waiting to be done.

Large organizations tend to take longer to fill positions because they have so many personnel issues to handle simultaneously, and may be trying to hire several individuals for different kinds of positions. Talking with a large number of diverse job applicants and trying to schedule interviews can take time. Even though the process can take longer, applications received after the first round of interviews has been scheduled are usually set aside and will be seriously considered only if circumstances require a second round. If an applicant is selected from the first round of interviews, your late application is out of luck.

Small organizations can concentrate on filling one job at a time. When they have a job opening, it usually means they are understaffed and are under pressure to hire someone immediately. A number of small business owners have told us that they follow a simple hiring rule: the first qualified applicant they interview gets the job offer. No elaborate psychological screening, no series of interviews with key personnel, no procedures mandating consideration of at least three applicants, no extensive background checks. *They meet, they like, they hire.* If you are slow to apply, the candidate selected may already be on the job by the time your resume floats in.

4. It is possible that you would have been the perfect match for the position as originally advertised. However, since you did not apply promptly, the employer did not have the opportunity to review your qualifications and has reconsidered and revised the nature of the position. Unfortunately, you are not a perfect match for the reissued vacancy announcement. Once employers change their minds concerning the nature of a position, they rarely reverse course. They usually think the revised course of action is a better one.

▶ Failing to Meet Application Deadlines ◀

Unless a position is listed as having no deadline for the receipt of applications, or as "open until filled," "open continuously," or something similar, it will usually have **a specified closing date by which applications must be received.** The only exception to this is when the listing indicates that the closing date is the date by which applications must be **postmarked.**

Government agencies--Federal, state, and local--frequently advertise jobs with specific closing dates. Unfortunately, many job hunters either do not take these dates seriously or delay mailing or delivering their applications until the last minute. Late applications are often discarded or returned because of their failure to meet the deadline.

Occasionally there is a very good reason why you cannot meet a specific deadline. Perhaps you only became aware of the vacant position close to the last day applications would be accepted. If you find yourself in this predicament, and the job in question sounds ideal, contact the employer and try your utmost to speak to the person directly responsible for accepting applications for that specific job. Explain your problem, indicate that you are in the process of sending in your application, and ask the official to accept it anyway. This approach frequently succeeds and your application may then be considered even if it arrives a little late.

The best approach, of course, is to keep informed about available jobs and to apply for them as soon as you see them advertised, regardless of their announced closing date.

► Making Sure Your Application Gets There ◄

If you do run across the job of your dreams, the one where, when you read the job description, your pulse quickens with excitement because you know the job was meant for none other than you and you were meant for the job, *make sure your application gets there*. There are plenty of ways to guarantee this. Regular first-class mail service is not one of them. Use an overnight delivery service and have someone at the receiving end sign for your package. Occasionally when we suggest this to clients, they balk because it will cost them more than the price of a first-class postage stamp. If your application does not get there at all, it will cost you a great deal more than that.

✓ Mistake No. 88: Keeping Your Whereabouts a Secret

Dinah Myte was a chemistry student at a well known university. She applied for a prestigious summer internship with a Federal Government agency, hoping to show through her summer performance that she merited a full time job upon graduation. She put her home telephone number on her application form. Unfortunately, as a busy, ambitious student, she could only be reached at that number when she went home to sleep. She spent most the day in classes, and then went to her part-time job at the local hospital. She was selected for the job from more than 80 applicants, but when the agency tried to call Ms. Myte at her home number, they could never reach her. After several days of futile attempts, they gave up and hired their second choice for the position. Ms. Myte lost the only summer job she really wanted.

In this competitive job market, how are you going to get a job offer if the employer can't find you?

You're not. With lots of qualified applicants for the really good jobs, employers will not wait for you to resurface. Instead, they will just go on to the next name down the list.

This means you have got to be covered at all times. (No, don't run out and rent a mobile telephone or even a beeper.) Just make certain that your resume contains **all** the telephone numbers through which you can be reached. This includes, in addition to your home and work numbers, (1) the number at your school where you can be reached or where messages may be left for you, and (2) the number at your parents or other permanent address if you live in temporary quarters, such as a dormitory or a military barracks.

If you have a fairly regular schedule, you should also include in your application the times when you may be reached at each number.

Naturally, if you indicate a number where messages may be left for you, you should check those places regularly to see if any messages have in fact been left for you.

If you're conducting your job hunt from home, it is advisable to get an answering machine or subscribe to a telephone answering service. *NOTE:* When you tape your answering machine message to callers, keep it brief and conventional. Forego being amusing or cute. No employer will be favorably impressed by a message given by an Elvis Presley or Mae West sound-alike.

When placing (or receiving) job hunting calls from home, make sure there is no distracting noise in the background--such as children's voices, music, the radio, or the TV.

Many individuals at the executive level have found it valuable to have an extra phone installed temporarily in their homes, with a separate number, to maintain an aura of professionalism. It is then this phone number which is listed on the resume and with which the answering machine or answering service is associated.

If you will be away for a while during the job hunting period, advise the employer where you can be contacted during your trip.

If you move or change jobs after you have submitted your resume/application form, advise your prospective employer of your new address and telephone number.

✔ Mistake No. 89: Not Keeping Records

The typical job hunter scatters resumes and cover letters to the four winds and then sits back and waits. Let's say a few of the cover letters were "personalized," that is, targeted specifically at particular employers. Two weeks later, Amalgamated Corp. writes back, inviting Typical for an interview. In closing, the Vice President for Marketing of Amalgamated says:

> I read with a great deal of interest the points you raised in your letter accompanying your resume. When we talk, I want to focus our discussion on these interesting items.
>
> Looking forward to meeting you, I am
>
> Very truly yours,
>
> *Martin Mogul*
> Martin Mogul
> VP, Marketing

Very flattering. Only one problem: *Typical never made a copy of the letter he sent Amalgamated (or anyone else) and now does not remember a single one of the "interesting items" VP Mogul wants to discuss.* How impressive do you think Typical will be at the interview?

A slight variation on this scenario is something that has happened to us (and probably every other employer) from time to time: We read an interesting resume and contact the candidate, who does not recollect who we are, what our company does, the nature of the advertised job, which resume we were mailed, etc. Needless to say, we do not proceed further with people who cannot manage their own job hunting. Therefore,

> **Keep Careful And Meticulous Records Of Your Job Search.**

Records should include *copies of everything you send to any employer*. This does not mean, of course, that you need keep a separate copy of each standard resume you submit. One copy of a resume you sent to more than one employer will do. However, if you have crafted a series of targeted resumes, make sure to keep a careful record of which resume you submitted to each employer. The same procedure holds true for cover letters (or market letters).

Such records will not only serve to refresh your recollection of what you told a prospective employer when you pursue follow-up calls, but will also serve as a resource when you (inevitably) change jobs again at some future date. Since the average member of the U.S. workforce changes jobs every four years, it is highly likely you will have reason to refer back to your prior successful strategy in years to come. When job hunting time rolls around again, you will be thankful that you practiced good recordkeeping habits.

✓ Mistake No. 90: Not Following Up Your Application

If you have done your homework and targeted your job search to a well-researched market, what should you do after you have submitted your application?

Wait...but for how long?

That depends on the employer. As a rule, the larger the organization, the longer it takes to process job applications. Smaller employers do it faster because they have fewer bureaucratic hoops to jump through before arriving at a decision. A large organization may take six to eight weeks to process applications; a smaller one may process applications in a few days.

OK, you've waited a suitable length of time. Now what do you do? Not what most applicants do, which is nothing. Like sheep, they bleat around the meadow waiting passively for something, **anything** to happen.

If a reasonable time (based on your assessment of the size of the employing organization) has passed, **you should contact the employer in order to get a status report on your application.** Of course, the best person to talk to is the individual responsible for the ultimate hiring decision. However, in a large organization, that is not easy to do. Often, if you explain the purpose of your call to that individual's secretary or assistant, you may be able to discover a great deal about where you stand. Make sure to identify yourself in connection with the position for which you have applied. Above all, be courteous to **everyone** with whom you speak.

Polite persistence in contacting an organization--to try to schedule an interview or to obtain an update on your status--is frequently taken by the employer as a sign of serious interest and initiative, and may even help your chances of getting hired.

Note: The best times to telephone an organization are weekdays between 10:30 a.m. and 11:30 a.m., or between 2:00 p.m. and 4:00 p.m. Try to avoid calling any time Monday morning or Friday afternoon. The "missing" hours are typically devoted to re-entry syndrome (early morning), lunch-hour rituals, or preparation for departure (late afternoon).

▶ Being a Pest ◀

The applicant who begins calling immediately after submitting an application and continues to nag the employer for a decision quickly becomes labeled as an annoying pest. Frustration builds on both sides. You want to talk with the decision-maker, and the staff's instructions are to shield the decision-maker from the constant calls of overly zealous job applicants. You think the staff is surly and incompetent; the staff members begin to characterize you as curt and aggressive.

This is not good "applicant-etiquette." It's best to assume every person in an office has the power to veto your application for employment. Comments from members of the support staff with whom you have been dealing (i.e., "She's a pain in the xxx" or "He's an arrogant xxxxxxx") can effectively ruin any chances you may have had with their boss. In every dealing with an office, remember the following: *support staff can't hire you, but their negative comments can keep you from being hired!*

Good applicant-etiquette requires you to be polite and understanding. You know how busy everyone in the office is, and you do not want to distract them from their important duties, but you want to touch base with them periodically to check on how the applicant review process is coming along. Explain that you would like to call back in a few days for an update, it if would not be too much trouble. Make "friends" with the support staff with whom you have been dealing; address them formally (Ms. Roadblock, Mr. Brickwall) until they have given you permission to call them by their first names; always ask if they have a few moments to talk with you or, if this is not a good time, if you could call back later. If you can identify the key staff member who is the personal assistant to the decision-maker, that is the individual to target. Whenever you call, ask to speak with that person in particular.

A final word of warning concerning the workplace of the '90s. Never assume that the woman who answers the phone is someone's secretary or receptionist. She might be an executive who happened to be next to the phone when it rang. If you treat her in a peremptory or condescending manner while explaining you're a job applicant, your chances for employment there have just hit zero.

✓ Mistake No. 91: Starving While Job Hunting

One of the worst job search management pitfalls is watching your financial resources dwindle to practically nothing while you're job hunting. This is not managing. It is sliding down the slippery slope toward financial disaster. Estimates vary on the average amount of time it takes to land a new management or professional position, but none is very encouraging. Some say the average is three to five months; some say six months or longer. For women, ethnic minorities, or those over 50 years old, the search may take even longer.

Do not wait until you can't meet a mortgage payment or are eating peanut butter sandwiches every night for dinner before seeking some temporary source of income. There are many firms which specialize in short-term or temporary employment opportunities. Many companies seek qualified individuals for limited assignments. They may be working on a contract deadline; they may be temporarily understaffed due to an employee's illness or maternity leave; they may have just encountered a problem they are not staffed to handle; they may be preparing a proposal or are facing an audit; or they may be developing a new product. The reasons why a company could suddenly need an employee with special skills are endless. Realizing that the need is for a limited period of time, management wants someone to fill that need and then depart.

This kind of assignment is perfect for someone between full-time jobs. It provides a source of income, it presents an opportunity to make new contacts, and it looks good on a resume. An added bonus for the job seeker is that many short-term assignments do not involve a full 40 hours a week, allowing time to pursue other job hunting leads during the off-hours.

Look around in your area for temporary help firms that handle short-term assignments and watch the Sunday classifieds for ads placed directly by the companies themselves.

If you would like to obtain a list of temporary help firms located in your own geographic area (or one to which you would like to move), send a stamped, self-addressed envelope indicating the geographic area in which you are interested, to:

National Association of Temporary Services
119 S. Saint Asaph Street
Alexandria, VA 22314
Telephone: 703/549-6287

According to the National Association of Temporary Services (NATS), the estimated percentages among temporary help industry segments are as follows:

- 63% of all temporary help jobs consist of office/clerical positions.

- 15% of jobs involve light and heavy industrial skills ranging from assembly line work to product demonstrations to janitorial services.

- 11% of jobs encompass technical and professional positions such as engineers, accountants, draftsmen, computer programmers, writers, lawyers, and managers.

- 10% of jobs are in the medical area which includes registered and licensed practical nurses, therapists, nursing aides, and lab technicians for hospital staffing and home health services.

Some temporary help firms specialize in certain substantive areas, such as accountants or medical support staff; others handle a broad range of temporary assignments. If the name of the firm does not reflect its area of expertise, you will have to contact it directly to see if it handles temporary professional jobs that would be appropriate for you.

Of course, while working on a temporary assignment you would not be a regular full-time employee eligible for many traditional employee benefits, such as participation in the company retirement plan. But you would be working, you would have money coming in, you would be making contacts, and you would not wind up with a huge time gap on your resume that might look as though no one wanted to hire you.

CHAPTER NINE: Interview Mistakes

If you have avoided most of the mistakes we have examined up to now, you are probably in line for a series of job interviews. This is make-or-break time in your job search. Consequently, the same effort that went into your job hunting effort up to this point must be applied to your forthcoming interviews.

This is no time to relax, to assume that your chances of winning the job are any greater than before. In fact, for a variety of reasons, the trend among many employers (especially large employers) is to do **more** interviewing, not less, in order to have more insurance against making a hiring mistake. Not only are hiring organizations interviewing a **greater number** of candidates for a particular job than they have in the past, they are also interviewing job finalists **more than once**--sometimes involving different individuals or teams of individuals. This means you have to be prepared...and *preparation is more essential to interviewing success than it is at any other stage of the job hunting process.* It is also a great confidence-builder, something that you can lean on when the butterflies hit you in the reception area as you wait for your interview to begin.

✓ Mistake No. 92: Not Preparing for an Interview

Not preparing for an interview is one of the worst possible mistakes you can make. You may think you are prepared because you have thoroughly rehearsed the answers to the standard questions--How did you do in school? What do you want out of your career? Why do you want to work for our firm? What are your strengths?--but this is not enough. It is just scratching the surface. Don't get us wrong, this kind of preparation is fine, as far as it goes, but in no way does it really prepare you or help distinguish you from every other candidate for the job, several of whom (if not all) are also able to rattle off the same kind of standard responses to the same standard questions.

What the vast majority of interviewees overlook is the other side of the interview preparation coin--**familiarizing themselves with the employer**.

Here are some of the things you should do to prepare for an interview:

1. *Learn as much as you can about the employer.* There is a great deal of **background information** publicly and readily available about any sizable organization. For example: If you are interviewing with a corporation whose stock is publicly traded on a stock exchange or "over-the-counter," you will be able to examine its

latest annual report, business analyses issued by stock brokerages, articles in business journals, etc. We have included in our *Bibliography* some of the most easily accessible sources that can be tapped for this kind of background information, most of which can be found in libraries.

2. *Study the latest news about the company, its competitors, and the industry in general.* For example: You do not want to walk into a real estate office the day after there's been a steep rise in mortgage interest rates and have that dismal information revealed to you for the first time by the interviewer. Thousands of job hunters have been sorely embarrassed by such revelations. Do whatever is necessary to avoid factual surprises.

There are many excellent sources of timely information about industry and company developments. The newspapers are one of them. Whatever you do, make certain you *read at least one daily newspaper consistently.* And not just the Sports or the Lifestyle sections, either. Beyond the daily papers, there are *specialized sources* that you should examine. Read the business and trade press. The <u>Wall Street Journal</u> is a must, at least during the time you are in the job market. In addition, many metropolitan areas have weekly business journals that are superb sources of information about local companies, including the impact of economic trends and political decisions on these companies.

Virtually every industry in the U.S. has at least one *trade publication*. These journals monitor industry happenings and are also "must" reading for an interview. Many of these are available in larger public libraries and, if not there, from the trade association that publishes the journal. You can find the names of these associations, and the names of the trade publications, in the <u>Encyclopedia of Associations</u>, <u>National Trade and Professional Associations of the United States</u>, or the <u>Associations Yellow Book</u>. These excellent references are available in most libraries (see *Bibliography*).

There may even be a commercial newspaper or journal that monitors the industry and its members either on a nationwide basis, regionally, or both. For instance, the legal industry is ably covered by such newspapers as <u>American Lawyer</u>, <u>National Law Journal</u>, or <u>Legal Times</u>. These types of publications often contain articles examining individual law firms or corporate legal offices, from which a prospective employee can learn a great deal. There are few industries in the U.S. that are exempt from this type of in-depth scrutiny.

Beyond these sources, there are several other, more sophisticated (and, consequently, more expensive) sources of excellent information. Several computerized data bases, updated daily, can provide you with more detailed information than you may ever want to know about companies and industries. DIALOG, for example, is a data base maintained by the Lockheed Corporation. It is perhaps the most comprehensive available and can be used in many public and school libraries. Mead Data Central's NEXIS data base can also be accessed through a library.

3. *Familiarize yourself with the company's "product line."* For companies that actually produce a tangible product, this is easy. Go to a store where the product(s) is sold, see how it's marketed, try to analyze its customer base and its competition. Contact a marketing representative and request information about the product. If possible, buy some of the product and use it.

4. *If the company markets a service, learn what you can about the service and its customers.* While there is plenty of information available about publicly traded service firms from the same sources cited earlier, if it is a small, private organization such as a dry cleaner, printer, publisher, baker, equipment repair company, etc., you may have to do a little spade work on your own. Depending on the nature of the organization, some of the points to consider are: What are the components of the service? How much does it cost? How frequently does each customer use it? How is it marketed? What is the geographical spread of the company's market? What is its profit margin? What companies are its competition and what are they doing? What does the economic future hold for such a service?

5. *If you're interviewing for a job in the public sector, with a local, state, or Federal government office*, get information on the agency mission and structure. This is all public information, easily obtained in most public libraries. For the Federal Government, at least look at the U.S. Government Manual, which is a standard source for this kind of information. Further, the Code of Federal Regulations often contains agency and office mission statements at the beginning of each agency's section. These descriptions of organizational objectives are very useful when preparing for an interview. At the state level, every state issues some kind of manual or directory describing state agencies and organizations. Formal documents may be more difficult to obtain at the city or county level, but budget requests (at **all** governmental levels) are frequently accompanied by descriptions of offices and their missions in order to justify their existence and continued need for public funding. Further, every government agency has a **public information office** which can always send you a description of that agency's functions and responsibilities.

The impression your knowledge of the employer will make on the interviewer cannot be overstated:

- *The more you know about the organization, the greater will be your confidence during the interview.* Confidence is a trait looked for by all employers.

- *Your knowledge will impress the interviewer.* You are demonstrating that you do your homework and that you care.

145

- *You will distinguish yourself in a positive way when compared to most, if not all, of the other applicants for the position.* An employer will remember the well-prepared applicant.

We are always surprised by the number of people who go into an interview after **hours** of preparing answers to tough questions about themselves, and ask the employer: "What is it, exactly, that you do?" It's hard to relate how annoying this is...and what a **negative** impression this deliberate ignorance projects. We have interviewed MANY people for positions in our own organization, but have never hired anyone who had not made the slightest attempt to learn what we did before coming for an interview.

✓ Mistake No. 93: Not Seeking Out Practice Interviews

Most job candidates only go to interviews for jobs they are seriously pursuing. This is a big mistake.

A job interview is a unique phenomenon. It does not resemble any other life experience. If you really want the job for which you are interviewing, try not to go into that interview as a novice. After all, if you were a professional athlete, you would practice, practice, practice until you maximized your professional proficiency. The same rigor should be applied to job interviews.

A good rule of thumb is: never go into your first interview for a job you **really** want without at least one practice interview under your belt. No, practicing with a friend is not a substitute for the real thing. Does your friend make your pulse race and your palms sweat? Come on, we're not talking about **that** kind of a friend-- we're talking tongue-tied in an executive suite, not in a social setting.

While an employer may be aghast at the thought of spending valuable time interviewing applicants who may be only semi-interested in the job being offered, that is not your worry. After all, who do you think it is that puts all of those job vacancy announcements in the paper merely to comply with the equal employment opportunity laws, knowing all the time they have someone in mind to fill the position? If you said employers, you were right. But you don't know that when you see the ad and get excited and then spend your precious time and money getting your application in to the employer by the deadline. So, don't feel guilty about using employers a tiny bit to your own advantage for a change.

This does not mean that you should not take every interview seriously. You should. Even if you have little desire to work there, go into the interview and try to make a good impression. The best practice interview is one that conditions you well for the serious interviews that you will go to subsequently. Of course, the practice interview may surprise you. More than once an applicant has been so favorably impressed during a "practice" interview--and has, in turn, made such a positive impression--that the interview became a serious one.

In the case of job interviews, practice breeds relaxation and confidence, two attributes that can go a long way towards getting you the job you want.

✓ Mistake No. 94: Failing to Prepare for the Tough Interview Questions

This book talks a lot about human nature and everyone's natural inclination to avoid difficult and uncomfortable situations. One such source of discomfort is the tough questions that inevitably arise during a job interview. When preparing for an interview, candidates frequently neglect to practice their responses to this kind of probing inquiry.

What are the tough interview questions? While there can, of course, be no generic definition, there are some obvious candidates that have attained the status of virtual "sure things" as a result of the frequency with which they crop up. Among these are:

- Will you tell me a little about yourself?
- Why do you want to leave your current job?
- Why did you leave your last job?
- What do you like/dislike the most about your current job?
- What did you like/dislike the most about your last job?
- What are your strengths (and/or weaknesses)?
- Aren't you overqualified for this position?
- What kind of a job do you really want?
- Are you a good team player?
- What are the qualities of a good manager?
- What is the biggest problem you've been asked to solve?
- Where do you see yourself in five years?
- Would you be prepared to make a geographic move?
- What can you contribute to this company?
- Why should I hire you?

147

This is not to say that you are certain to face all of these questions during each interview...but you are apt to be confronted with at least one of them at every session. So, you should take time to think through your answers **before** the questions are asked.

While preparing your answers to these questions, make sure to keep them brief. In the first place, no one really wants to hear a 10 or 15 minute explanation of why you left your last job. In the second place, in such a lengthy explanation you are almost certain to reveal information **that should be left unstated**. You should practice presenting explanations that do not exceed two or three minutes. Sometimes a sentence or two will suffice. If the interviewer wants more information, he or she will ask for it...allowing you to focus your response on the particular point raised. Above all, listen to exactly what is being asked and the key words being used.

Keep in mind that many interviewers are human resource **professionals** who have academic training (many times including advanced degrees) and extensive experience in asking questions to find the right person for the job. Spotting the weak point in a resume or a poor answer to a tough question is child's play for these interviewers...**don't underestimate them!**

✔ Mistake No. 95: Criticizing Your Current or Former Employer

---

"Why did you leave Happy Times Inc., Ms. Perfect?"

"My boss was an idiot and I couldn't stand working for such a jerk!"

We have heard similar refrains from job applicants all too often. We have **never** hired anyone who made that kind of a negative statement about a former employer. Even if the employer was a Beast From Hell, there are many reasons you could use to explain your departure (see Mistake No. 3) that would not immediately raise questions about **your** judgment, **your** maturity, **your** ability to be part of a team. Further, no one wants to be saddled with a person who has a bad attitude. All employers enjoy working with positive, "sunny" people, not ones walking around under a dark cloud all day long.

Complaining about a former employer--organization, supervisor, even co-workers--is a guaranteed way to blow a job opportunity. Put yourself in the shoes of the interviewer--your prospective boss. He or she will inevitably identify with the management you are vilifying, not with you, and will wonder about the **employer's**

version of the situation. Any employer would inevitably think: "Do I really want to hire someone who speaks about her boss this way?"

✓ Mistake No. 96: Failing to Ask Good Questions at an Interview

---

A traditional interview concludes with the following question from the interviewer: "Do you have any questions?" Unfortunately, many job seekers are so frazzled at that point they say "No." They either want to exit quickly or want the interviewer to think all relevant information has been so thoroughly discussed that there is nothing left to say. This is a big mistake. *The moment when questions can be asked provides another chance to make your mark.* You want the interviewer's final impression of you to be positive, that you have been listening carefully and are interested in the position and the company. Some of these questions could include:

- How would you describe the ideal applicant for this job?

- What are the most important qualities you're seeking in that ideal applicant?

- Is this a new position you're seeking to fill? (If not, inquire about what happened to the person who used to hold the position...the answer will be an important factor in your consideration of a job offer.)

- What are the key responsibilities of this position?

- What are going to be the biggest challenges I would face in the position?

- Where does this position fit in the organizational hierarchy? Or, To whom would I be reporting?

- If you're seeking a managerial position, you could also ask questions relating to the company's current competitive edge in the market and plans to increase its market share...always reflecting your familiarity with the company's products or services as well as its competition.

149

- If you're being interviewed for a position as manager of a division or unit, ask how many individuals you would be supervising and what goals the company hopes the division or unit will achieve in a year's time.

- Finally, always ask for a timetable on when they anticipate the position will be filled...How soon could I start working? They might want someone who could start next week--or next year.

Remember, no matter how exhausted or unnerved you might be at the end of an interview, *you must always have a good question or two to ask when given the opportunity*. You know your skills and the kind of position you're seeking, so only **you** can craft the most appropriate kinds of questions for the interviews you'll have. The final impression you're striving to leave with the interviewer is that you're enthusiastic about the position, understand the company, and can communicate this information effectively.

► Asking Dreadful Questions ◄

Everyone's interviewing nightmare is to inadvertently make the fatal blunder. There are many to avoid, but this section will address the kinds of questions which can undermine your credibility as an applicant. Over the years, through our own interviews with many individuals for a variety of positions in our company, we have developed a list of classically dreadful questions...questions which immediately eliminated the applicant from serious consideration. This **Dreadful Questions Hall of Fame** includes:

- What does your company do?
- How much money can I make?
- Will I have my own office?
- Would my boss be a woman?
- How much sick leave will I earn?
- When will I be able to take my first vacation?
- How soon can I get in on the pension plan?
- What did you say a few minutes ago about this position's responsibilities?
- When will I get a raise?
- When will I get promoted?
- I won't have to work overtime, will I?
- Do people always work this hard around here?

There are obviously ways to elicit some of this information in a more positive way. For example:

"I just want you to know that I'm not afraid of overtime. An important part of any job is doing it well and meeting deadlines. If this position involves working late or on weekends to make that happen, I'm ready and willing to accept that responsibility."

For all you know, the position involves absolutely no overtime at all...but if you frame the question in such a way that you sound lazy and bored, you've already lost it.

It is also natural to express interest in your career path within an organization. Ask whether doing a good job and performing well means you would be assigned increased responsibility. Allow the interviewer to use the word "promotion" in his response, if it is appropriate. You're supposed to be interested in the **position being offered**, not one the next rung up the ladder.

So often, job applicants do not realize the impression they're making. No one wants to hire someone who is already dissatisfied with the job's duties or its salary, who wants to know about vacation time and sick time, who will not be a team player, or who does not care about the company's needs. The interviewer wants to know what **you have to offer the company,** and is turned off when you concentrate on **what the company can offer you.**

✔ Mistake No. 97: Ignorance of Salary/Compensation Levels

For some unfathomable reason, many job hunters are unprepared for questions concerning compensation that are usually raised at serious interviews. Prepared as they might be to handle all the other tough questions with great aplomb, they fall flat on their faces when asked the obvious question: "What kind of salary are you seeking?" Answers typically range from the ridiculous to the sublime. Many job seekers actually tell the interviewer: "I don't know...what did you have in mind?" Or, "I haven't given it much thought!"

If the salary question comes up at the beginning of an interview, try to postpone the discussion of compensation until later--after you have been able to present your qualifications. Explain that while salary is important, you think it's more important to discuss the nature of the position and what you could contribute to the organization.

When you're pressed for an answer, state a salary range. If you're now making $32,000, you might give the range of $35,000-$40,000. If you're now making $52,000, you might give the range of $55,000-$60,000. Whenever a salary range comes up on either side of the employment equation, it frames the parameters of the issue and usually inclines all parties to a consideration of a mid-point within the range when negotiations get serious.

• *If the salary then turns out to be less than what you're currently making,* it might be possible to explain the extent to which your qualifications would allow the employer to **expand** the job description and thus raise the salary offered for the position with additional responsibilities.

• *If the salary turns out to be much higher then expected* (which rarely happens), then your "salary range" approach would permit you to slip in at a higher level.

• *When you're asked directly what you're currently earning* (and keep in mind that this figure can be verified immediately), state $XX,XXX **plus benefits**. In some organizations "benefits"--even at modest salary levels--can have a cash value of $4,000-$10,000.

Above all, try to be prepared. People "leave money on the table" every day by not realizing the salary level of the position they're seeking. Try to do a little research into what people in the industry in comparable positions are making.

• *Organizations large enough to issue job vacancy announcements always state the salary range in the announcement.* Check these out. They are frequently posted on bulletin boards or kept in notebooks in the Human Resources/Personnel Department. Smaller organizations in the same geographical area usually have salaries which are competitive with those offered by the larger organizations or are slightly lower.

• *Do a little phone work.* Do you know anyone in that organization or a comparable organization? They can usually tell you what the salary range is for a certain kind of position--secretary, computer programmer, accountant, etc. Of course, you cannot call someone and ask about **their** salary or the salary range for **their position**, but you might be surprised at how much salary information people stockpile in their memory banks. Almost any mid-level manager in any company can give you a salary range for every kind of position in the company.

• *Consult salary information sources.* There are a number of excellent up-to-date sources of salary information. The <u>Occupational Outlook Handbook</u>, compiled by the U.S. Department of Labor and published by the U.S. Government Printing Office, is available at most public and school libraries. It contains entry-level, average or median, and Federal Government salary information for many occupations. Civil service organizations at all governmental levels publish detailed salary scales. For the private sector, publications such as the <u>National Business Employment Weekly</u> frequently include articles on average salary levels for individual occupations nationwide. For information on each of these publications, see *Bibliography*.

• *Contact trade and professional associations.* Often, more detailed salary data can be obtained from industry trade or professional associations. Many of these associations conduct annual salary surveys of their membership and publish the results in their periodical publication or in special reports. Many of these surveys are broken down by geographic regions.

• *If all else fails, at least check out the Help Wanted/Employment ads in the Sunday newspapers* in the city/region where the job is located. Look for positions comparable to the one for which you will be interviewed and see what salary is being offered.

✔ Mistake No. 98: Arriving Late (Or Too Early) for an Interview

If you are ever going to be somewhere at the appointed hour, an interview is the place. Nothing will annoy and upset an interviewer more than a job applicant who arrives late for the interview. If you get there late (unless you have an **outstanding** excuse), that will probably end your chances of getting the job.

So, plan ahead. If there is any possibility whatsoever of running into a delay, make certain that you leave early enough to give yourself ample time to make the appointment. If you run into unanticipated transportation problems during your trip, call the interviewer **before** the time established for the interview and explain that you have been delayed, but are on the way.

Arrive at the interview early enough to sit quietly in the reception area for a few minutes. Identify yourself to the receptionist, try to absorb the general tone/ambience of the office, and focus on your goals for the interview.

Arriving "early enough" means around 15-20 minutes before your appointment is scheduled to begin, not one hour (or more). Most interviewers have heavy appointment schedules and the *extremely early* arrival of an appointment can be disruptive and annoying. Many people feel uncomfortable having individuals with whom they have scheduled appointments (of any kind) waiting outside their offices for extensive periods of time...it seems rude and unprofessional. As a result, the interviewer feels compelled to adjust his or her schedule to accommodate the early arrival and is generally not happy about doing so.

✓ Mistake No. 99: Making a Poor First Impression

Several years ago the authors interviewed two finalists for an intern position. The one with the most impressive resume walked in wearing a glossy college windbreaker. In addition, he also sported very long, unkempt hair, a shirttail that hung out over one side of his belt, as well as a belt end which flapped from side-to-side as he walked. After shaking his hand, we were astonished to observe him plop down heavily into a chair, uninvited.

After our mercifully brief interview with this candidate, the second applicant came in wearing a well-fitting suit and conservative tie. He was very well-groomed, looked us in the eye as he firmly shook hands, and remained standing until he was invited to be seated. Despite his decidedly inferior resume, there was no doubt that he was the candidate for us.

Because you like to wear casual or punk clothes in your leisure time is not a justification to wear them to a job interview. Assuming that you are not trying to get a job at a New Wave hair salon or with a heavy metal band, of course. The overwhelming majority of employers like to hire people who are well-groomed and neatly and conservatively dressed. You will rarely find an exception to this tendency. Consequently, dress for the percentages.

If you feel that you HAVE TO reflect your political philosophy in your dress, and that to do otherwise would be hypocritical, that's fine. But be prepared for rejection if that philosophy is out of sync with the people you're trying to impress. The desk clerks at the Unemployment Office won't care how you dress or groom yourself.

If you are interviewing with a firm that you suspect has a strict dress code and are having trouble fine-tuning your wardrobe, visit the company offices before your interview to reconnoiter. Or, have lunch during the work week at a restaurant located near the office to see what company employees are wearing. If neither is possible, then obtain a copy of the organization's annual report and study the pictures of company officers and employees. That will tell you a great deal about how to dress.

Years of extensive research by psychologists and behavioral scientists demonstrate unequivocally that first impressions are absolutely critical to success in any encounter. Communications experts say that during an initial encounter between two people, more than 70 percent of the message is communicated by appearance alone. No matter what kind of meeting you are preparing for--employment interview, business meeting, negotiating session--you should make your appearance as impressive as possible. This means going to job interviews well-groomed and in appropriate attire.

For some excellent advice on making a strong, positive first impression, we recommend First Impression, Best Impression by Dr. Janet Elsea (see *Bibliography*).

✓ Mistake No. 100: Being Too Agreeable (Or Too Argumentative) at the Interview

---

In virtually all life situations where one party is dealing from a position of relative strength and the other party is dealing from a position of relative weakness, the weaker one tells the stronger one what he thinks the stronger one wants to hear. This is the way life works, right?

Right. But don't confuse employment interviews with living. Interviews are at least a partial exception to this rule, for a very good reason.

An interview is an opportunity for an employer to **test** you. Often, interviewers engage in a considerable amount of role-playing...that is, they play devil's advocate, purposely coming on strong or being argumentative in order to test how you respond. Typical challenges could range from politics to affirmative action, from comments about your former employer to generalizations about foreign competition. If this happens to you, you have several options:

1. *You can say nothing.* Surprisingly, this is the strategy chosen by a great many interviewees in this kind of situation. For some, the sheer intellectual shock stuns them to silence. However, be advised that selecting this approach gives a strong signal to the employer that you cannot think "on your feet."

2. *You can be agreeable, acquiescing in even the most extreme statements.* However, unless you are being interviewed by a madman who actually believes the outrageous statements he is making, you will be doing yourself a disservice. *Whatever you do, don't grovel.* Regardless of their darkest fantasies about the ideal employee, employers generally despise grovelers and "yes-men."

155

3. *You can become overly defensive.* If disparaging, critical, or probing comments are made about your current or former employer, don't fall into the trap of revealing confidential information while fending off the attack. Respond with positive statements highlighting general corporate progress or achievements...nothing more. A spirited, detailed defense might win the debate but lose the job. No one wants an employee who lacks discretion or the ability to distinguish between public and private information.

4. *You can state your own point of view clearly and firmly.* This is always the best approach. A polite disagreement, if well-reasoned, will enhance your chances for the job. But be careful to avoid being overly argumentative. If an interviewer states that you did poorly in school, cite the mitigating factors that caused your relatively low grades, i.e., you worked while in college in order to pay the tuition, you have since matured and applied yourself diligently in all your other pursuits, etc. Emphasize your good points and strengths.

Remember, *the interviewer wants to see if you can rise to the challenge.* Many corporate interactions involve resolving differences to achieve a consensus. If you cannot express an opposing or dissenting view in a non-confrontational manner, your value to the company is diminished. An antagonistic attitude exacerbates problems... never contributes to their resolution.

✓ Mistake No. 101: Boring the Interviewer

Interviews make most applicants nervous, and nervous people often tend to expand their responses to avoid periods of silence. Droning on--and on--and on-- about **any** subject is never a good idea. It inevitably begins to bore the interviewer, who has a number of points to cover, and gives the impression that you cannot communicate in a clear, concise manner.

So, keep your statements brief, concise, and to the point. Don't ramble. Stay alert. Look for opportunities to wax anecdotal in a context the interviewer will understand and appreciate. For example: If the interviewer invites an opening such as: "We have to do something to counteract foreign competition," don't respond with a polite nod of your head and say something innocuous like: "You're right. We do." Try to use this obvious opening to articulate your well-reasoned views on this timely topic. If you have prepared for the interview and are reasonably up on current events and the employer's industry, this or any other business topic will not catch you by surprise.

Interviewers are evaluating much more than your credentials when you are in front of them. They also want to assess how your mind works and how your thought processes translate into language. We live in a society and an economy in which the ability to communicate is ever more critical. A job interview is as much about communication skills as anything else.

✓ Mistake No. 102: Ignoring Interview Etiquette

Everyone has nervous habits or mannerisms that project a non-professional image. Many of us also tend to ignore basic etiquette. An interview is not the stage on which to exhibit either tendency. For example, during an interview:

• *Don't smoke.* Even if the interviewer invites you to smoke, refrain from doing so...unless you're interviewing with a tobacco company.

• *Don't drink alcohol or take drugs.* Alcohol makes people less inhibited and promotes indiscrete comments. No one hires a substance abuser. This also applies to any legal drugs for which you have a prescription or purchase "over-the-counter," if those drugs might cause you to behave in a non-customary manner. A case in point: Some allergy drugs make people very drowsy. If you are beset with allergies and cannot do without an antihistamine, ask your doctor beforehand if there is an alternative to one that might impede your performance at a job interview.

• *Don't fuss with your clothes or hair.* Fidgeting is extremely distracting.

• *Don't slouch.*

• *Don't sit with your legs crossed, swinging one leg.*

• *Don't look at the floor or ceiling when you're being addressed.* Maintain good eye contact as much as possible.

• *Don't make any religious, political, ethnic, or sexual comments or jokes.*

• *Don't ask for a pen and paper so you can take notes.* Arrive prepared. Bring your own.

• *Don't ask for the correct spelling of the interviewer's name.* You should already have basic facts before entering the building, much less the interview. If you are unexpectedly introduced to someone who participates in the interview process, and you feel unsure of that person's name or position in the organization, telephone later (to the receptionist or someone's assistant) to verify that person's name and title.

• *If a third person, a professional colleague, enters the office during the interview and you're introduced to that person, stand up immediately and shake that person's hand firmly.*

• *Don't address the interviewer (or anyone else to whom you have been introduced) by his or her first name*...unless specifically requested to do so.

• *Don't keep glancing at your watch.* Is your time too valuable to sit through an interview? If you have something else scheduled that you have to do, you have not planned your interview schedule carefully enough. What if the interviewer is 30 minutes late? Or an hour late? What will you do, walk out? If so, wave good-bye to the job. We once interviewed a gentleman who entered our offices, sat down, took off his watch, and positioned it in front of him on a flat surface so that he could see it at all times during the interview! All during the interview, we could not take our eyes or our minds off that watch. Naturally, we did not consider him a serious candidate for the job.

• *If the interview has been arranged during your lunch hour, indicate that fact when you're setting it up.* Then, restate the fact that you're on your lunch hour **the moment you begin the interview**. This is a well understood phenomenon in the business world and your work schedule will be respected.

• *If the interviewer has to take a phone call during the interview,* immediately offer to leave the office to allow that person privacy during the call.

• *Take along at least six copies of your resume.* There is always the possibility that you may be meeting with more than one person. Taking along only one copy of your resume is usually a mistake. If you should need a second copy, what are your alternatives? Grabbing it out of the interviewer's hands and running outside to get a copy? Hoping the interviewer will pick up the phone, call a staff assistant, and ask that person to come to the office, get the resume, take it to the copier, and then come back with the copies? This would not create the impression of an organized, efficient, thoughtful person.

• *If you are asked to supply references,* reach in your briefcase or notebook and hand the interviewer a typed sheet (headed by your name, address, and phone number) listing at least three professional references. This should include, for each one, the person's full name, professional title, name of organization, address, and a phone number at which the individual can be reached during working hours. Do not take out a pen or pencil and try to scribble down this information from memory.

• *Before leaving, always thank the interviewer for taking the time to meet with you and express your interest in the position.* You can never assume that the interviewer knows beyond any doubt that you want the job. Make certain that you indicate, unequivocally, that you are **eager to be hired by the employer.** Do not act casual or blase about the job at any point during the interview. Make sure the interviewer knows that this company--and this job--is **your first choice.**

• *Follow up the interview with a letter* that once again thanks the interviewer for meeting with you, briefly restating your qualifications for the position and interest in joining the organization in that capacity. This is a terrific way to drive home the point that you take the job opportunity seriously and that you would be a conscientious employee if hired. More likely than not, such a letter will also set you apart from the crowded candidate field and leave a favorable impression in the employer's mind.

• *If you have been interviewed by more than one person,* make sure you write **individual follow-up letters** thanking each person. These people will probably **compare your letters** so make sure each one is different, reflecting the different topics covered during each conversation.

✓ Mistake No. 103: Leaving the Interview Without Knowing Where You Stand

---

When the interview ends, most job seekers get up, shake hands, say "thank you," and walk out the door. Make sure you do one more thing before departing. *Ask the interviewer for an immediate reaction:* "Do you consider me a serious candidate for this position?"

Of course, keep in mind that even if the answer is "yes," that does not mean that a commitment has been made or that you have been assured a job. It only means that on the basis of your resume and interview, you are still under serious consideration.

If the interviewer adds a "but," *listen carefully.* For example: "You are still a viable candidate for this job, but we were hoping to find someone with more computer programming experience on XXX equipment." Comments such as this one represent a yellow "caution" flag. If the very next applicant has the desired experience, you may well be eliminated. If such an applicant does not appear on the scene, you may be hired.

Or, once you discover the importance of a particular skill, you may be able to suggest how you can correct the deficiency. Many a job has been won at the last moment by a job hunter offering to take a course or training in a certain area. Such an offer always makes a positive impression and it shows how much you want the job.

Or, the interviewer may be *mistaken* in the impression that you lack a certain kind of skill or experience. Perhaps your resume omitted some relevant information and the interviewer took its absence at face value. Perhaps you *did* mention that skill and the interviewer, momentarily distracted, missed it. Whatever the reason, this exchange would give you the opportunity to *clarify* your background and the extent to which it *does* represent a good match with the job requirements.

The point of asking this kind of leading question is to try to determine where you stand...and why. Remember, from the prospective employer's point of view, the fact that you *asked* the question confirms your interest in the position and willingness to continue competing for it.

✓ Mistake No. 104: Failing to Follow Up an Interview

Once the interviewing process is over, the employer generally takes some time to review interview notes and resumes in order to narrow the field of candidates for the position. In your case, the employer should also be reviewing the thank-you letter that you wrote shortly after the initial interview.

Now, how are you going to follow up that interview? If you really want the job, you should follow it up with a phone call about a week or ten days later. Call the person who interviewed you and ask how the recruiting process is coming along. Restate your interest in the position and ask if there is any information which you could add as a supplement to your application. You may be surprised at the response. If you are a serious contender, and if the field of applicants has been narrowed down to two or three, you may be asked to supply additional data. For example: If your references have been difficult to contact, you may be asked to provide alternative phone numbers. Or, you may be asked to supply an academic transcript or writing sample. Or, your obvious interest alone may prompt an invitation for a second interview.

It's always wise to assume that employers are BUSY people with a thousand things to do. If there has been a glitch in verifying your employment, your educational background, or reaching a reference, you may be passed over simply because of that difficulty. Or, if only three applicants are to be asked back for a second interview, your call might be the easy way for an employer to decide in your favor.

If you receive a *negative* reaction from your follow-up phone call, at least you can cross that particular employment possibility off your list. Everybody always hears "we'll call you" and too many candidates actually sit around waiting for the call. Don't do it. Take charge of your job hunt. Be assertive, be enthusiastic, show that you have the skill to GET the job.

✓ Mistake No. 105: Job Fair Failure

Over the years we have spoken with a number of employers who have participated in job fairs. Do not let the term used for these events, "job fair," give you the impression that these are casual events at which people are expected to have a good time. Employers take such events seriously and those attending should do so as well.

If you decide to attend a job fair, some of the guidelines for a successful encounter are:

1. *Arrive early.* The recruiters or personnel specialists handling the booths tend to get frazzled by the end of the day and may not feel as patient or as sympathetic as they did earlier. They are all trained to listen and observe carefully, but their ability to concentrate wears thin after long periods of noisy, disorganized conversations.

2. *Dress well, just as though you were going to a scheduled interview.* Those who wear jeans or other casual attire may not be taken seriously.

3. *Take at least 30-40 copies of your application document with you,* whether it is a resume or an SF-171, Application for Federal Employment. Do not risk running short.

161

4. *If you have two or three "targeted" versions of your application material, keep them in separate folders or sections of your briefcase* so you can reach easily and quickly for the one you want. Don't remove a copy, scan it, put it back, and then shuffle through your papers for a different version. Anyone would wonder what the other, hidden version contained and might conclude that you are not what you seem to be.

5. *Speak just as courteously and as carefully as you would in a private interview for a job.* Be prepared to give succinct answers to standard interview questions. Be prepared to state briefly the kind of position you seek (a statement which you can subtly adjust according to the nature of each organization and the kinds of job opportunities being offered).

6. *Take a briefcase to hold the company or agency information you collect.* Don't stuff wads of paper in your pockets or in a shopping bag.

7. *Ask for the recruiters' business cards* and attach them to the appropriate material for future reference.

8. *Take pens to make notes of your impressions to facilitate follow-up.* Later, sort out the information you have collected and decide which opportunities should be pursued by a telephone call or letter.

One job applicant we know went to a job fair because he knew a specific employer would be represented there, seeking applicants for the kind of job he wanted. Unfortunately, he was extremely curt with the personnel specialist at the company's booth because she was young and not familiar with his professional field. He was subsequently called for an interview, and found himself faced with the same personnel specialist who had been at the fair. He hoped she would not remember him; much to his regret, she did. He had misjudged the situation and ruined his chances. Remember, resumes do not get jobs; people do.

The natural inclination once you have been job hunting for a while is to get down on your knees in gratitude when you receive an offer. You should feel gratified, of course, that someone feels you are a worthy person. However, you must not let your gratitude get in the way of cold-blooded analysis and sound decision-making about the position. Many people have talked themselves into being so desperate that they grab at any employment crumb thrown their way. All too often, they soon come to regret their eagerness to leap at the first job offered.

✔ Mistake No. 106: Growing Discouraged If You Receive No Immediate Job Offers

The hiring process usually takes a long time. This is particularly true in today's tight job market, where a mistake in a hiring decision can have substantial economic consequences for the employer. Moreover, the keen competition for many jobs makes the process take even longer, since many resumes have to be reviewed and checked out, usually by more than one person. Subsequently, interviews have to be arranged (it is not uncommon to hold three or four interviewing sessions for some professional jobs at large organizations), references must be contacted, and a hiring decision, usually involving more than one person, must be made.

It is easy to become discouraged when job offers are not quickly forthcoming. The general rule concerning the time it takes to get a new job is as follows: hiring decisions concerning the lowest level, lowest paying jobs can be made quickly; hiring decisions for key executive positions are made slowly, with great care. Clerk typists can be offered jobs within 24 hours of being interviewed; the search for a CEO or General Counsel can take many months. Most jobs fall somewhere in between.

The best thing to be when job hunting is a realist. The ultimate reality is that the process takes much more time than you think it will. Try to use that time as constructively as possible: use it to learn more about the job market and about individual employers, to hone your resume and application forms, and to develop more expertise in your chosen field.

The time involved in the job hunting process should be considered to be a long-term investment--in your economic and professional future. If a job is worth having, it is worth enduring the time it will take to get it.

✔ Mistake No. 107: Accepting the First Job Offer that Comes Along

Job hunting is a nerve-wracking undertaking. Visions of unemployment and economic disaster often consume every waking moment and even invade dreams during the job hunting process. Self-doubt rises. Will I ever find a job? How many times will I be passed over at interviews? The whole affair tends to make marshmallows out of otherwise poised and self-confident people. These negative traits are reinforced as more and more time passes without a favorable response. Some people become so desperate that, when they do get a job offer, they grab it right away. In a disturbing number of cases, they jump at a job that, earlier in their job search, they would not have touched with a 10-foot pole.

If you give up too quickly and accept something for which you feel overqualified, you will make yourself miserable. Not only does this mean you are once again back in the job hunting business, but by taking off from that inadequate, lower-level position it may be even *more* difficult to land the kind of job you aspired to in the first place. It will certainly raise questions about your ability and ambition.

Desperation leads to mistakes; mistakes throw you back in the job market. Then you're not climbing a ladder to success, and not even maintaining a firm grip on your own rung of the ladder...you're slowly slipping backward.

✔ Mistake No. 108: Not Evaluating Job Offers Thoroughly

When you are offered a job, you are naturally excited and flattered by this reaffirmation of your worth. You have warm feelings toward the offeror, and feel kindly toward your prospective employer. But don't let your warm feelings overcome the need for cold-blooded analysis of the offer.

Here are some of the factors you should consider when evaluating a job offer:

1. *Money.* Do not merely look at the salary. Rather, examine the total compensation package. This includes salary, bonuses, health insurance and other benefits, deferred compensation, retirement plans, stock options, and perks, such as membership in the local health spa or day care for the children. At the same time,

consider state and local property taxes if you are moving out-of-state. Relocation and home buying/selling expenses should also be factored into the equation.

2. *Type of Work.* Is this the kind of job that will make you eager to go to work each morning? Will it energize and motivate you?

3. *Working Conditions.* Will you be working around dangerous equipment? Toxic substances? High noise levels? People who smoke? Will you have a private office? An office with 20 other people? A cubicle? A desk in the hall?

4. *Corporate "Culture."* Would you be comfortable in that particular corporate environment? Does it seem to be conservative, formal, highly structured, deliberate? Or casual, informal, hectic, energetic?

5. *Co-workers.* Are they a sullen lot? Do they party all the time? Find out as much as you can about them before accepting the job. You will, after all, be spending at least 40 hours of every week with them. If possible, talk to former employees of the organization. They can be immensely valuable sources of inside information.

6. *Immediate Supervisor.* Do you think you could get along well with this person? Do you seem to have the same attitude and goals? Does he or she have an "open door" policy indicating easy access and willingness to communicate? Every supervisor has a "reputation" inside the company; see if you can determine what the consensus of opinion is on the person who would be supervising your work. If your gut instinct signals a potential problem, proceed with caution...no matter how charming the CEO or director of human resources might be.

7. *Challenge.* Will the job be stimulating? Will it give you a personal sense of accomplishment? Nothing is worse than a boring job, regardless of the remuneration.

8. *Personal Opportunity.* Will you be able to grow professionally in the job, both in terms of compensation and promotion possibilities? Will your responsibilities increase? What happened to the person whose position you are taking? Was he or she promoted? Fired for poor job performance? Quit in disgust? See if you can have an off-the-record discussion with that person and then use your good judgment about what you learn.

9. *Life-style.* Will the demands of the job require changes in your life-style? Will it involve working long or unusual hours? Will it involve extensive and frequent out-of-town trips? Is geographic mobility a condition of employment?

10. *Time Limit.* Is the position being funded under a special project or new contract? Determine the anticipated length of that project or contract and form your opinion of the position accordingly. Despite corporate reassurances that a permanent place can always be found for employees who perform well, many professionals have found themselves out of a job when contract or project funding ends.

11. *Non-Compete Agreements.* How broadly is the agreement written? Can it be limited in terms of time and geography? Most such agreements can be legally challenged, but the best course is to restrict any agreement to as narrow a focus as possible. If you're inexperienced in such matters, seek legal advice.

12. *Corporate Future.* What are the prospects for the company and for the industry? Is the company growing? Is it stable? Are there rumors of the company being taken over or acquired? Here is where you can draw on the spadework you did in targeting the job market and in preparing for your interview.

> We once offered an Office Administrator position to an impressive candidate who turned us down for a 20 percent higher salary and a free parking space at a much larger company. While our offer could not compare, the applicant went into his new job mindful that his employer's industry was declining. Within a month, he contacted us to see if our position was still open. His new employer was in an economic squeeze and had already begun laying people off.

13. *Location.* Is this where you really want to live? Make a site visit if the job you have been offered is located in another community. Talk to the local people and assess the community before committing yourself to a disruptive move.

14. *Severance.* In the event that you're terminated, does the company have a policy on severance payments and outplacement assistance? Although a difficult subject to bring up, such topics are frequently covered in printed material that discusses a large organization's employment policies. Ask to review such material before signing on the dotted line. If you're structuring a specific employment agreement, such topics should always be addressed.

✓ Mistake No. 109: Losing a Job You've Been Offered

After a period of time in the job market, job offers are bound to occur. What if you're offered a job that interests you, but may not be your first choice. What do you do? Everyone would like to have a number of job offers made *simultaneously* so that they can all be compared and the best one chosen. This seldom happens. You are forced to made a decision on the basis of the immediate job being offered, not knowing if any other offers will ever be made.

There are two key points to consider: (1) how long can you delay making a decision; and (2) what do you say when postponing that decision. Unfortunately, we know of several people who have LOST a job at this stage because of a strategic error. In a sudden burst of honesty, they stated they were waiting to have other job offers confirmed and would get back to the first employer when the other offers had been considered. The employer, insulted that the job hunter did not immediately accept the job with delight and enthusiasm, rescinded the offer. Yes, this really happens...and it happens more often than you would like to think. Look at the situation from the employer's point of view: there are usually several top applicants for every position, all of whom have interviewed well, so why hire the one who is not sure about you or the company? All employers want dedication and a lively interest in the organization's future, so why would they hire anyone who was hesitant, lukewarm, or indicated that the job offered was not a first choice but would be accepted if nothing better came along?

In an ideal world, you should accept the job offer immediately...with enthusiasm. In the real world, it is accepted practice to *express* enthusiasm and THEN state that you would like to consider the job offer for a few days (preferably no more than two or three) and will contact the employer on an exact date with a decision. For example: If the job offer is made on a Tuesday, say that you will contact the employer on the following Friday morning with your decision. This indicates that you take the offer, the position, and the decision seriously. What it does not say is what you are going to be doing in the intervening period of time, which might be scrambling around trying to nail down another offer.

If you're not happy with the job offered in terms of salary or benefits, be careful when deciding whether to attempt a negotiation for more favorable terms. If you really feel that you're being offered a salary way out of line with what you're reasonably worth on the job market, you should speak up. Perhaps you could suggest expanding the job's responsibilities so the organization could feel justified in paying a higher salary. If you **knew** the job's salary (and responsibilities) from the

167

beginning, the employer will feel sandbagged. Many people entertain visions of Lee Iacocca or Donald Trump at the bargaining table and think they'll gain respect by playing hard-ball. This can work for some, but not many. If you're really willing to gamble on losing the job, go ahead...but the time for such negotiations is usually during the **interview stage** when both sides are clarifying their expectations.

If the position had been discussed in terms of a **salary range** and you're offered the position at the lower end of the range, then of course it's time to negotiate...carefully. Restate how well qualified you feel you are for the position and cite the exact salary figure you were hoping to receive. It is not uncommon for the employer to make a counteroffer that is somewhere in between the two figures which you can both live with. For example: Let's say you knew the salary offered was in the low-to-mid $30's. You're offered $31,000; you state why your experience qualifies you to receive $35,000; the counteroffer is for $33,500 and the deal is made. Both sides feel they have won a little.

A final note: Accepting a job offer and then calling back at a later date to say you've changed your mind can be a dangerous game. There can always be circumstances which force you into this kind of unfortunate action, but professional circles tend to be smaller than most people imagine and memories are long. Treat a potential employer as fairly as you expect to be treated yourself.

✓ Mistake No. 110: Operating on a Handshake

Operating on a handshake is never a good idea, regardless of the situation. It is a terrible idea when we are talking about a job. Never work for someone without a signed piece of paper in the nature of an agreement that specifies, to your satisfaction, the conditions under which you are accepting the position. Such an agreement should, at a minimum, cover compensation, position title, the date when you would begin working, a description of what is expected of you on the job, your place in the organizational hierarchy, benefits, and relocation costs if you have to move. It is not necessary that this be an agreement drawn up by lawyers for both parties (although if the stakes are high enough, e.g., an entertainer or professional athlete, you should have legal representation). It is perfectly acceptable and legally enforceable if the agreement is in the form of a letter to you signed by the employer.

Many large organizations have company-wide "conditions of employment" concerning employee rights and benefits that are automatically included in employment agreements (or in the fine print on company application forms). Make sure to obtain a copy of these conditions and read them carefully. They may be incorporated into your particular agreement only by reference (manual title, paragraph numbers, etc.); it is up to you to learn the details.

More than one person has accepted a new job, given two weeks' notice to a current employer, and perhaps even made a geographical move, only to find that the new job **had disappeared**. If you don't have something in writing from your future employer, you will have a serious problem if the company you think you're joining suddenly decides, for any number of unfortunate reasons, to freeze hiring and rescind all outstanding job offers.

We live in difficult and volatile times. You never know when you may have to assert your rights in a formal judicial or administrative setting in order to get what's rightfully coming to you. Make sure you have the evidence on file.

* *

A Final Point

Jobs are an important part of life. Prepare for the job hunt as though your future depended on the outcome. It does. Most people don't fall into great jobs through good fortune or sheer luck. They work at finding and winning them.

We hope this discussion of job hunting mistakes will help you avoid some of the pitfalls so prevalent in the job hunting process.

If we have drawn your attention to *even one idea* that can help you focus your efforts, save you time, provide encouragement, or increase your confidence, we think we will have succeeded. Now all the rest, the real work, is up to you.

169

APPENDIX A

The following is a list of Federal Job Information Centers (FJIC's) maintained by the U.S. Office of Personnel Management throughout the United States and its possessions. FJIC's compile and publish listings of Federal job vacancies and registers for the areas that they serve. They also provide SF-171's, any additional application forms required for the vacancy or register for which you are applying, and administer written tests. Many FJIC's are only open certain hours of the day and certain days of the week so you may have to call more than once to get the information you are seeking.

Alabama
520 Wynn Drive NW
Huntsville, AL 35816-3426
(205) 837-0894

Alaska
222 W. 7th Avenue, #22, Room 156
Anchorage, AK 99513-7572
(907) 271-5821

Arizona
3225 N. Central Avenue, Room 1415
Phoenix, AZ 85012
(602) 640-4800

Arkansas
[See San Antonio listing.]
(405) 231-4948

California
Los Angeles:
9650 Flair Drive, Suite 100A
El Monte, CA 91731
(818) 575-6510

1029 J Street, Room 202
Sacramento, CA 95814
(916) 551-1464

Federal Building, Room 4218
880 Front Street
San Diego, CA 92101-8821
(619) 557-6165

211 Main Street, Room 235
San Francisco, CA 94120
(415) 744-5627

Colorado
12345 W. Alameda Parkway
Lakewood, CO 80215
(303) 969-7050
For forms, call (303) 969-7055.

Connecticut [See Massachusetts listing.]

Delaware [See Philadelphia listing.]

District of Columbia Metro Area
1900 E Street N.W., Room 1416
Washington, DC 20415
(202) 606-2700

Florida
Claude Pepper Federal Building
51 S.W. 1st Avenue, Room 1222
Miami, FL 33130
(305) 536-6738

Commodore Building, Suite 125
3444 McCrory Place
Orlando, FL 32803-3701
(407) 648-6148

Georgia
Richard B. Russell Federal Building
Room 940A, 75 Spring Street, S.W.
Atlanta, GA 30303
(404) 331-4315

Hawaii
[Honolulu and other Hawaiian Islands and Overseas.]
Federal Building, Room 5316
300 Ala Moana Blvd
Honolulu, HI 96850
(808) 541-2791
Overseas Jobs: (808) 541-2784

Idaho [See Washington listing.]

Illinois
175 W. Jackson Blvd, Room 530
Chicago, IL 60604
(312) 353-6192
[For Madison & St. Clair Counties, see St. Louis listing.]

170

Indiana
Minton-Capehart Federal Building
575 N. Pennsylvania Street, Room 368
Indianapolis, IN 46204
For additional information services in Indiana, see Michigan (313) 226-6950. [For Clark, Dearborn, & Floyd Counties, see Ohio listing.]

Iowa
[For Scott County, see Illinois listing. For rest of state, see Kansas City, MO listing.]
(816) 426-7757

Kansas
One-Twenty Building, Room 101
120 S. Market Street
Wichita, KS 67202
For additional information services in Kansas, see Kansas City, MO listing.]
(816) 426-7820

Kentucky
[See Ohio listing; for Henderson County, see Michigan listing.]

Louisiana
1515 Poydras Street, Suite 608
New Orleans, LA 70112
(504) 589-2764

Maine [See Massachusetts listing.]

Maryland
300 West Pratt Street
Baltimore, MD 21201
(410) 962-3822

Massachusetts
Thomas P. O'Neill, Jr. Federal Bldg
10 Causeway Street
Boston, MA 02222-1031
(617) 565-5900

Michigan
477 Michigan Avenue, Room 565
Detroit, MI 48226
(313) 226-6950

Minnesota
1 Federal Drive, Room 501
Bishop Henry Whipple Federal Building
Ft. Snelling, Twin Cities, MN 55111
(612) 725-3430

Mississippi [See Alabama listing.]

Missouri
Federal Building, Room 134
601 E. 12th Street
Kansas City, MO 64106
(816) 426-5702
[For counties west of and including Mercer, Grundy, Livingston, Carroll, Saline, Pettis, Benton, Hickory, Dallas, Webster, Douglas, and Ozark.]

400 Old Post Office Building
815 Olive Street
St. Louis, MO 63101
(314) 539-2285
[For all other Missouri counties not listed under Kansas City above.]

Montana [See Colorado listing.]
(303) 969-7052

Nebraska
[See Kansas City, MO listing.]
(816) 426-7819

Nevada
For Clark, Lincoln, and Nye Counties, see Los Angeles listing. [For all other Nevada counties not listed above, see Sacramento listing.]

New Hampshire
[See Massachusetts listing.]

New Jersey
Rodino Federal Building
970 Broad Street, 2nd Floor
Newark, New Jersey 07102
[For additional information services in Atlantic, Burlington, Camden, Cape May, Cumberland, Gloucester, Mercer, Monmouth, Ocean, and Salem Counties, see Philadelphia listing.]

New Mexico
505 Marquette Avenue, Suite 910
Albuquerque, NM 87102
(505) 766-2906

New York
Jacob K. Javits Federal Building
26 Federal Plaza, 2d Floor, Room 120
New York, NY 10278
(212) 264-0422/0423

New York cont.
100 S. Clinton Street
Syracuse, NY 13202
(315) 423-5660

North Carolina
4407 Bland Rd, Suite 202
Raleigh, NC 27609-6296
(919) 790-2822

North Dakota [See Minnesota listing.]

Ohio
Federal Building, Room 506
200 W. 2nd Street
Dayton, OH 45402
(513) 225-2720
[For Van Wert, Auglaize, Hardin, Marion,
Crawford, Richland, Ashland, Wayne, Stark,
Carroll, Columbiana, Counties and all coun-
ties north of these, see Michigan listing.]

Oklahoma [See San Antonio listing.]
(405) 231-4948

Oregon
Federal Building, Room 376
1220 S.W. Third Avenue
Portland, OR 97204
(503) 326-3141

Pennsylvania
Federal Building, Room 168
P.O. Box 761
Harrisburg, PA 17108
(717) 782-4494

Wm. J. Green, Jr. Federal Building
600 Arch Street
Philadelphia, PA 19106
(215) 597-7440

Federal Building
1000 Liberty Avenue, Room 119
Pittsburgh, PA 15222
[Walk-in only; for mail or telephone, see
Philadelphia listing.]

Puerto Rico
U.S. Federal Building, Room 340
150 Carlos Chardon Avenue
Hato Rey, PR 00918-1710
(809) 766-5242

Rhode Island [See Massachusetts listing.]

South Carolina
[See North Carolina listing.]

South Dakota [See Minnesota listing.]

Tennessee: [Walk-in only]
200 Jefferson Avenue, Suite 1312
Memphis, TN 38103-2335
[For mail or telephone, see Alabama listing.]

Texas
Corpus Christi [See San Antonio listing.]
(512) 884-8113

1100 Commerce Street, Room 6B10
Dallas, TX 75242
(214) 767-8035

Harlingen [See San Antonio listing.]
(512) 412-0722

Houston [See San Antonio listing.]
(713) 759-0455

8610 Broadway, Room 305
San Antonio, TX 78217
(210) 805-2423
For forms, call (210) 805-2406.
24-hour Job Information: (210) 805-2402

Utah [See Colorado listing.]
(303) 969-7053

Vermont [See Massachusetts listing.]

Virgin Islands [See Puerto Rico listing.]
(809) 774-8790

Virginia
Federal Building, Room 220
200 Granby Street
Norfolk, VA 23510-1886
(804) 441-3355

Washington
Federal Building, Room 110
915 Second Avenue
Seattle, WA 98174
(206) 220-6400

West Virginia [See Ohio listing.]
(513) 225-2866

Wisconsin
For Dane, Grant, Green, Iowa, Rock, La-
fayette, Jefferson, Walworth, Milwaukee,
Waukesha, Racine, and Kenosha Counties,
see Illinois listing (312) 353-6189.
[For all other Wisconsin counties not listed
above, see Minnesota listing.] (612) 725-3430

Wyoming [See Colorado listing.]
(303) 969-7052

State Central Personnel Offices

These offices can be contacted for information regarding state government jobs (as well as jobs with comparable U.S. jurisdictions, such as Puerto Rico).

Alabama
Director
State Personnel Department
64 N. Union Street, Room 402
Montgomery, AL 36130

Alaska
Director
Division of Personnel
Department of Administration
P.O. Box C-0201
Juneau, AK 99802-0201

Arizona
Director
Division of Personnel
Department of Administration
1831 W. Jefferson, Room 100
Phoenix, AZ 85007

Arkansas
Administrator
Personnel Management
Finance and Administration Department
P.O. Box 3278
Little Rock, AR 72203

California
Executive Officer
State Personnel Board
P.O. Box 944201
Sacramento, CA 94244-2010

Colorado
Director
Department of Personnel
1313 Sherman Street, Room 123
Denver, CO 80203

Connecticut
Deputy Commissioner
State Personnel and Labor Relations
165 Capitol Avenue
State Office Building
Hartford, CT 06106

Delaware
Acting Director
State Personnel Office
P.O. Box 1401
Dover, DE 19903

Florida
Secretary
Department of Administration
435 Carlton Building
Tallahassee, FL 32399-1550

Georgia
Commissioner
Merit System of Personnel Administration
5th Floor W Tower
Suite 504
200 Piedmont Avenue
Atlanta, GA 30334

Hawaii
Director
Department of Personnel Services
830 Punchbowl Street
Honolulu, HI 96813

Idaho
Director
Personnel Commission
700 W. State Street
Boise, ID 83720

Illinois
Acting Manager
Bureau of Personnel
Central Management Services
503 William G. Stratton Building
Springfield, IL 62706

Indiana
Director
State Personnel Department
GCS Room W161
402 W. Washington
Indianapolis, IN 46204

Iowa
Director
Department of Personnel
Grimes State Office Building
East 14th Street and Grand Avenue
Des Moines, IA 50319

Kansas
Director
Division of Personnel Services
Department of Administration
Landon State Office Building, Room 951-S
9th and Jackson
Topeka, KS 66612-1251

Kentucky
Commissioner
Department of Personnel
Capitol Annex
Room 373
Frankfort, KY 40601

Louisiana
Director
Department of State Civil Service
P.O. Box 94111
Baton Rouge, LA 70804-9111

Maine
Director
Bureau of Human Resources
State Office Building
2nd Floor
State House, Station #4
Augusta, ME 04333

Maryland
Secretary
Department of Personnel
301 W. Preston Street, Room 609
Baltimore, MD 21201

Massachusetts
Deputy Administrator
Department of Personnel Administration
1 Ashburton Place, Room 213
Boston, MA 02108

Michigan
Director
Department of Civil Service
400 S. Pine Street
P.O. Box 30002
Lansing, MI 48909

Minnesota
Commissioner
Department of Employee Relations
658 Cedar, 2nd Fl Centennial Building
St. Paul, MN 55155

Mississippi
Director
State Personnel Board
301 N. Lamar Street, Suite 100
Jackson, MS 39201

Missouri
Director
Division of Personnel
Office of Administration
P.O. Box 388
Jefferson City, MO 65102

Montana
Administrator
State Personnel Division
Mitchell Building, Room 130
Helena, MT 59634

Nebraska
Director
Department of Personnel
301 Centennial Mall South
P.O. Box 94905
Lincoln, NE 68509-4905

Nevada
Director
Personnel Department
209 E. Musser Street
Carson City, NV 98710

New Hampshire
Director
Division of Personnel
State House Annex, Room 1
25 Capitol Street
Concord, NH 03301

New Jersey
Commissioner
Department of Personnel
3 Station Plaza, CN 317
Trenton, NJ 08625

New Mexico
Director
Personnel Office
P.O. Box 26127
Santa Fe, NM 87502-6127

New York
Commissioner
Department of Civil Service
State Campus, Building #1
Albany, NY 12239

North Carolina
Director
Office of State Personnel
Department of Administration
116 W. Jones Street
Raleigh, NC 27603-8003

North Dakota
Director
Central Personnel Division
Office of Management and Budget
State Capitol, 14th Floor
600 E. Boulevard Avenue
Bismarck, ND 58505-0120

Ohio
Director
Personnel Division
Department of Administrative Services
30 E. Broad Street, 28th Floor
Columbus, OH 43215

Oklahoma
Administrator & Secretary of Human
   Resources
Office of Personnel Management
Jim Thorpe Building
2101 Lincoln Boulevard
Oklahoma City, OK 73105

Oregon
Administrator
Personnel and Labor Relations Division
155 Cottage Street, NE
Salem, OR 97310

Pennsylvania
Director
State Civil Service Commission
P.O. Box 569
Harrisburg, PA 17120

Rhode Island
Acting Personnel Administrator
One Capitol Hill
Providence, RI 02908

South Carolina
Director
Human Resource Management Division
1201 Main Street, Suite 1000
Columbia, SC 29201

South Dakota
Commissioner
Office of Executive Management
Bureau of Personnel
State Capitol Building
500 East Capitol
Pierre, SD 57501-5070

Tennessee
Commissioner
Department of Personnel
James K. Polk Building, Second Floor
Nashville, TN 37219-5185

Texas
Director
Job Bank and Personnel
201 E. 14th Street, Room 119
Sam Houston Building
Austin, TX 78711

Utah
Director
Department of Human Resource Management
2120 State Office Building
Salt Lake City, UT 84114

Vermont
Commissioner
Department of Personnel
110 State Street
Montpelier, VT 05602

Virginia
Director
Department of Personnel and Training
James Monroe Building
101 N. 14th Street, 12th Floor
Richmond, VA 23219

Washington
Director
Department of Personnel
521 Capitol Way S.
P.O. Box 1789
Olympia, WA 98504-7500

West Virginia
Director
Division of Personnel
Building 6, Room B-416
State Capitol Complex
Charleston, WV 25305

Wisconsin
Administrator
Division of Merit Recruitment & Selection
Department of Employment Relations
137 E. Wilson Street
P.O. Box 7855
Madison, WI 53707-7855

Wyoming
Administrator
Personnel Division
2001 Capitol Avenue
Emerson Building
Cheyenne, WY 82002-0060

District of Columbia
Acting Director
Office of Personnel
613 G Street NW
Room 306
Washington, DC 20001

American Samoa
Director
Department of Human Resources
Pago Pago, AS 96799

Guam
Director
Department of Administration
P.O. Box 884
Agana, GU 96910

Northern Mariana Islands
Management Officer
Civil Service Commission
P.O. Box 150, CHRB
Saipan, MP 96950

Puerto Rico
Director
Office for Personnel Administration
P.O. Box 8476
Fernandez Juncos Station
Santurce, PR 00910

Virgin Islands
Acting Director
Division of Personnel
Gers Complex, 3rd Floor
488-50C Kronprimdsene Gade
St. Thomas, VI 00802

Assistant Director
Division of Personnel
2205 Church Street, Suite 8
Christiansted
St. Croix, VI 00828

APPENDIX C

For matters regarding discrimination in employment because of race, color, sex, age, national origin, religion or disability, contact the following state or comparable U.S. jurisdictional offices.

Alaska
Executive Director
Human Rights Commission
Office of the Governor
800 A Street, Suite. 202
Anchorage, AK 99501

Arizona
Chief Counsel
Civil Rights Division
Office of the Attorney General
1275 W. Washington
Phoenix, AZ 85007

California
Director
Fair Employment & Housing
2014 T Street, Suite 210
Sacramento, CA 95814

Colorado
Director
Civil Rights Division
Department of Regulatory Agencies
1560 Broadway, Room 1050
Denver, CO 80202

Connecticut
Director
Commission on Human Rights &
 Opportunities
90 Washington Street
Hartford, CT 06106

Delaware
Chairman
Human Relations Commission
Department of Community Affairs
820 N. French St., 4th Floor
Wilmington, DE 19801

Florida
Administrator
Office of Civil Rights
209 Berkeley Building
Tallahassee, FL 32399

Georgia
Executive Director
Human Relations Commission
100 Peachtree Street, Suite 350
Atlanta, GA 30303

Hawaii
Executive Director
Civil Rights Commission
Labor & Industrial Relations Dept.
888 Mililani Street, 2nd Floor
Honolulu, HI 96813

Idaho
Director
Human Rights Commission
Office of the Governor
450 W. State Street
Boise, ID 83720

Illinois
Director
Department of Human Rights
100 W. Randolph
Suite 10-100
Chicago, IL 60601

Indiana
Director
Civil Rights Commission
32 E. Washington Street
Suite 900
Indianapolis, IN 46204

Iowa

Acting Director
Civil Rights Commission
211 E. Maple Street, 2nd Floor
Des Moines, IA 50319

Kansas

Acting Executive Director
Human Rights Commission
Landon State Office Building, 8th Floor
Topeka, KS 66612

Kentucky

Executive Director
Commission on Human Rights
Capital Plaza Tower
Frankfort, KY 40601

Louisiana

Attorney General
Department of Justice
P.O. Box 94005
Baton Rouge, LA 70804

Maine

Executive Director
Maine Human Rights Commission
State House Station #51
Augusta, ME 04333

Maryland

Executive Director
Human Relations Commission
20 E. Franklin Street
Baltimore, MD 21202

Massachusetts

Chairman
Commission Against Discrimination
1 Ashburton Place, Room 601
Boston, MA 02108

Michigan

Director
Department of Civil Rights
303 W. Kalamazoo, 4th Floor
Lansing, MI 48913

Minnesota

Commissioner
Department of Human Rights
500 Bremer Tower
St. Paul, MN 55101

Missouri

Director
Commission on Human Rights
Labor & Industrial Relations Dept.
Truman Building, Box 1129
Jefferson City, MO 65102

Montana

Administrator
Human Rights Division
Dept. of Labor & Industry
Capitol Station
Helena, MT 59620

Nebraska

Executive Director
Equal Opportunity Commission
301 Centennial Mall S.
P.O. Box 94934
Lincoln, NE 68509

Nevada

Executive Director
Equal Rights Commission
1515 E. Tropicana, #590
Las Vegas, NV 89158

New Hampshire

Executive Director
Commission for Human Rights
163 Loundo Road
Concord, NH 03301

New Jersey

Executive
Division on Civil Rights
Department of Law & Public Safety
1100 Raymond Blvd.
Newark, NJ 07102

New Mexico
Executive Director
Human Rights Division
1596 Pacheco Street, Aspen Plaza
Santa Fe, NM 87503

New York
Commissioner
Division of Human Rights
Executive Department
55 W. 125th St.
New York, NY 10027

North Carolina
Director
Human Relations Council
Department of Administration
121 W. Jones Street
Raleigh, NC 27603

North Dakota
Commissioner
Department of Labor
State Capitol, 5th Fl.
600 E. Boulevard
Bismarck, ND 58505

Ohio
Director
Ohio Civil Rights Commission
220 Parsons Avenue
Columbus, OH 43266

Oklahoma
Chairman
Human Rights Commission
2101 N. Lincoln Blvd., Room 481
Oklahoma City, OK 73105

Oregon
Administrator
Civil Rights Division
Bureau of Labor & Industries
1400 SW 5th Avenue
Portland, OR 97201

Pennsylvania
Executive Director
Human Relations Commission
P.O. Box 3145
Harrisburg, PA 17105

Rhode Island
Executive Director
Human Rights Commission
10 Abbott Park Place
Providence, RI 02903

South Carolina
Commissioner
Commission on Human Affairs
P.O. Box 4490
Columbia, SC 29240

South Dakota
Acting Director
Division of Human Rights
Commerce & Regulations Department
910 E. Sioux, State Capitol
Pierre, SD 57501

Tennessee
Executive Director
Commission for Human Development
208 Tennessee Building
535 Church Street
Nashville, TN 37243

Texas
Executive Director
Texas Commission on Human Rights
P.O. Box 13493
Austin, TX 78711

Utah
Director
Division of Anti-Discrimination & Labor
   Industrial Commission
160 E. 300 S.
Salt Lake City, UT 84111

Vermont
Chief
Public Protection Division
Office of the Attorney General
109 State Street
Montpelier, VT 05602

Virginia
Director
Council on Human Rights
1100 Bank Street
Richmond, VA 23219

Washington
Executive Director
Human Rights Commission
711 S. Capitol Way
402 Evergreen Plaza Bldg, M/S: FJ-41
Olympia, WA 98504

West Virginia
Executive Director
West Virginia Human Rights Commission
East End Plaza, Morris & Lewis Streets
Charleston, WV 25301

Wisconsin
Administrator
Division of Equal Rights
Industrial Labor & Human Relations
P.O. Box 7946
Madison, WI 53707

Wyoming
Director
Department of Employment
Labor Standards Division
Herschler Building
Cheyenne, WY 82002

District of Columbia
Executive Director
Office of Human Rights
2000 14th St., NW, 3rd Floor
Washington, DC 20009

Guam
Attorney General
Office of the Attorney General
238 Archbishop Flores St., Suite 701
Agana, GU 96910

Northern Mariana Islands
Personnel Officer
Civil Service Commission
Personnel Management Office
Office of the Governor
Saipan, MP 96950

Puerto Rico
Executive Director
Civil Rights Commission
P.O. Box 2338
Hato Rey, PR 00919

U.S. Virgin Islands
Director
Virgin Islands Civil Rights Commission
P.O. Box 6645
St. Thomas, VI 00804

State Employment Security Agencies

These offices provide job placement and job counseling assistance to job seekers, as well as applicant assessment and applicant screening for employers. They also play a vital role in bringing veterans into the civilian workforce.

Alabama
Director
Department of Industrial Relations
649 Monroe Street, Room 204
Montgomery, AL 36130

Alaska
Director
Employment Security Division
Alaska Department of Labor
P.O. Box 25509
Juneau, AK 99802-5509

Arizona
Director
Department of Economic Security
P.O. Box 6123-010A
Phoenix, AZ 85005

Arkansas
Director
Employment Security Department
P.O. Box 2981
Little Rock, AR 72203-2981

California
Director
Employment Development Department
P.O. Box 826880, MIC 83
Sacramento, CA 94280-0001

Colorado
Executive Director
Department of Labor & Employment
600 Grant Street, Suite 900
Denver, CO 80203-3528

Connecticut
Executive Director
Employment Security Division
State Labor Department
200 Folly Brook Boulevard
Wethersfield, CT 06109-1114

Delaware
Secretary of Labor
State Department of Labor
820 North French Street, 6th Floor
Wilmington, DE 19801

Florida
Secretary
Department of Labor & Employment
  Security
2012 Capital Circle, SE
Suite 303, Hartman Building
Tallahassee, FL 32399-2152

Georgia
Commissioner
Georgia Department of Labor
148 International Blvd, NE, Suite 600
Atlanta, GA 30303

Hawaii
Director
Department of Labor & Industrial Relations
830 Punchbowl Street, Room 320
Honolulu, HI 96813

Idaho
Director
Department of Employment
317 Main Street
Boise, ID 83735

Illinois
Director
Department of Employment Security
401 South State Street, Room 615
Chicago, IL 60605

Indiana
Commissioner
Department of Workforce Development
10 North Senate Avenue, Room E204
Indianapolis, IN 46204

Iowa
Director
Department of Employment Services
1000 East Grand Avenue
Des Moines, IA 50319

Kansas
Secretary
Kansas Department of Human Resources
401 Topeka Boulevard
Topeka, KS 66603

Kentucky
Commissioner
Department for Employment Services
275 East Main Street
Frankfort, KY 40621

Louisiana
Assistant Secretary for the Office of
    Employment Security
Department of Employment & Training
P.O. Box 94094
Baton Rouge, LA 70804-9094

Maine
Executive Director
Bureau of Employment & Training Programs
Maine Department of Labor
State House Station 55
Augusta, ME 04330

Maryland
Assistant Secretary
Division of Employment & Training
Department of Economic & Employment
    Development
1100 North Eutaw Street, Room 600
Baltimore, MD 21201

Massachusetts
Commissioner
Department of Employment & Training
19 Staniford Street, 3rd Floor
Boston, MA 02114

Michigan
Director
Michigan Employment Security Commission
7310 Woodward Avenue
Detroit, MI 48202

Minnesota
Commissioner
Minnesota Department of Jobs & Training
390 North Robert Street
St. Paul, MN 55101

Mississippi
Executive Director
Mississippi Employment Security
    Commission
P.O. Box 1699
Jackson, MS 39215-1699

Missouri
Director
Division of Employment Security
P.O. Box 59
Jefferson City, MO 65104

Montana
Commissioner
Department of Labor & Industry
State Capitol
Helena, MT 59624

Nebraska
Commissioner of Labor
Department of Labor
550 South 16th Street
Lincoln, NE 68509-4600

Nevada
Executive Director
Nevada Employment Security Department
500 East Third Street
Carson City, NV 89713

New Hampshire
Commissioner
Department of Employment Security
32 South Main Street
Concord, NH 03301-4857

New Jersey
Assistant Commissioner
Employment Security & Job Training
New Jersey Department of Labor
CN 110
Trenton, NJ 08625-0110

New Mexico
Secretary
New Mexico Department of Labor
P.O. Box 1928
Albuquerque, NM 87103

New York
Commissioner
New York State Department of Labor
State Office Building Campus
Building 12, Room 592
Albany, NY 12240

North Carolina
Chairman
Employment Security Commission of
 North Carolina
P.O. Box 25903
Raleigh, NC 27611

North Dakota
Executive Director
Job Service North Dakota
P.O. Box 1537
Bismarck, ND 58502

Ohio
Administrator
Ohio Bureau of Employment Services
145 South Front Street
Columbus, OH 43215

Oklahoma
Executive Director
Employment Security Commission
2401 North Lincoln
215 Will Rogers Memorial Office Building
Oklahoma City, OK 73105

Oregon
Administrator
Employment Department
875 Union Street, NE
Salem, OR 97311

Pennsylvania
Executive Deputy Secretary
Department of Labor & Industry
Labor & Industry Building, Room 1700
Harrisburg, PA 17121

Rhode Island
Director
Department of Employment & Training
101 Friendship Street
Providence, RI 02903-3740

South Carolina
Executive Director
South Carolina Employment Security
 Commission
P.O. Box 995
Columbia, SC 29202

South Dakota
Deputy Secretary
South Dakota Department of Labor
700 Governors Drive
Pierre, SD 57501-2277

Tennessee
Commissioner
Tennessee Department of Employment
 Security
12th Floor - Volunteer Plaza
500 James Robertson Parkway
Nashville, TN 37245-0001

Texas
Administrator
Texas Employment Commission
15th & Congress Avenue, Room 656
Austin, TX 78778

Utah
Administrator
Utah Department of Employment Security
140 East 300 South
174 Social Hall Avenue
Salt Lake City, UT 84147-0249

Vermont
Commissioner
Department of Employment & Training
P.O. Box 488
Montpelier, VT 05601-0488

Virginia
Commissioner
Virginia Employment Commission
703 East Main Street
Richmond, VA 23219

Washington
Commissioner
Employment Security Department
212 Maple Park, Mail Stop KG-11
Olympia, WA 98504-5311

West Virginia
Commissioner
West Virginia Bureau of Employment
  Programs
112 California Avenue
Charleston, WV 25305-0112

Wisconsin
Secretary
Department of Industry, Labor and Human
  Relations
P.O. Box 7946
Madison, WI 53707

Wyoming
Director
Department of Employment
122 West 25th Street
Herschler Building, 2nd Floor East
Cheyenne, WY 82002

District of Columbia
Director
Department of Employment Services
500 C Street, NW, Room 600
Washington, DC 20001

Puerto Rico
Director
Bureau of Employment Security
505 Munoz Rivera Avenue
Hato Rey, PR 00918

Virgin Islands
Commissioner
Virgin Islands Department of Labor
2131 Hospital Street,
Christensted, St. Croix, VI 00820

The entries in this Bibliography have been divided into broad career categories. Each category identifies job bulletins and/or general reference books. Many of these books are quite expensive and can be found only in major libraries. We have included the current prices for all publications to help you decide which ones you may want to purchase for your own use and which ones to use in a library.

CAREERS IN GENERAL

Action Careers: Employment in the High-Risk Job Market. Ragnar Benson. 1988. Covers career opportunities such as river rafting guides, fire fighters, hunting and fishing guides, process servers, rodeo cowboys, U.S. Secret Service agents, skydiving instructors, FBI agents, explosives handlers, Peace Corps volunteers and private detectives.

Carol Publishing Group, 120 Enterprise Ave, Secaucus, NJ 07094. Tel: 201/866-0490. $9.95.

The Almanac of American Employers 1994. Jack W. Plunkett. 1993. A guide to America's 500 most successful large corporations, ranked and profiled by salaries, benefits, financial stability, and opportunities for job advancement.

Corporate Jobs Outlook, P.O. Drawer 100, Boerne, TX 78006-0100. Tel: 210/755-8810. $110 plus $5.00 postage.

America's Top 300 Jobs. 1990-91. Based on extensive research by the U.S. Department of Labor, provides detailed descriptions of 225 jobs. A special index covers an additional 125.

The Career Press Inc., 180 Fifth Ave, P.O. Box 34, Hawthorne, NJ 07507. Tel: 201/427-0229 or 1-800/CAREER-1. $17.95.

The Best Jobs for the 1990s and into the 21st Century. Drs. Ron and Caryl Krannich. 1992. Identifies the fastest growing jobs that also offer excellent salaries and job security. Sur-

veys numerous growing and declining jobs. Includes information on education, training, skill requirements, salaries, advancement opportunities, and future job outlook.

Impact Publications, 10655 Big Oak Circle, Manassas, VA 22111-3040. Tel: 703/361-7300. $12.95 plus $3.00 postage.

Career Opportunities News. Robert Calvert, Jr. and Mary B. French, eds. Published six times a year, this newsletter includes articles on the current outlook in various occupations, resources to aid job seekers, special opportunities for minorities, and free and inexpensive career materials.

Garrett Park Press, P.O. Box 190C, Garrett Park, MD 20896-0190. Tel: 301/946-2553. $30.00 (1 year); $25.00 (1 year prepaid).

Corporate Jobs Outlook. Each bimonthly issue contains Reports on 16 or 17 major firms, detailing growth plans, salaries, benefits, financial stability, training, hiring, advancement opportunities, and corporate culture.

Corporate Jobs Outlook, P.O. Drawer 100, Boerne, TX 78006-0100. Tel: 210/755-8810. $169.99 (annually).

Emerging Careers: New Occupations for the Year 2000 and Beyond. Norman Feingold and Norma Reno Miller. 1983. Identifies hundreds of new and emerging careers such as public affairs psychologist, robot technician, ocean engineer, and neutrino astronomist.

May be obtained through Garrett Park Press, P.O. Box 190C, Garrett Park, MD 20896-0190. Tel: 301/946-2553. $11.95.

Everybody's Business. Milton Moskovitz et al. 1990. A guide to 400 companies in virtually every major industry. Information includes ranking by size, market standing of specific products and services, sales and profits (1989), and names and addresses of owners, CEOs and other top managers. Also includes information on the company's workplace surroundings, its social responsibility, and its global presence.

Doubleday, 2451 South Wolf Road, Des Plaines, IL 60018. $22.50. Tel: 212/354-6500.

The How to Get a Job Series.
  How to Get a Job in Atlanta (1994).
  How to Get a Job in Chicago (1993).
  How to Get a Job in Dallas/Fort Worth
  (1994).
  How to Get a Job in Europe (1993).
  How to Get a Job in Houston (1993).
  How to Get a Job in Southern California
  (1993).
  How to Get a Job in New York (1993).
  How to Get a Job in San Francisco (1993).
  How to Get a Job in Boston (1994).
  How to Get a Job in the Pacific Rim (1992).
  How to Get a Job in Seattle/Portland (1990).
  How to Get a Job in Washington, DC (1993).
Each book contains the names and addresses
of over 1,500 major local firms arranged by
industry and includes the names of people to
contact.
  Surrey Books, 230 E. Ohio St, Ste 120, Chi-
cago, IL 60611. Tel: 312/751-7330 or 1-800/-
326-4430. $15.95-$17.95 plus $3.00 postage per
book.

The Job Finder. Monthly listing of approximately 20 job vacancies in such areas as budget
and finance, engineering and public works,
general administration, personnel services, and
labor relations.
  Western Governmental Research Association, c/o Graduate Center for Public Policy and
Administration, 1250 Bellflower Blvd, Long
Beach, CA 90840. Tel: 213/985-5419. $20.00
annually.

The Job HUNTER. A biweekly national job vacancy publication that lists approximately 350
positions in such categories as: arts, business,
communications, health, human services, public affairs, science, and international.
  University of Missouri-Columbia, 305 Noyes
Building, Columbia, MO 65211. Tel: 314/882-
2097. $40.00 (6 months); $50.00 (12 months).

Job Hunter's Sourcebook. Michelle LeCompte,
ed. 1993. A combination handbook, "how-to,"
and directory focusing on sources of employment leads available for more than 150 specific
careers. Lists sources of help-wanted ads,
employer directories, employment agencies,

placement services, and other specific information sources.
  Gale Research Inc., P.O. Box 33477, Detroit, MI 48232-0577. Tel: 1-800/877-4253.
$57.00.

Job Seekers Sourcebooks
  Boston & New England (1992). $13.95
  Chicago & Illinois (1992). $13.95
  Los Angeles & Southern California (1992).
  $14.95
  Mid-Atlantic (1993). $14.95
  Mountain States (1993). $13.95
  New York & New Jersey (1993). $14.95
  Northern Great Lakes (1992). $14.95
  Ohio Valley 1993). $14.95
  Pacific Northwest (1992). $14.95
  Plains States (1993). $13.95
  Southern Atlantic Coast (1992). $14.95
  Southern States (1993). $13.95
  Southwest (1993). $14.95
Donald D. Walker and Valerie A. Shipe. Each
book identifies employment agencies, execu-
tive search firms, database/network/referral ser-
vices, career counselors, outplacement firms,
and resume preparation firms (with names,
addresses, and phone and fax numbers) located within a specified geographical area. Tips
for interviewing, networking, and overall preparation and organization of a job search are
also included.
  Independent Publishers Group, 814 North
Franklin Street, Chicago, IL 60610. Tel: 312/-
337-0747.

Jobs Available. A monthly bulletin of current
public sector job opportunities in the South-
western and Western states.
  Jobs Available, P.O. Box 1040, Modesto,
CA 95353-1040. Tel: 209/571-2120. $22.00
(annually).

Jobs and Careers for the 1990s. This career
catalogue contains over 1100 resources, including career books, videos, audiocassettes, and
computer software designed to help find jobs
and/or change careers.
  Impact Publications, 10655 Big Oak Circle,
Manassas, VA 22111-3040. Tel: 703/361-7300.
Free of charge.

Jobs for People Who Love to Travel. Drs. Ron & Caryl Krannich. 1993. Identifies numerous jobs and careers that enable individuals to travel both at home and abroad. Surveys hundreds of jobs in business and government, including summer jobs abroad, international careers, jobs in the travel industry, import/export opportunities, and sales and training positions.

Impact Publications, 10655 Big Oak Circle, Manassas, VA 22111-3040. Tel: 703/361-7300. $12.95 plus $3.00 postage.

National Business Employment Weekly. Weekly newspaper listing of hundreds of professional level positions available in the U.S. and abroad.

Dow Jones & Company, Inc., P.O. Box 435, Chicopee, MA 01021-0435. Tel: 413/592-7761 or 1-800/562-4868. $35.00 (8 weeks prepaid; all other subscriptions by phone order); $52.00 (12 weeks).

Occupational Outlook Handbook 1992-1993. 1992. Describes what workers do on the job, working conditions, the training and education required, earnings, and expected job prospects in a wide range of occupations covering over 100 million jobs.

Superintendent of Documents, U.S. Government Printing Office, Washington, DC 20402. Tel: 202/783-3238 or Bureau of Labor Statistics, Publication Sales Center, P.O. Box 2145, Chicago, IL 60690. Tel: 312/353-1880. $23.00.

Offbeat Careers. Al Sacharov. 1988. An alphabetical directory of approximately 100 unusual occupations ranging from acupuncturist to wine steward. Job source references follow each description.

Ten Speed Press/Celestial Arts, P.O. Box 7123, Berkeley, CA 94707. Tel: 510/845-8414 or 1-800/841-2665. $6.95 plus $2.50 postage.

The Outdoor Careers Guide. Gene R. Hawes and Douglas L. Brownstone. 1986. Profiles jobs for outdoor enthusiasts in occupations ranging from agricultural extension agent to yacht captain. Lists entry requirements, income levels, and job outlook.

Facts on File, 460 Park Avenue South, New York, NY 10016-7382. Tel: 212/683-2244 or 1-800/322-8755. Out of print but available in libraries.

The Professional's Private Sector Job Finder. Daniel Lauber. 1992. New edition available January 1994. Details over 1,500 of the best sources of private sector job vacancies from accounting to zoology. Includes sections on job hotlines, job-matching services, specialty periodicals with job ads, and directories.

Planning/Communications, 7215 Oak Ave, River Forest, IL 60305-1935. Tel: 708/366-5200 or 1-800/829-5220. $18.95 plus $3.75 postage. Includes one update sheet.

The Search Bulletin. Bimonthly 25-30 page newsletter. Each issue features 85-150 senior-level jobs available through executive search organizations and companies in fields such as general management, finance and accounting, marketing and sales, and consulting/corporate planning. Salary ranges are $60,000-$250,000+ per year. Includes some overseas positions and some part-time positions.

The Beacon Group, The Village Centre, P.O. Box 641, Great Falls, VA 22066. Tel: 703/759-4900 or 1-800/486-9220. $97.00 (6 issues); $177.00 (12 issues).

VGM Career Books. This catalogue includes the "Careers for You Series" detailing careers in such industries as business and management, building, industrial and mechanical services, computers, communications, health care, sports, art and design, public and social services, ecology and the environment, and engineering and the sciences. Names and addresses of associations connected with each career are also included.

VGM Career Horizons, NTC Publishing Group, 4255 West Touhy Avenue, Lincolnwood, IL 60646-1975. Tel: 708/679-5500 or 1-800/323-4900. Free of charge.

Where the Jobs Are: A Comprehensive Directory of 1200 Journals Listing Career Opportunities. Norman Feingold and Glenda Ann Hansard-

Winkler. 1989. Lists over 1,200 journals that announce job openings in hundreds of fields. A comprehensive index helps to identify periodicals with listings of potential interest.

May be obtained through Garrett Park Press, P.O. Box 190C, Garrett Park, MD 20896-0190. Tel: 301/946-2553. $15.00.

CAREERS IN GENERAL
► REFERENCE BOOKS ◄

Directory of Executive Recruiters. 1993. Annual publication identifying search firms and the industries served. Includes over 3,600 offices of 2,500 firms in the U.S., Canada, and Mexico.

Kennedy Publications, 21 Templeton Road, Fitzwilliam, NH 03447. Tel; 603/585-6544 or 1-800/531-0007. $39.95 plus $5.00 shipping.

Dun's Directory of Service Companies. 1994. Provides information on approximately 50,000 of the largest service enterprises with 50 or more employees, covering a broad range of service industries. Includes facts on the companies that derive their primary income from a service activity plus the top 500 companies that perform a service as a secondary line of business.

Dun and Bradstreet Information Services, Three Sylvan Way, Parsippany, NJ 07054-3896. Tel: 201/605-6000 or 1-800/526-0651. $495.00.

Dun's Employment Opportunities Directory/The Career Guide. 1993. Details more than 5,000 U.S. companies that have indicated that they plan to recruit during the publication year. Use the *Guide* to: locate prospective employers; gain knowledge of a company's employment requirements, its career development opportunities, and other benefits; identify personnel consultants nationwide; and target employers in desired industries or geographic regions.

Dun and Bradstreet Information Services, Three Sylvan Way, Parsippany, NJ 07054-3896. Tel: 201/605-6000 or 1-800/526-0651. $475.00.

First Impression, Best Impression. Dr. Janet Elsea. 1986. Intended as a self-evaluation course for persons going through the interviewing process. Suggests a strategy to help make a positive first impression by using interpersonal communication skills.

Simon and Schuster, 200 Old Tappan Rd, Old Tappan, NJ 07675. Tel: 201/767-5000 or 1-800/223-2336. $6.95.

Job Seeker's Guide to Private and Public Companies, Peggy Kneffel Daniels and Susan E. Edgar, eds., 1993. 4 vols. Includes 16,000 entries with contact data (human resources contacts and other corporate officials), description, application procedures, internship availability, benefits, and more.

Gale Research Inc., P.O. Box 33477, Detroit, MI 48232-0577. Tel: 1-800/877-4253. $365.00/set. Volumes are divided geographically (Vol. 1: The West. Vol. 2: The Midwest. Vol. 3: The Northeast. Vol. 4 The South.) and may be purchased individually for $99.00 each. Also available in softcover abridgment under the title, *Job Seekers Guide to 1,000 Top Employers* for $22.95.

Million Dollar Directory Series: America's Leading Public and Private Companies. 1993. This comprehensive five-volume *Series* profiles over 160,000 of America's most productive publicly- and privately-held companies each having either 1) $25 million dollars in sales annually, 2) 250 employees, or 3) a net worth of over $750,000. The first three volumes list all 160,000 businesses alphabetically by company name. The fourth and fifth are cross-reference volumes designed to maximize convenient use of the *Series*.

Dun and Bradstreet Information Services, Three Sylvan Way, Parsippany, NJ 07054-3896. Tel: 201/605-6000 or 1-800/526-0651. $1350.00.

Professional Careers Sourcebook. Kathleen M. Savage and Joseph M. Palmisano, eds. 1993. Presents over 115 professional career profiles, including information on general career guides, professional associations, standards and certification agencies, directories of educational programs, basic reference guides, and handbooks related to the profession.

Gale Research Inc., P.O. Box 33477, Detroit, MI 48232-0577. Tel: 1-800/877-4253. $85.00.

VGM's Careers Encyclopedia. 1991. Examines 200 careers, from accounting to word processing, with special emphasis on aptitudes required, qualifications needed, training, competition for future jobs, and potential growth of each profession. Lists the names and addresses of professional associations in the U.S. and Canada where additional information can be obtained.

VGM Career Horizons, NTC Publishing Group, 4255 W. Touhy Ave., Lincolnwood, IL 60646-1975. Tel: 708/679-5500 or 1-800/323-4900. $39.95.

ADVERTISING AND PUBLIC RELATIONS

Advertising Career Directory. Bradley J. Morgan, ed. 1992. Provides information on what it's like to work in the industry and includes articles by experts on getting started as a copywriter, preparing a portfolio, radio and television advertising, direct mail, database marketing, corporate advertising, getting started at an agency, and more.

Gale Research Inc., P.O. Box 33477, Detroit, MI 48232-0577. Tel: 1-800/877-4253. $17.95 (paperback).

Career Opportunities in Advertising and Public Relations. Shelly Field. 1990. Provides the job seeker with in-depth information about how to "break into" these fields.

Facts On File, Inc., 460 Park Avenue South, New York, NY 10016-7382. Tel: 212/683-2244 or 1-800/322-8755. $14.95.

BUSINESS AND FINANCE

The 50 Best Low-Investment, High-Profit Franchises. Robert L. Perry. 1990. Details 50 lucrative franchises with investments starting as low as $2,500. Spells out pros and cons, start-up

costs, the franchiser's package of services and products, support and training, and potential earnings.

Prentice Hall Mail Order Processing Center, P.O. Box 11071, Des Moines, IA 50336-1071. Tel: 515/284-6751. $12.95.

Job Opportunities in Business 1994. 1993. Details over 2,000 organizations that hire employees with business and liberal arts backgrounds.

Peterson's, Dept. 1423, 202 Carnegie Center, P.O. Box 2123, Princeton, NJ 08543-2123. Tel: 609/243-9150 or 1-800/338-3282. $18.95.

BUSINESS AND FINANCE
▶ REFERENCE BOOKS ◀

Best's Insurance Reports. Contains in-depth information on the history, financial condition, and operating methods of over 2,400 major property/casualty companies in the U.S. and Canada. Evaluates the various factors affecting the overall performance of an insurance company in order to form an opinion as to the company's relative financial strength.

A.M. Best Company, Ambest Road, Oldwick, NJ 08858-9988. Tel: 908/439-2200. $750.00 (Full service includes one year subscription to both *Best's Review* and *Best's Insurance Management Reports*); $570.00 (Regular service includes one year subscription to *Best's Review*).

Business Organizations, Agencies, and Publications Directory. Michael Huellmantel, ed. 1993. The 26,000 entries describe 39 types of business information sources arranged in five broad categories: U.S. and International Organizations, Government Agencies and Programs, Facilities and Services, Research and Education Facilities, and Publications and Information Services.

Gale Research Inc., P.O. Box 33477, Detroit, MI 48232-0577. Tel: 1-800/877-4253. $345.00.

The Corporate Directory of U.S. Public Companies 1993. 2 vols. Details the essential facts on more than 9,500 publicly-traded firms having at least $5 million in assets.

Published by Walker's Western Research. Available from Gale Research Inc., P.O. Box 33477, Detroit, MI 48232-0577. Tel: 1-800/877-4253. $360.00.

Corporate Yellow Book. Quarterly directory with complete data on the top manufacturing, service, and utility companies traded on the major U.S. stock exchanges. Lists key executives and their direct-dial telephone numbers. Describes each business, its product lines, and annual revenues.

Monitor Publishing Company, 104 Fifth Ave, 2nd Floor, New York, NY 10011. Tel: 212/627-4140. $215.00.

Financial Yellow Book. Annual directory listing over 32,000 top executives at the leading financial institutions in the U.S., their major subsidiaries and divisions, assets and business description, and addresses and phone numbers.

Monitor Publishing Company, 104 Fifth Ave, 2nd Floor, New York, NY 10011. Tel: 212/627-4140. $165.00.

NASDAQ Yellow Book. Annual directory listing over 20,000 key executives in companies traded over-the-counter. Includes business descriptions, product lines and annual revenue estimates, and addresses and phone numbers of domestic and foreign subsidiaries.

Monitor Publishing Company, 104 Fifth Ave, 2nd Floor, New York, NY 10011. Tel: 212/627-4140. $165.00.

Standard & Poor's Register of Corporations, Directors and Executives. 3 vols. 1992. This well known guide to the business community and executives who run it, covers over 55,000 U.S. companies and major companies in Canada and abroad. Vol. 1 (Corporate Listings) includes the names of over 55,000 corporations with addresses; telephone numbers; names, titles, and function of approximately 500,000 officers, directors and other principals. Vol. 2 (Individual Listings) includes the names of over 70,000 individuals serving as officers, directors, trustees, and partners and provides principal business affiliations with official titles, business addresses, residence addresses and other per-

tinent information on each individual. Vol. 3 (Indexes) is a seven-section index including the Standard Industrial Classification Index, Standard Industrial Classification Codes, Geographic Index, and Corporate Family Indexes.

Standard & Poor's Corporation, 25 Broadway, New York, NY 10004. Tel: 212/208-8786 or 1/800-221-5277. $575.00 (3 volumes).

Standard & Poor's Stock Report. Presents facts, figures, and business trends for over 4,000 publicly-held U.S. corporations. The service includes over 1,700 individual reports on all companies listed on the New York Stock Exchange, reports on over 800 companies listed on the American Stock Exchange, and over 1,500 individual reports on those stocks most actively traded Over-the-Counter and on Regional Exchanges.

Standard & Poor's Corporation, 25 Broadway, New York, NY 10004. Tel: 212/208-8805 or 1/800-221-5277. Annual prices range from $880.00 to $1,350.00 depending on daily, weekly, or quarterly service.

U.S. Industrial Outlook '93. 1993. Provides estimates for major industry sectors of the gross national product (GNP) in 1993 and industry forecasts through the 1990s. Covers natural resources and energy, construction and related industries, industrial materials and components, production and manufacturing equipment, information and communications, consumer economics, transportation and travel, health care, financial services, and business and professional services. Includes the international outlook for 1993, a glossary of terms, and an index.

Superintendent of Documents, U.S. Government Printing Office, Washington, DC 20402. Tel: 202/783-3238. $37.00.

Value Line Investment Survey. A three-part weekly publication reporting on shares traded on the New York Stock Exchange. Part 1 (Summary and Index) includes information on stocks ranked highest for probable performance in the upcoming 12 months. Part 2 (Selection and Opinion) includes stock highlights, market monitor, industry price performance, and changes in financial strength ratings. Part 3 (Ratings & Reports) includes timely reports on various stocks within several industries.

Value Line Publishing, Inc, 711 Third Ave, New York, NY 10017-4064. Tel: 212/687-3965 or 1-800/833-0046. $525.00 annually.

Ward's Business Directory of U.S. Private and Public Companies 1994. 5 vols. Provides data on more than 142,000 businesses--over 90% of which are privately held. Vols. 1-3 list companies in alphabetical order with financial information, employee figures, and 4-digit SIC codes. Vol. 4, the Geographic Section, includes a regional analysis of the top 1,000 U.S. employers ranked by number of employees, the top 1,000 publicly-held companies ranked by sales, the top 1,000 privately-held companies ranked by sales, and other pertinent information. Vol. 5, available separately or as part of the set, ranks companies by sales volume within 4-digit SIC classifications.

Gale Research Inc., P.O. Box 33477, Detroit, MI 48232-0577. Tel: 1-800/877-4253. $1,400.00 (Vols. 1-5); $1,250.00 (Vols. 1-4); $795.00 (Vol. 5).

COMMUNICATIONS

Broadcasting. Weekly magazine with a classified help wanted section covering such areas as management, technical, news directing, programming production, and directing in both radio and television. Approximately 80 jobs listed in each issue.

Broadcasting, 1705 DeSales Street, NW, Washington, DC 20036. Tel: 202/659-2340 or 1-800/554-5729. $85.00 annually (52 issues).

Career Opportunities in Television, Cable and Video. Maxine K. Reed and Robert M. Reed. 1991. Details 95 job titles with information about employment prospects, salary ranges, and educational and experience requirements.

Facts On File, Inc., 460 Park Avenue South, New York, NY 10016-7382. Tel: 212/683-2244 or 1-800/322-8755. $14.95.

Careers in Radio and *Careers in Television*, 1991. These two booklets prepared by the National Association of Broadcasters (NAB) describe key jobs found in radio and television stations. Careers such as announcer, camera operator, salesperson, studio engineer, and sports writer are described along with required education and experience.

NAB Services, 1771 N Street, NW, Washington, DC 20036. Tel: 202/429-5376 or 1-800/368-5644. $3.50 per copy. (NAB member price: $3.00 per copy.)

Current. A public telecommunications newspaper issued 23 times per year. Includes a classified section listing jobs available in radio, television, and engineering.

Current, 1612 K Street, NW, Suite 704, Washington, DC 20006. Tel: 202/463-7055. $70.00 annually.

Looking for Employment in the Broadcasting Industry: Getting Started. 1991. A directory of joblines, referral services, upcoming industry meetings, salary data, a bibliography, and other sources helpful to those looking for a job in broadcasting.

National Association of Broadcasters (NAB) Library and Information Center, 1771 N Street, NW, Washington, DC 20036. Tel: 202/429-5490. $15.00. (NAB member price: $10.00).

NAB Employment Clearinghouse. A program designed by the National Association of Broadcasters (NAB) to collect resumes of minorities and women (non-minority males are not excluded) for referral to broadcast stations for jobs ranging from entry-level to managerial positions. Counseling is also available. This service is free.

NAB Services, 1771 N Street, NW, Washington, DC 20036. Broadcast job-seekers may also use "Jobline" by calling 202/429-5498, Monday-Friday (6 p.m.-8:30 a.m.); and Saturday, Sunday, and holidays all day. Openings in a particular job category are featured each day.

Newspapers Career Directory. Bradley J. Morgan, ed. 1993. Covers internships, opportunities for minorities, reporting, editing, photojournalism, art and graphics, circulation, news-paper research, classified advertising sales, and national account sales.

Gale Research Inc., P.O. Box 33477, Detroit, MI 48232-0577. Tel: 1-800/877-4253. $17.95.

Radio and Television Career Directory. Bradley J. Morgan, ed. 1993. Industry professionals describe opportunities in radio, TV news, broadcast meteorology, radio programming, radio marketing, writing for television, cable TV, and other specialties. Includes detailed entries for radio, television, cable, and communications companies.

Gale Research Inc., P.O. Box 33477, Detroit, MI 48232-0577. Tel: 1-800/877-4253. $17.95 (paperback).

TV News: Building a Career in Broadcast Journalism. Ray White. 1989. Guide to entry and advancement in broadcast journalism with a discussion of educational and training requirements and the various jobs and responsibilities in a TV newsroom.

Focal Press. Distributed by Butterworth & Heinemann, 80 Montvale Avenue, Stoneham, MA 02180. Tel: 1-800/544-1013. $19.95 plus $3.75 postage.

COMMUNICATIONS
▶ REFERENCE BOOKS ◀

Gale Directory of Publications and Broadcast Media 1994. Karen Troshynski-Thomas and Deborah M. Burek eds. 1993. 3 vols. Includes more than 38,000 listings, which provide address, phone and fax numbers, description, frequency, and key personnel, for radio and television stations, and cable companies, geographically arranged in the U.S., Puerto Rico, and Canada. Information on magazines and newspapers is also included. A new Publishers Index is included in Vol. 3.

Gale Research Inc., P.O. Box 33477, Detroit, MI 48232-0577. Tel: 1-800/877-4253. $340.00 (update included).

News Media Yellow Book of Washington and New York. Semi-annual directory offering access to 19,000 journalists and opinion-makers at over 2,700 media organizations in Washington, DC and the New York metropolitan area. Journalists are listed by title and alphabetically by assignment for each organization--many with direct-dial phone numbers.

Monitor Publishing Company, 104 Fifth Ave, 2nd Floor, New York, NY 10011. Tel: 212/627-4140. $165.00.

Publishers Directory 1994. Wendy S. Van de Sande, ed. 1993. Details 19,000 major publishing firms as well as small, independent presses and 600 distributors in the U.S. and Canada.

Gale Research Inc., P.O. Box 33477, Detroit, MI 48232-0577. Tel: 1-800/877-4253. $275.00.

Telecommunications Directory 1994-95. John Krol, ed. 1993. Details more than 2,300 national and international communications systems and services, voice and data communication services, local area networks, teleconferencing facilities, video-tex and teletext operations, electronic mail services, facsimile services, telegram and telex services, interactive cable television, satellite services, and electronic transactional services.

Gale Research Inc., P.O. Box 33477, Detroit, MI 48232-0577. Tel: 1-800/877-4253. $325.00.

CONSULTING ORGANIZATIONS

CONSULTING ORGANIZATIONS
▶ REFERENCE BOOKS ◀

Consultants and Consulting Organizations Directory 1994. Janice McLean, ed. 1993. 2 vols. Details 20,000 firms and individuals arranged alphabetically under 14 general fields of consulting activity, ranging from agriculture to marketing.

Gale Research Inc., P.O. Box 33477, Detroit, MI 48232-0577. Tel: 1-800/877-4253. $470.00/set; $390.00 (March 1994 supplement).

COUNSELING

Careers in Counseling and Human Development
Brooke B. Collison and Nancy J. Garfields, eds. 1990. Successful professionals provide invaluable insights into 90 different career options. Includes where to find career opportunities, starting salaries and prerequisites, and an index of occupations.

American Counseling Association, 5999 Stevenson Ave, Alexandria, VA 22304-3300. Tel: 703/823-9800 or 1-800/347-6647. $17.95 (Member price: $14.95) plus $2.50 postage.

DISABLED PERSONS

Careers and the Disabled. A quarterly magazine designed for people with disabilities. Includes a special braille section, advertisements from companies that hire the disabled, and an affirmative action career directory.

Equal Opportunity Publications, Inc., 150 Motor Parkway, Suite 420, Hauppauge, NY 11788-5145. Tel: 516/273-0066. $10.00 annually (prepaid); $12.00 (with invoice).

ECONOMICS

Career Choices for the 90's for Students of Economics. 1990. Provides current information on job opportunities for economists, highlighting the job outlook, competition for openings, where and who the employers are, salary levels, working environment, and new job opportunities. Includes a geographic job index, and names and addresses of professional associations.

Walker and Company, 720 Fifth Avenue, New York, NY 10019. Tel: 212/265-3632 or 1-800/289-2553. $8.95.

Job Openings for Economists. Published seven times a year, this bulletin lists approximately 500 academic and non-academic jobs available for economists.

American Economic Association (AEA), P.O. Box 307026, Nashville, TN 37230-7026. Annual subscription (7 issues): $15.00 for AEA members; $25.00 for non-members.

EDUCATION

Chronicle of Higher Education. A weekly newspaper containing interesting articles and information about grants and fellowships. The "Bulletin Board" section lists hundreds of positions for individuals with experience in librarianship, sports/coaching, computers, public relations/fundraising, campus printing and publishing, personnel management, career development/counseling, risk management, security, and other aspects of academic administration. Positions are available in the U.S. and abroad.

Chronicle of Higher Education, 1255-23rd Street, NW, Washington, DC 20037. Tel: 202/466-1000 or 1-800/347-6969. $3.25 per issue; $75.00 annually.

Personnel Service Newsletter. A monthly newsletter available to the members of the American Political Science Association listing approximately 100 academic jobs each issue. Includes positions in academic and applied settings, fellowships, and faculty exchange programs.

American Political Science Association, 1527 New Hampshire Ave, NW, Washington, DC 20036. Tel: 202/483-2512. Annual membership dues are based on salary. *Newsletter* is $30.00 annually.

ENVIRONMENT

The Complete Guide to Environmental Careers. edited by New Environmental Careers Organization. 1993. Provides essential information needed to plan career search: job outlook, salary levels, entry-level requirements, and volunteer and internship opportunities.

Island Press, Box 7, Covelo, CA 95428. Tel: 1-800/828-1302. $15.95.

Environmental Career Directory. Bradley J. Morgan and Joseph M. Palmisano, eds. 1993. From forestry and fish and wildlife management to air and water quality control, this directory gives practical information on finding a job in the environmental preservation industry.

Gale Research Inc., P.O. Box 33477, Detroit, MI 48232-0577. Tel: 1-800/877-4253. $17.95 (paperback).

Environmental Career Guide. Nicholas Basta. 1991. Explores careers in this new growth field, explaining key skills required and how to find employers and get the job.

John Wiley & Sons Publishers, 1 Wiley Dr, Somerset, NJ 08875-1272. Tel: 908/469-4400. $14.95.

Environmental Opportunities. Sanford Berry, ed. Monthly bulletin listing environmental jobs throughout the U.S. and abroad. Includes positions in administration, ecology and fisheries, education, environmental science, forestry, research, and horticulture.

Environmental Opportunities, P.O. Box 4957, Arcada, CA 95521. Tel: 603/756-4553. $24.00 (6 months); $44.00 (annually).

Job Opportunities in the Environment, 1994. 1993. Lists 1,500 companies and government agencies that are hiring, including Federal and state agencies, advocacy groups, and environmental design groups.

Peterson's, Dept. 1423, 202 Carnegie Center, P.O. Box 2123, Princeton, NJ 08543-2123. Tel: 609/243-9150 or 1-800/338-3282. $18.95.

The Job Seeker. A bimonthly 16-page publication of current vacancies in the environmental and natural resource fields. Job titles range from entry-level through senior executive including: permanent, seasonal, part-time, and internships and cover vacancies from private, local, state, and Federal employers across the nation.

The Job Seeker, Route 2, Box 16, Warrens, WI 54666-9501. Tel: 608/378-4290. $36.00 (12 issues); $60.00 (24 issues).

National Parks Trade Journal. 1991. Cites over 100,000 positions (service, volunteer, educational, and environmental) with national parks and ski resorts in this country and abroad.

Published by Taverly-Churchill. May be obtained through Garrett Park Press, P.O. Box 190C, Garrett Park, MD 20896-0190. Tel: 301/946-2553. $14.95.

ENVIRONMENT
▶ REFERENCE BOOKS ◀

Canadian Environmental Directory 1992. Details the entire network of individuals, agencies, firms, and associations active in environment-related activities in Canada. The Information Services section details legal, ecological, and management consultants and provides information on resource centers and databases available.

Published by Canadian Almanac & Directory Publishing Company Ltd. Available from Gale Research Inc., P.O. Box 33477, Detroit, MI 48232-0577. Tel: 1-800/877-4253. $175.00.

Conservation Directory. Lists the names and addresses of organizations, agencies, and officials concerned with natural resource use and management in the U.S. and Canada.

National Wildlife Federation, 1400 Sixteenth Street, NW, Washington, DC 20036-2266. Tel: 1-800/432-6564. $18.00 plus $4.85 postage.

Gale Environmental Sourcebook. Karen Hill and Annette Piccirelli, eds. 1992. Lists full contact data on 8,634 environmental organizations, information services, programs, and publications involved in all aspects of the environment including advocacy and education, policy and enforcement, research and development, and consumer issues/products.

Gale Research Inc., P.O. Box 33477, Detroit, MI 48232-0577. Tel: 1-800/877-4253. $80.00.

The Nature Directory. Susan D. Lanier-Graham. 1991. This concise guide covers 130 major environmental organizations, national and regional, with key facts about each. Includes a brief history of each organization, its achievements, major projects under way, and name, address, and phone number of contact persons.

Walker and Company, 720 Fifth Avenue, New York, NY 10019. Tel: 212/265-3632 or 1-800/289-2553. $12.95.

GOVERNMENT AND LAW

The Complete Guide to Public Employment. Drs. Ron and Caryl Krannich. 1990. New edition available January 1994. Discusses how to find jobs with Federal, state, and local governments; associations; contractors; consultants; foundations; and research and political groups.

Impact Publications, 10655 Big Oak Circle, Manassas, VA 22111-3040. Tel:703/361-7300. $19.95 plus $3.00 postage.

Federal Careers for Attorneys, Second Edition. 1991. A comprehensive guide to legal careers with over 300 U.S. Government general counsel and other legal offices throughout the Federal system. Discusses each office from the standpoint of the agency's mission, the work of the office, its divisions/structure, number of attorneys, hiring procedures, special recruitment programs, application addresses, and locations of any regional/field offices. Includes a subject index and a geographic index.

Federal Reports, Inc., 1010 Vermont Ave, NW, Suite 408, Washington, DC 20005. Tel: 202/393-3311. $29.95; $75.00 institutional rate.

Federal Jobs Digest. A biweekly newspaper devoted to jobs openings in the Federal Government. Lists thousands of new jobs nationwide and includes special sections on senior executive and overseas jobs, as well as instructions on filling out the U.S. Government application form.

Federal Jobs Digest, Box 594, Millwood, NY 10546. Tel: 1-800/824-5000. $29.00 (six biweekly issues); $54.00 (12 biweekly issues).

Federal Law-Related Careers Directory, Third Edition. 1994. This completely revised edition describes in detail careers that are not desig-

nated "attorney" positions but which, under a variety of occupational titles, require a strong legal background. Includes a detailed explanation of the Government-wide "Administrative Careers with America" recruitment and testing program; updated descriptions of each of the 150+ law-related careers; a new index of all of the Federal law-related careers; and the addresses of more than 1,000 Federal recruiting offices.

Federal Reports, Inc., 1010 Vermont Ave, NW, Suite 408, Washington, DC 20005. Tel: 202/393-3311. $24.95; $50.00 institutional rate.

The Government Job Finder. Daniel Lauber. 1992. New edition available January 1994. Where to find professional and non-professional positions in local, state, and Federal government. Lists over 1,128 sources of government vacancies.

Planning/Communications, 7215 Oak Ave, River Forest, IL 60305-1935. Tel: 708/366-5200 or 1-800/829-5220. $16.95 plus $3.75 postage. Includes one update sheet.

National and Federal Legal Employment Report. A monthly detailed listing of hundreds of current attorney and law-related job opportunities with the U.S. Government and other public/private employers in the Washington, DC area, throughout the U.S., and abroad. Includes 500-600 new jobs each issue.

Federal Reports, Inc., 1010 Vermont Ave, NW, Suite 408, Washington, DC 20005. Tel: 202/393-3311. $34.00 (3 months); $58.00 (6 months); $104.00 (one year).

The Paralegal's Guide to U.S. Government Jobs. 1993. The first Federal job hunting manual written exclusively for paralegal professionals, designed for both entry-level and experienced paralegals. Explains U.S. Government hiring procedures, describes 70 law-related Federal careers for which paralegals qualify, outlines special hiring programs, and provides detailed instructions on how to fill out the SF-171 (Application for Federal Employment). Also contains a directory of the 1000-plus Federal agency personnel offices that hire the most paralegal talent.

Federal Reports, Inc., 1010 Vermont Ave, NW, Suite 408, Washington, DC 20005. Tel: 202/393-3311. $15.00.

GOVERNMENT AND LAW
▶ REFERENCE BOOKS ◀

County Executive Directory. 1993. Published twice a year. Lists the names, addresses, and phone numbers of primary managers for all U.S. counties, including council members for counties with populations over 50,000. Information capsule for counties with populations over 25,000 gives locator phone number, county seat, and population.

Carroll Publishing Company, 1058 Thomas Jefferson Street, NW, Washington, DC 20007. Tel: 202/333-8620. $130.00 plus $8.00 postage.

Federal Executive Directory. 1993. Updated six times a year. More than 75,000 entries cover the Executive Office of the President, Cabinet departments, major Federal administrative agencies, and Congress. Names, titles, addresses, and phone numbers are listed by agency, office or department. Names are indexed alphabetically with phone numbers, and office functions. Includes committee assignments and brief biographical profiles of members of Congress, plus areas of responsibility for their legal and administrative assistants.

Carroll Publishing Company, 1058 Thomas Jefferson Street, NW, Washington, DC 20007. Tel: 202/333-8620. $180.00 plus $10.00 postage.

Handbook of Occupational Groups and Series. 1993. Annual Office of Personnel Management guide for positions in the General Schedule of the Federal Government. Lists the occupational groups and series of classes, defines them, and assigns a number to each.

Superintendent of Documents, U.S. Government Printing Office, Washington, DC 20402. Tel: 202/783-3238. $4.00.

Official Congressional Directory, 1993-94: 103rd Congress. 1993. This comprehensive and detailed resource contains an alphabetical list of the Members of Congress with their addresses, rooms, and phone numbers; biographical sketches of members, including description of congressional districts and ZIP codes; boards, commissions, and advisory organizations; Capitol officers and officials; committees, and committee assignments. Also includes the names and phone numbers of key officials in the Executive and Judicial Branches, international organizations, and foreign embassies.

Superintendent of Documents, U.S. Government Printing Office, Washington, DC 20402. Tel: 202/783-3238. $20.00.

Qualifications Standards Handbook for General Schedule Positions (formerly known as *Handbook X-118: Qualifications Standards for Positions under the General Schedule*). 1993. Subscription service consists of the *Handbook*, reprinted to incorporate changes through Transmittal Sheet 229, and monthly revised pages for an indeterminate period. Furnishes current qualification standards for various grade-level occupations under the General Schedule.

Superintendent of Documents, U.S. Government Printing Office, Washington, DC 20402. Tel: 202/783-3238. $93.00.

State Administrative Officials Classified by Function 1993-94. 1993. Lists 147 state functions together with the names, addresses and phone numbers of the highest ranking officials, elected or appointed, in their respective states, who bear direct responsibility for each function.

The Council of State Governments, P.O. Box 11910, Lexington, KY 40578-1910. Tel: 606/231-1939 or 1-800/800-1910. $30.00.

State Executive Directory. 1993. Published three times a year. Lists the executive and legislative officials of the 50 states, the District of Columbia, Puerto Rico, and the U.S. territories. Includes more than 33,000 names (with titles, addresses, and phone numbers) of key officials of executive branch departments, boards, and commissions, as well as state legislative members/officials.

Carroll Publishing Company, 1058 Thomas Jefferson Street, NW, Washington, DC 20007. Tel: 202/333-8620. $160.00 plus $10.00 postage.

The United States Government Manual 1993/94. 1993. Official handbook of the Federal Government which provides comprehensive information on the agencies of the legislative, judicial, and executive branches. Also includes information on quasi-official agencies; international organizations in which the U.S. participates; and boards, commissions, and committees. Each agency description includes a list of principal officials, a summary statement of the agency's purpose and role in the Federal Government, a brief history of the agency, a description of its programs and activities, and a "Sources of Information" section which provides information on consumer activities, contracts and grants, employment, publications, and other areas of public interest.

Superintendent of Documents, U.S. Government Printing Office, Washington, DC 20402. Tel: 202/783-3238. $30.00.

HEALTH CARE

Healthcare Career Directory--Technologists and Technicians. Bradley J. Morgan and Joseph M. Palmisano, eds. 1993. Describes educational requirements and career expectations in jobs such as nuclear medical, surgical, or laboratory technicians, radiology specialists, and many more.

Gale Research Inc., P.O. Box 33477, Detroit, MI 48232-0577. Tel: 1-800/877-4253. $17.95 (paperback).

Healthcare Career Directory--Therapists and Allied Health Professionals. Bradley J. Morgan and Joseph M. Palmisano, eds. 1993. Provides information on a variety of professional healthcare careers, including chiropractor, dietician, optometrist, pharmacist, physical therapist, and more.

Gale Research Inc., P.O. Box 33477, Detroit, MI 48232-0577. Tel: 1-800/877-4253. $17.95 (paperback).

Job Opportunities in Health Care, 1994. 1993. Lists 1,500 companies hiring health care pro-

fessionals for skilled nursing care facilities, hospitals, medical laboratories, home health care, and pharmaceuticals.

Peterson's, Dept. 1423, 202 Carnegie Center, P.O. Box 2123, Princeton, NJ 08543-2123. Tel: 609/243-9150 or 1-800/338-3282. $18.95.

Mental Health and Social Work Career Directory. Bradley J. Morgan and Joseph M. Palmisano, eds. 1993. Provides information on careers such as family therapist, marriage counselor, substance abuse counselor, behavioral psychologist, and many more. Includes tips on how to locate entry-level positions.

Gale Research Inc., P.O. Box 33477, Detroit, MI 48232-0577. Tel: 1-800/877-4253. $17.95 (paperback).

120 Careers in the Health Care Field. 2nd ed. 1991. Describes the occupations and training requirements of all allied health personnel, listing 5,435 accredited training programs/schools.

U.S. Directory Service, Publishers, 121 Chanlon Road, New Providence, NJ 07974. Tel: 1-800/521-8110. $45.00 plus $4.75 postage.

HEALTH CARE
► REFERENCE BOOKS ◄

Dun's Healthcare Reference Book. 1992/93. Details 27,000 businesses and institutions in the healthcare industry, approximately 18,000 of which are suppliers and 9,000 of which are providers. Cross-referenced by name of business, by geographic location, by industry classification, and by brand name of manufactured product.

Dun and Bradstreet Information Services, Three Sylvan Way, Parsippany, NJ 07054-3896. Tel: 201/605-6000 or 1-800/526-0651. $410.00.

Encyclopedia of Medical Organizations and Agencies. Karen Backus, ed. 1993. Provides information on more than 12,000 major public and private agencies in medicine and related fields.

Gale Research Inc., P.O. Box 33477, Detroit, MI 48232-0577. Tel: 1-800/877-4253. $220.00.

Medical and Health Information Directory. Karen Backus, ed. 3 vols. 1992. (1994 editions will be available in June 1994.) Vol. 1): Describes 16,400 state, national, and international professional and voluntary associations, Federal and state agencies, foundations and grant-awarding organizations, research centers, medical and allied health schools, and more. Vol 2: details more than 9,700 libraries, audiovisual producers and services, publications, publishers, and databases. Vol. 3: contains data on over 23,000 clinics, treatment centers, care programs, counseling/diagnostic services, and other health services.

Gale Research Inc., P.O. Box 33477, Detroit, MI 48232-0577. Tel: 1-800/877-4253. $485.00/set; $195.00 per volume.

1993 Nursing Job Guide. Annual employment directory for professional nurses and nursing students in the U.S.
1993 Canada Nursing Job Guide. Annual employment directory for professional nurses and nursing students in Canada.

Prime National Publishing Corporation, 470 Boston Post Rd, Weston, MA 02193. Tel: 617/899-2702. $75.00 each.

INTERNATIONAL

The Almanac of International Jobs and Careers. Drs. Ron and Caryl Krannich. 1992. New edition available January 1994. Provides contact information for hundreds of public and private organizations offering international job opportunities at home and abroad. Includes government agencies; international organizations, associations, societies and research institutes; businesses; foreign firms operating in the U.S.; contracting and consulting firms; private voluntary organizations; nonprofits and foundations; and colleges and universities.

Impact Publications, 10655 Big Oak Circle, Manassas, VA 22111-3040. Tel: 703/361-7300. $19.95 plus $3.00 postage.

Careers in International Affairs. Maria P. Carland and Daniel H. Spatz, Jr., eds. 1991. Identifies 350 Federal agencies and private organi-

zations that hire in the field of international affairs.

School of Foreign Service, Georgetown University, P.O. Box 344, Mt. Vernon, VA 22121. $15.00 (mail orders only).

The Complete Guide to International Jobs and Careers. Drs. Ron and Caryl Krannich. 1990. Guide to help job seekers understand the what, where, and how of working abroad.

Impact Publications, 10655 Big Oak Circle, Manassas, VA 22111-3040. Tel:703/361-7300. $13.95 plus $3.00 postage.

The Directory of Jobs and Careers Abroad 1993. A guide to career opportunities abroad for persons of all levels of educational and professional achievement. Details the top trades and professions in Europe, Australia, and New Zealand.

Peterson's, Department 1423, 202 Carnegie Center, P.O. Box 2123, Princeton, NJ 08543-2123. Tel: 609/243-9150 or 1-800/338-3282. $16.95.

Guide to Careers in World Affairs. 1993. Describes more than 250 organizations in international business, banking and finance; international law, journalism and consulting; nonprofit organizations; the U.S. Government; the United Nations and other international organizations. Includes size of professional staff, required qualifications, internships (when available), and the application procedure and address for each organization.

Foreign Policy Association, 729 Seventh Ave, New York, NY 10019. Tel: 212/764-4050 or 1-800/477-5836. $14.95 plus $1.75 postage.

The International Consultant. H. Peter Guttmann. 1988. A complete orientation for aspiring international consultants covering topics such as spotting and pursuing foreign prospects; writing proposals; negotiating a contract overseas; financing and administering overseas work, joint ventures, foreign partners and representation; and terminating contracts, disputes, and international arbitration.

John Wiley & Sons Publishers. 1 Wiley Dr, Somerset, NJ 08875-1272. Tel: 908/469-4400. $24.95.

International Employment Gazette. A biweekly newspaper (24 pages minimum) listing 400 or more current job openings in Africa, Asia, Australia/New Zealand, Europe, Latin America, and the Middle East in professions such as business, agriculture, transportation, education, communication and the arts, construction and trades, liberal arts and social sciences, public and social services, science and technology, health care and medicine, and computer technology. Jobs listed are with American companies with overseas operations, foreign companies, government agencies, nonprofit and relief agencies, and religious organizations.

International Employment Gazette, 1525 Wade Hampton Blvd, Greenville, SC 29609. Tel: 803/235-4444 or 1-800/882-9188. 3 months (6 issues), $35.00; 6 months (12 issues), $55.00; 12 months (24 issues), $95.00.

International Employment Hotline. A monthly eight-page newsletter that monitors the international job market and reports on hundreds of current overseas openings in the Federal Government and private industry for U.S. citizens.

International Employment Hotline, P.O. Box 3030, Oakton, VA 22124. Tel: 703/620-1972. $25.00 (six months); $36.00 (one year).

International Jobs: Where They Are/How to Get Them. 4th ed. Eric Kocher. 1993. Lists over 500 kinds of international jobs, such as those with businesses, publishing companies, schools, law firms, nonprofit organizations, and government agencies, all over the world.

Addison Wesley, Route 128, Redding, MA 01867. Tel: 617/944-3700 or 1-800/447-2226. $14.38.

The ISS Directory of Overseas Schools. 1993. Annually updated directory of the International Schools Services (ISS) organization describes individual overseas schools that educate the dependents of local business and government leaders, and the international diplomatic community. All schools hire American teachers and classes are taught in English. Information provided on each of the approximately 500 schools includes complete contact names and addresses; number of teaching staff and specialists; student nationalities, grade levels, and enrollment; curriculum, special programs and extracurricular activities; and types of schools and facilities.

International Schools Services. Available from World Wise Books, P.O. Box 3030, Oakton, VA 22124. Tel: 703/620-1972. $32.00.

Looking for Employment in Foreign Countries. 1992. Outlines the current employment situation in 46 countries, how to obtain a work permit, and the number of U.S. multinational corporations with branches in each country.

World Trade Academy Press Inc., 50 East 42nd Street, Suite 509, New York, NY 10017-5480. Tel: 212/697-4999. $16.50 plus $3.50 postage.

Overseas Employment Newsletter. A biweekly listing describing in detail at least 300 currently available job opportunities for a broad range of skills, careers, and positions in many developing nations and industrialized countries around the world. Positions in professions such as banking, nursing, physical education, advertising, electronic printing, marketing, engineering, and education are available in Europe, Asia, the Middle East, Africa, South America, Mexico, Australia/New Zealand, Bermuda, and the Caribbean.

Overseas Employment Services, P.O. Box 460, Town of Mount Royal, Quebec, Canada H3P 3C7. Tel: 514/739-1108. 3 months (6 issues), $39.00; 6 months (12 issues), $65.00; 12 months (24 issues), $105.00

Passport to Overseas Employment, Dale Chambers. 1990. Provides comprehensive information on over 100,000 job opportunities abroad, including volunteer work; international careers; Federal employment; careers with U.S. companies abroad; Third World opportunities; and airline, tourist, and cruise line sources. Cites work permit requirements, sources for grants and independent study, and U.S. and foreign embassy and consular office addresses. Includes addresses, phone numbers, and names (when appropriate) for each entry.

Simon and Schuster, 200 Old Tappan Rd, Old Tappan, NJ 07675. Tel: 201/767-5000 or 1-800/223-2336. $15.00.

INTERNATIONAL
▶ REFERENCE BOOKS ◀

American Jobs Abroad. Edward Knappman, ed. Available March 1994. A guide to American firms and organizations that employ Americans abroad. Describes more than 800 companies and organizations with overseas operations, listing key contact information, a brief company profile, types of jobs available abroad, and countries of operations. Also includes 110 country profiles listing key statistics, important government contacts, social services available, and more.

Gale Research Inc., P.O. Box 33477, Detroit, MI 48232-0577. Tel: 1-800/877-4253. $55.00.

Associations Canada 1992. Over 20,000 entries cover English and French language organizations, with details on professional staff, elected officials, membership profiles, services provided, resource centers, and publications.

Published by Canadian Almanac & Directory Publishing Company. Available from Gale Research Inc., P.O. Box 33477, Detroit, MI 48232-0577. Tel: 1-800/877-4253. $175.00.

The Blue Book of Canadian Business 1993. Annual directory that ranks major Canadian companies by sales, assets, net income, advertising expenditures and stock trading, and features in-depth profiles on scores of the top-ranked Canadian firms. Includes the Canadian Business Index, featuring the most recent information available on over 2,500 top Canadian companies, with ownership information, addresses, business descriptions, and names of officers and directors.

The Blue Book of Canadian Business, 65 Overlea Blvd, Suite 207, Toronto, Ontario, Canada M4H 1P1. $159.95.

Craighead's International Business, Travel, and Relocation Guide to 71 Countries, 1994-95. 1993. Includes information about the economies, customs, communications, and other invaluable data for relocation purposes.

Gale Research Inc., P.O. Box 33477, Detroit, MI 48232-0577. Tel: 1-800/877-4253. $460.00.

Directory of American Firms Operating in Foreign Countries. 1993. 3 vols. Identifies some 2,600 American companies with 19,000 subsidiaries and affiliates in 127 foreign countries. Includes information on number of employees, principal product and/or services, and the countries in which foreign operations are located.

World Trade Academy Press Inc., 50 East 42nd Street, Suite 509, New York, NY 10017-5480. Tel: 212/697-4999. $200.00 plus $7.50 postage.

Eastern European Business Directory 1991. Frank Didak, ed. More than 7,000 entries detailing the largest business enterprises in seven Eastern European countries: Romania, Bulgaria, Czechoslovakia, Hungary, Poland, parts of the Soviet Union (countries formerly recognized as the Soviet Union), and former East Germany.

Gale Research Inc., P.O. Box 33477, Detroit, MI 48232-0577. Tel: 1-800/877-4253. $275.00.

Encyclopedia of Associations: International Organizations, 1994. Grant Eldridge, ed. 1993. 2 vols. A guide to over 13,500 international organizations, including over 5,000 national organizations of countries other than the U.S. Details organizations with international memberships, binational organizations, and national organizations in more than 180 countries around the world. Complete factual information included. Supplement includes over 700 additional multinational and national organizations.

Gale Research Inc., P.O. Box 33477, Detroit, MI 48232-0577. Tel: 1-800/877-4253. $475.00/set with supplement.

International Corporate Yellow Book. Annual directory of over 30,000 chief executives, managing directors and officers, as well as subsidiary and division executives, including a description of product lines, annual revenue estimates and assets, and addresses and phone numbers.

Monitor Publishing Company, 104 Fifth Ave, 2nd Floor, New York, NY 10011. Tel: 212/627-4140. $165.00.

International Encyclopedia of Foundations. 1990. Edited by Joseph C. Kiger. Lists the history and operation of 146 of the most significant non-profit foundations in 31 countries including Japan, Canada, Mexico, Germany, and the U.S.S.R. (those countries formerly known as the Soviet Union).

The Foundation Center, 79 Fifth Ave, Dept. ZE, New York, NY 10003-3050. Tel: 212/620-4230 or 1-800/424-9836. $75.00 plus $4.50 postage.

International Research Centers Directory, 1994-95. Thomas Cichonski, ed. 1993. Lists more than 7,600 government, university, independent, nonprofit, and commercial research and development activity areas in more than 150 countries worldwide. Includes name and acronym, address, telecommunication access, name of director, organizational notes, research activities, and more.

Gale Research Inc., P.O. Box 33477, Detroit, MI 48232-0577. Tel: 1-800/877-4253. $410.00.

Japan Company Handbooks. Quarterly directory consisting of two sets. *Japan Company Handbook-First Section* deals with major Blue Chip Japanese companies listed on Japan's major stock exchanges. *Japan Company Handbook-Second Section* describes the country's newer growth companies. Financial analyses and historical data are provided for all companies, which are categorized by industry and cross-referenced alphabetically.

Toyo Keizai America Inc, 380 Lexington Ave, Room 4505, New York, NY 10168. Tel: 212/949-6737. $204.00 annually *(First Section)*; $204.00 annually *(Second Section)*.

Japan Trade Directory 1993-94. 1993. Profiles 3,000 Japanese companies that import or ex-

port products and services. Gives full information on trade contacts, corporate structure, and financial data.

Published by the Japan External Trade Organization. Available from Gale Research Inc., P.O. Box 33477, Detroit, MI 48232-0577. Tel: 1-800/877-4253. $245.00.

Japanese-Affiliated Companies in the USA and Canada 1993-94. 1993. Contact information for more than 9,500 Japanese firms, restaurants, and other resources.

Published by the Japan External Trade Organization. Available from Gale Research Inc., P.O. Box 33477, Detroit, MI 48232-0577. Tel: 1-800/877-4253. $190.00.

Major and Medium Companies of Europe 1993-94. 1993. 6 vols. Provides crucial company data on both major and medium-sized companies in Europe.

Published by Graham & Trotman, London. Available from Gale Research Inc., P.O. Box 33477, Detroit, MI 48232-0577. Tel: 1-800/877-4253. $1,950.00/set.

Major Companies of the Arab World 1993-94. 1993. Details nearly 6,000 major companies in 20 Arab countries with information on finances, personnel, structure, products, and profitability.

Published by Graham & Trotman, London. Available from Gale Research Inc., P.O. Box 33477, Detroit, MI 48232-0577. Tel: 1-800/877-4253. $720.00.

Major Companies of the Far East and Australasia, 1993-94. 1993. 3 vols. Identifies nearly 4,500 major companies and their key decision-makers and executives. Includes details on each company's finances, personnel, structure, products, and profitability.

Published by Graham & Trotman, London. Available from Gale Research Inc., P.O. Box 33477, Detroit, MI 48232-0577. Tel: 1-800/877-4253. Vol. 1, South East Asia: $420.00; Vol. 2, East Asia: $420.00; Vol. 3, Australia and New Zealand: $300.00. $1,140.00/set.

Major Energy Companies of Europe 1992-93. 1993. Details the finances, personnel, structure, products, and profitability of over 1,000 major energy companies of Western Europe.

Published by Graham & Trotman, London. Available from Gale Research Inc., P.O. Box 33477, Detroit, MI 48232-0577. Tel: 1-800/877-4253. $323.00.

Major Financial Institutions of Continental Europe 1993-94. 1993. Details more than 1,100 leading financial institutions of Europe arranged within country chapters.

Published by Graham & Trotman, London. Available from Gale Research Inc., P.O. Box 33477, Detroit, MI 48232-0577. Tel: 1-800/877-4253. $370.00.

LAW ENFORCEMENT

Law Enforcement Careers. Ron Stern. 1988. How to choose a law enforcement agency, what types of physical and written exams to expect, and information on police academies, government agencies, and other organizations that offer careers in law enforcement.

Lawman Press, P.O. Box 934, Montague, CA 96064. Tel: 916/459-0232. $12.95.

Law Enforcement Employment Guide. 1990. Contains 76 agency names, addresses, entrance requirements, salaries and benefits, number of officers/reserves, and types available positions.

Lawman Press, P.O. Box 934, Montague, CA 96064. Tel: 916/459-0232. $19.95.

National Employment Listing Services (NELS) Bulletin. A monthly national listing of approximately 80 job opportunities in the criminal justice system, covering such areas as academics and research, community services and corrections, courts, institutional corrections, and law enforcement and security.

NELS, Criminal Justice Center, Sam Houston State University, Huntsville, TX 77341-2296. Tel: 409/294-1692. $17.50 (6 months); $30.00 annually.

LIBERAL ARTS/FINE ARTS

Alternative Careers for Teachers. Sandy Pollack. 1984. Transfer teaching skills such as communication, management, and organization, into other spin-off careers in a variety of other occupations.

Harvard Commons Press. Distributed by National Book Network, 4720 Boston Way, Lanham, MD 20706. Tel: 1-800/462-6420. $8.95.

ARTJOB. Bimonthly publication of the Western States Arts Federation that provides information on current job vacancies, internships, workshops, and publications, including a small number of listings for opportunities abroad.

Western States Arts Federation, 236 Montezuma Avenue, Santa Fe, NM 87501. Tel: 505/-988-1166. $24.00 (6 months/12 issues); $36.00 (1 year/24 issues).

ArtSEARCH. This national employment service bulletin for the arts is published 23 times a year and contains current job vacancies available nationwide in the areas of administration, performance, production, and education. A career development section lists apprenticeships, internships, and fellowships.

Theatre Communications Group, Inc., 355 Lexington Avenue, New York, NY 10017. Tel: 212/697-5230. $48.00 (23 issues).

Aviso. This newsletter of the American Association of Museums (AAM), which is issued 12 times a year, provides timely information on news in the museum world, Federal legislation, AAM activities and services, upcoming seminars and workshops, and grant deadlines. Includes a job bank, with an average of 100 job listings in each issue.

American Association of Museums, P.O. Box 40, Washington, DC 20042-0040. Tel: 202/289-1818. $33.00 (annually).

Career News. Monthly newsletter from the Maryland Institute, College of Art. Includes news of current exhibition opportunities, internships, fellowships/grants, and full-time/-part-time employment.

Maryland Institute, College of Art, 1300 Mount Royal Avenue, Baltimore, MD 21217. Tel: 410/225-2420. Free of charge.

Career Opportunities in the Music Industry. Shelly Field. 1986. Offers realistic information on 84 different job titles within the music field and related industries, describing employment prospects, salary ranges, and education and experience requirements.

Facts On File, Inc., 460 Park Avenue South, New York, NY 10016-7382. Tel: 212/-683-2244 or 1-800/322-8755. $27.50 (hardbound only).

Careers in Museums: A Variety of Vocations, Resource Report. 1992. Describes 15 museum careers, suggested experience and educational requirements, a job placement resource list, and annotated bibliography.

American Association of Museums, 1225 Eye Street, NW, Washington, DC 20005. Tel: 202/289-1818. $10.00 (members); $12.00 (non-members).

History News Dispatch. A monthly publication for members of the American Association for State and Local History (AASLH) that contains a listing of current job openings and also defines qualifications, education, and experience required for certain positions in the history field.

American Association for State and Local History, 530 Church Street, Suite 600, Nashville, TN 37219. Tel: 615/255-2971. $30.00 (annual membership fee).

How to Be a Working Actor: The Insider's Guide to Finding Jobs in Theater, Film and Television. M.L. Henry & L. Rogers. New edition available April, 1994. Includes names, addresses, and audition material, both commercial and dramatic.

M. Evans & Co., Distributed by National Book Network, 4720 Boston Way, Lanham, MD 20706. Tel: 1-800/462-6420. $9.95.

Liberal Arts Jobs: The Job Idea Book for Liberal Arts Majors. Burton J. Nadler. 1989. Describes more than 300 specific jobs in over 60 occupations, including job requirements, work environment, and career paths and prospects.

Peterson's, Department 1423, 202 Carnegie Center, P.O. Box 2123, Princeton, NJ 08543-2123. Tel: 609/243-9150 or 1-800/338-3282. $9.95.

The Music Business: Career Opportunities and Self-Defense. Dick Weissman. 1990. Explores careers for both performers and those behind the scenes: managers, producers, music publishers, and others.

Crown Publishing, Inc., 400 Hahn Road, Westminster, MD 21157. Tel: 212/572-2068 or 1-800/733-3000. $12.00.

National Arts Placement. Montly Newsletter published August through May with a combined September and October issue. Includes employment opportunities, fellowships/grants, and internships in the arts.

National Arts Placement, 1915 Association Drive, Reston, VA 22091-1590. Tel: 703/860-8000. $45.00 annually.

LIBRARY SERVICES

Guide to Library Placement Sources. Margaret Myers. 1993. This extensive guide, prepared by the Office for Library Personnel Resources of the American Library Association, lists sources which primarily give assistance in obtaining professional positions. Included are general sources for library job opportunities, library joblines, specialized library associations and groups, state library agencies, state and regional library associations, library education programs, Federal library jobs, and overseas opportunities.

American Library Association, Office for Library Personnel Resources, 50 East Huron Street, Chicago, IL 60611. Tel: 312/944-6780. Free of charge.

NON-PROFIT

Careers for Dreamers and Doers. Lilly Cohen and Dennis R. Young. 1989. A comprehensive guide about management opportunities in the nonprofit world, offering practical advice on job hunting strategies tested by successful managers in the field.

The Foundation Center, Department QK, 79 Fifth Avenue, New York, NY 10003-3076. Tel: 1-800/424-9836. $24.95 plus $4.50 postage.

Careers for Good Samaritans & Other Humanitarian Types. Marjorie Eberts and Margaret Gisler. 1991. Inventories careers for people who seek jobs in humanitarian or service organizations such as the Red Cross, Goodwill, the Salvation Army, VISTA, the Peace Corps, and UNICEF, as well as selected agencies at all levels of the government. An appendix lists organizations to contact.

VGM Career Horizons, NTC Publishing Group, 4255 W. Touhy Ave., Lincolnwood, IL 60646-1975. Tel: 708/679-5500 or 1-800/323-4900. $9.95.

The Chronicle of Philanthropy. A biweekly publication dedicated to the nonprofit sector. Includes a "Professional Opportunities" section listing approximately 60 jobs available.

The Chronicle of Philanthropy, 1255-23rd Street NW, Washington, DC 20037. Tel: 202/-466-1200 or 1-800/347-6969. $67.50 annually.

Community Jobs: The Employment Newspaper for the Non-Profit Sector. Monthly listing of over 200 positions in all types of non-profit organizations including environmental, international, arts, health, youth, labor, civil rights, housing and human services.

Access, 50 Beacon Street, Fourth Floor, Boston, MA 02108. Tel: 617/720-5627. $25.00 (6 months); $69.00 (one year).

Great Careers: The Fourth of July Guide to Careers, Internships, and Volunteer Opportunities in the Nonprofit Sector. Devon Cottrell Smith, ed. 1990. Developed by a team of 50 college career counseling directors and others. De-

scribes various fields, cites hundred of organizations and their programs.

May be obtained through Garrett Park Press, P.O. Box 190C, Garrett Park, MD 20896-0190. Tel: 301/946-2553. $35.00.

Invest Yourself: The Catalogue of Volunteer Opportunities. 1993. An annually updated directory of non-governmental full-time worldwide voluntary service opportunities through North American-based organizations. Includes nearly 200 organizations and a general orientation to the profession of volunteering as a way of life.

The Commission on Voluntary Service and Action, Inc., P.O. Box 117, New York, NY 10009. Tel: 1-800/356-9315. $9.50.

Jobs and Careers with Nonprofit Organizations. Drs. Ron & Caryl Krannich. 1993. Identifies the major domestic and international nonprofit organizations that provide attractive job alternatives and includes contact information in areas such as education, public affairs, medicine, consumer advocacy, public assistance, charities, arts, museums, women and minorities, public utilities, civil rights, and Federal, state, and local governments.

Impact Publications, 10655 Big Oak Circle, Manassas, VA 22111-3040. Tel: 703/361-7300. $15.95 plus $3.00 postage.

The NonProfit Times. Monthly publication for nonprofit news, marketing and management. Includes a listing of approximately 20-30 jobs available in the nonprofit sector.

The NonProfit Times, 190 Tamarack Circle, Skillman, NJ 08558. Tel: 609/921-1251. $59.00 annually.

The Non-Profits' Job Finder. Daniel Lauber. 1992. New edition available January 1994. Learn how to find jobs in the non-profit sector, including schools, medical facilities, social services, foundations, political organizations, and the arts by using job-matching services, directories, specialty periodicals with job ads, and job hotlines.

Planning/Communications, 7215 Oak Ave, River Forest, IL 60305-1935. Tel: 708/366-5200 or 1-800/829-5220. $16.95 plus $3.75 postage.

NON-PROFIT
▶ REFERENCE BOOKS ◀

Encyclopedia of Associations: Regional, State, and Local Organizations, 1993-94. 5 vols. A guide to more than 50,000 U.S. non-profit membership organizations with interstate, state, intrastate, or local scope and interest. The regions are separated into Vol 1. Great Lakes States; Vol. 2. Northeastern States; Vol 3. Southern and Middle Atlantic States; Vol 4. South Central and Great Plains States; and Vol. 5. Western States.

Gale Research Inc., P.O. Box 33477, Detroit, MI 48232-0577. Tel: 1-800/877-4253.

Finding a Job in the Nonprofit Sector. 1991. Presents an overview of employment trends in the nonprofit sector and includes a directory listing contacts and other employment information for approximately 5,000 of the largest nonprofit organizations in the U.S. Includes subject matter and geographic indexes.

The Taft Group, 12300 Twinbrook Parkway, Suite 450, Rockville, MD 20852. Tel: 301/816-0210 or 1-800/877-8238. $95.00.

The Foundation Directory. 1993. Annual edition identifies over 6,300 foundations in the U.S. that hold assets of $2 million or distribute at least $200,000 in grants annually. Includes more than 1,600 grant sources. $185.00.
The Foundation Directory Supplement. 1993. This complete update, published six months after the *Directory*, ensures current data. $110.00.
The Foundation Directory, Part 2. 1993. Biennial edition identifies over 4,300 foundations with grant programs between $50,000-$200,000. $160.00.

The Foundation Center, 79 Fifth Ave, Dept. ZE, New York, NY 10003-3050. Tel: 212/620-4230 or 1-800/424-9836. $415.00 if purchased as a three-volume set.

National Directory of Nonprofit Organizations. 1993. Includes names, addresses phone numbers, and income figures for 273,000 private, nonprofit organizations. Includes index of 260 areas of activity. Three volumes: two volumes listing organizations with over $100,000 in annual revenues; one volume listing organizations with $25,000-99,999 in annual revenues.

The Taft Group, 12300 Twinbrook Parkway, Suite 450, Rockville, MD 20852. Tel: 301/816-0811 or 1-800/877-8238. $415.00 (3 volumes); $296.00 (2-volume set for organizations with annual revenues over $100,000); $182.00 (1 volume for organizations with annual revenues of $25,000-99,000). $469.00/set. Volumes are sold separately for $99.00 each.

PUBLIC AFFAIRS

PUBLIC AFFAIRS
▶ REFERENCE BOOKS ◀

1994 Directory of Corporate Public Affairs. Annually revised directory of 13,500 public relations/public affairs professionals from 1,700 corporations with active public affairs programs.

Columbia Books, Inc., 1212 New York Avenue, NW, Suite 330, Washington, DC 20005. Tel: 202/898-0662. $90.00 plus $5.00 postage.

RESEARCH CENTERS

RESEARCH CENTERS
▶ REFERENCE BOOKS ◀

Earth and Astronomical Sciences Research Centers. Jennifer M. Fitch, ed. 1991. Details industrial, official, and academic laboratories, organizations, and observatories throughout the world that conduct or finance research in the earth and astronomical sciences.

Published by Longman. Available from Gale Research Inc., P.O. Box 33477, Detroit, MI 48232-0577. Tel: 1-800/877-4253. $475.00.

Electronic Research Centers. 1991. Includes nearly 3,500 profiles of corporate and academic laboratories and testing houses active in over 60 countries.

Published by Longman. Available from Gale Research Inc., P.O. Box 33477, Detroit, MI 48232-0577. Tel: 1-800/877-4253. $475.00.

Government Research Directory, 1992-93. Annette Piccirelli, ed. 1992. Describes over 3,700 Federal and non-Federal research facilities and programs of the U.S. Government. Every parent agency connected with an individual research unit is indexed separately, making it possible to find a specific program or facility.

Gale Research Inc., P.O. Box 33477, Detroit, MI 48232-0577. Tel: 1-800/877-4253. $405.00.

Pacific Research Centres. 1993. Details 3,500 scientific, technological, agricultural, and medical research centers located in Japan, the People's Republic of China, and other countries of the western Pacific region.

Published by Longman. Available from Gale Research Inc., P.O. Box 33477, Detroit, MI 48232-0577. Tel: 1-800/877-4253. $375.00.

SALES

Marketing and Sales Career Directory. Bradley J. Morgan, ed. 1992. Covers direct sales, industrial sales, consulting, services marketing, brand management, database marketing, and market research.

Gale Research Inc., P.O. Box 33477, Detroit, MI 48232-0577. Tel: 1-800/877-4253. $17.95.

The 100 Best Companies io Sell For. Philip et al. 1989. Surveys sales careers at leading U.S. companies covering salary ranges, bonus potential, benefits, and perks. Includes qualifications required, training offers, and opportunities for advancement in every type of industry from high tech to producers of raw materials.

John Wiley & Sons Publishers, 1 Wiley Dr, Somerset, NJ 08875-1272. Tel: 908/469-4400. $22.95.

Who's Who in Direct Selling. 1993. This directory lists 130 companies that are involved in direct selling.

Direct Selling Association, 1776 K St, NW, Washington, DC 20006. Tel: 202/293-5760. Free with self-addressed, stamped #10 envelope.

SCIENCE AND TECHNOLOGY

Employment Information in the Mathematical Sciences. Published five times a year, contains information on positions available in the mathematical sciences.

American Mathematical Society. P.O. Box 5904, Boston, MA 02206-5904. Tel: 401/455-4000 or 1-800/321-4267. $96.00 ($40.00 if student and unemployed).

Employment Review. A monthly employment newspaper that focuses on current job vacancies in engineering, data processing, management information, and health care. Editorial articles on job prospects in these fields and other professions, as well as a calendar of events throughout the U.S. are also included.

Recourse Communications, 334 Knight Street, P.O. Box 1040, Warwick, RI 02887-1040. Tel: 401/732-9850. $9.95 (6 months); $19.95 (annually).

Job Opportunities in Engineering and Technology 1994. 1993. Describes over 1,500 manufacturing, research, consulting, and government organizations that hire technical graduates.

Peterson's, Department 1423, 202 Carnegie Center, P.O. Box 2123, Princeton, NJ 08543-2123. Tel: 609/243-9150 or 1-800/338-3282. $18.95.

Job Referral Service. A resume data bank service of the American Institute of Chemical Engineers (AIChE) that will match member qualifications and preferences with the requirements of job openings at companies, universities, government agencies, consulting firms, etc. AIChE also maintains a list of approximately 15,000 companies in the U.S. and Canada that employ chemical engineers.

American Institute of Chemical Engineers, 345 E. 47th Street, New York, NY 10017. Tel: 212/705-7523. *Job Referral Service*: $35.00 for AIChE members currently employed; $25.00 for all other AIChE members; $70.00 for nonmembers. List of companies may be ordered for $50.00 (AIChE members); $100.00 (nonmembers).

SCIENCE AND TECHNOLOGY
▶ REFERENCE BOOKS ◀

Aerospace Technology Centers. 1991. In-depth profiles of more than 700 public and private research and technical laboratories in 70 countries.

Published by Longman. Available from Gale Research Inc., P.O. Box 33477, Detroit, MI 48232-0577. Tel: 1-800/877-4253. $475.00.

The Complete Computer Career Guide. Judith Norback. 1987. Assesses 25 major computer career options ranging from technician, systems programmer/analyst to software engineer, hardware designer, and computer salesman/consultant. Covers educational and job requirements, salaries, and how to get started on a successful job search.

Tab Books, Inc. Out of print but available in libraries.

The Complete Electronics Career Guide. 1989. Assesses 30 different career paths detailing education and training required, pay scales, and advancement pointers. Also includes extensive listings of professional associations, manufacturers, publications, and educational organizations.

Tab Books, Inc. Out of print but available in libraries.

Corporate Technology Directory. 4 vols. 1993. An annually updated directory listing over 33,000 U.S. entities that manufacture or develop high technology products in fields such as advanced materials, automation, biotechnology, chemicals, computers, defense materials, energy, medicine and pharmaceuticals, photonics, software, subassemblies and components,

telecommunications, and transportation. Included in company description is employment growth, number of government contracts, female/-minority ownership. A Non-U.S. Parent Company Index lists all foreign companies that have U.S. operating units profiled in the *Directory*.

Corporate Technology Information Services, Inc., 12 Alfred Street, Suite 200, Woburn, MA 01801-9998. Tel: 617/932-3939 or 1-800/333-8036. $445.00.

The Hidden Job Market 1994. 1993. Annual directory profiling 2,000 emerging companies in industries such as environmental consulting, genetic engineering, supercomputers, home health care, and telecommunications.

Peterson's, Department 1423, 202 Carnegie Center, P.O. Box 2123, Princeton, NJ 08543-2123. Tel: 609/243-9150 or 1-800/338-3282. $16.95.

Information Industry Directory 1994. Annette Novallo, ed. 1993. 2 vols. Vol. 1 enables users to contact nearly 5,000 producers and vendors of electronic information and related services in the U.S. and 70 other countries. Vol. 2 is a separate index on specific databases, publications, software, individuals, and services.

Gale Research Inc., P.O. Box 33477, Detroit, MI 48232-0577. Tel: 1-800/877-4253. $495.00/set; $335.00 (1994 supplement).

Space Industry International. Geoffrey K.C. Pardoe, ed. 1987. Handbook of companies, organizations, agencies, and similar bodies active in the space industry.

Published by Longman. Available from Gale Research Inc., P.O. Box 33477, Detroit, MI 48232-0577. Tel: 1-800/877-4253. $155.00.

SPORTS

Almanac of Sports Contacts. Greg J. Cylkowski. 1993. Lists over 7,500 professional, amateur, international, and collegiate sports with names and addresses of contact persons from leagues, teams, and organizations worldwide.

Athletic Achievements, 3036 Ontario Rd, Little Canada, MN 55117. Tel: 612/484-8299. $18.95 plus $3.75 postage.

Career Opportunities in the Sports Industry. Shelly Field. 1992. Offers a complete range of information, including descriptions and career paths in jobs ranging from sportscasting to physical therapy.

Facts On File, Inc., 460 Park Avenue South, New York, NY 10016-7382. Tel: 212/683-2244 or 1-800/322-8755. $14.95.

Careers for Horse Lovers. Ronald Trahan. 1981. Explores 39 different horse-related careers.

Houghton-Mifflin, Wayside Rd, Burlington, MA 01803. Tel: 617/272-1500 or 1-800/225-3362. $21.95 (hardbound only).

Careers for Sports Nuts. William Heitzmann, 1991. Explores careers in sports marketing, equipment sales, writing and photography, management, medicine, physical education and coaching, and others.

VGM Career Horizons, NTC Publishing Group, 4255 W. Touhy Ave., Lincolnwood, IL 60646-1975. Tel: 708/679-5500 or 1-800/323-4900. $9.95.

Developing a Lifelong Contract in the Sports Marketplace. Greg J. Cylkowski. 1993. Details networking opportunities and how to develop job contacts and acquire experience in a number of sports-related careers, with a special section on women in sports.

Athletic Achievements, 3036 Ontario Rd., Little Canada, MN 55117. Tel: 612/484-8299. $19.95 plus $3.75 postage.

Sports Careers. The Advantage Program membership includes a monthly newsletter with career information and listings of more than 100 sports-related jobs in media, administration, marketing, representation, and business ventures. Membership also includes a guidance consulting and resume bank service.

Stratford American Sports Corp., P.O. Box 10129, Phoenix, AZ 85064. Tel: 1-800/776-7877. $149.00 (six months), $199.00 annually.

TRADE AND PROFESSIONAL ASSOCIATIONS

TRADE AND PROFESSIONAL ASSOCIATIONS
► REFERENCE BOOKS ◄

Associations Yellow Book. A semi-annual publication designed to provide accurate, timely, and useful information on over 25,000 officers, directors, managers, professional staff and top administrators of the major trade and professional associations. Provides detailed information on over 900 of the leading national associations with budgets over $1 million and includes six specialized indexes.

Monitor Publishing Company, 104 Fifth Ave, 2nd Floor, New York, NY 10011. Tel: 212/627-4140. $165.00.

Encyclopedia of Associations 1994. Carol A. Schwartz, ed. 3 vols. Annual edition describes over 22,400 associations, with complete names, addresses, phone numbers, membership purpose and activities, national and international conferences, budget information, and more.

Gale Research Inc., P.O. Box 33477, Detroit, MI 48232-0577. Tel: 1-800/877-4253. $340.00/set.

National Trade and Professional Associations of the United States. Annual directory listing over 7,000 national trade associations, labor unions, professional, scientific or technical societies, and other national organizations.

Columbia Books Inc., 1212 New York Avenue, NW, Suite 330, Washington, DC 20005. Tel: 202/898-0662. $75.00.

TRANSPORTATION

Airline Job Bulletin. Monthly publication listing job openings by airline, including the skills, training, and experience required by a particular airline. Includes suggestions for applying for these positions.

Air Line Employees Association, 5600 S. Central Ave, Chicago, IL 60638. Tel: 312/767-3333. Associate membership required: $40.00 annually.

Airline Pilot. Future Aviation Professionals of America (FAPA). 1990. Covers job qualifications, requirements, and training programs.

Simon and Schuster, 200 Old Tappan Rd, Old Tappan, NJ 07675. Tel: 201/767-5900 or 1-800/223-2336. $16.00.

Travel Agent. Wilma Boyd. 1989. Entry-level introduction to the travel business, including operations, sales techniques, computer applications, and career strategies.

Simon and Schuster, 200 Old Tappan Rd, Old Tappan, NJ 07675. Tel: 201/767-5000 or 1-800/223-2336. $14.95.

Travel and Hospitality Career Directory. Bradley J. Morgan, ed. 1992. Describes a wide variety of career options in this industry. Essays discuss breaking into the hotel and motel industry, working for a local travel and tourism board, becoming a travel agent, convention and meeting planning, working for an airline, and more.

Gale Research Inc., P.O. Box 33477, Detroit, MI 48232-0577. Tel: 1-800/877-4253. $17.95 (paperback).

WOMEN AND MINORITIES

Minority Organizations: A National Directory. 1992. Lists the names and addresses of 9,700 Black, Hispanic, Asian, and Native American organizations including professional and trade associations, networking groups, and research organizations dealing with minorities.

May be obtained through Garrett Park Press, P.O. Box 190C, Garrett Park, MD 20896-0190. Tel: 301/946-2553. $50.00; $45.00 prepaid.

WOMEN AND MINORITIES
► REFERENCE BOOKS ◄

National Directory of Minority-Owned Business Firms 1992. Details 40,000 minority business enterprises. Nearly 50% of the data has been changed since the 1990 edition.

Published by Business Research Services. Available from Gale Research Inc., P.O. Box 33477, Detroit, MI 48232-0577. Tel: 1-800/877-4253. $225.00.

National Directory of Women-Owned Business Firms 1992. Information on 25,000 women-owned business enterprises.

Published by Business Research Services. Available from Gale Research Inc., P.O. Box 33477, Detroit, MI 48232-0577. Tel: 1-800/877-4253. $225.00.

WRITING/EDITING

Career Opportunities for Writers. Rosemary E. Guiley. 1992. Details more than 100 separate job descriptions within eight industries: arts and entertainment; journalism and news services; book publishing, advertising and marketing; government; business communications and public relations; education and nonprofit; and the free-lance market.

Facts On File, Inc., 460 Park Avenue South, New York, NY 10016-7382. Tel: 212/683-2244 or 1-800/322-8755. $14.95.

Careers for Bookworms and Other Literary Types. Marjorie Eberts and Margaret Gisler. 1990. Describes dozens of jobs for people who like to work with words, focusing on areas where reading, writing, editing, or research skills are vital.

VGM Career Horizons, NTC Publishing Group, 4255 W. Touhy Ave., Lincolnwood, IL 60646-1975. Tel: 708/679-5500 or 1-800/323-4900. $9.95.

ScienceWriters. A quarterly magazine for members of the National Association of Science Writers which includes the "Bulletin Board," a listing of job openings (approximately eight per issue), fellowships, and awards.

National Association of Science Writers, Inc., P.O. Box 294, Greenlawn, NY 11740. Tel: 516/757-5664. Annual dues: $60.00.

WRITING/EDITING
▶ MANUALS ◀

The Associated Press Stylebook and Libel Manual. 1993.

The Associated Press, 50 Rockefeller Plaza, New York, NY 10020. Tel: 212/621-1500. $9.75 plus $2.50 postage.

The Chicago Manual of Style. 1993.

The University of Chicago Press, 11030 South Langley Avenue, Chicago, IL 60628. Tel: 312/568-1550. $40.00.

The Elements of Style. William Strunk Jr, and E.B. White. 1979.

Macmillan Publishing Co., Inc, 100 Front St, Box 500, Riverside, NJ 08075-7500. Tel: 609/-461-6500 or 1-800/257-5755. $5.95.

A Manual for Writers. Kate L. Turabian. 1987.

University of Chicago Press, 11030 South Langley Ave, Chicago, IL 60628. Tel: 312/568-1550. $8.95.

The Right Word III. 1990.

Houghton-Mifflin, Wayside Rd, Burlington, MA 01803. Tel: 617/272-1500 or 1-800/225-3362. $3.95.

Style Manual. 1984.

Superintendent of Documents, U.S. Government Printing Office, Washington, DC 20402. Tel: 202/783-3238. $15.00.

A Uniform System of Citation. 1991.

The Harvard Law Review Association, Gannett House, Cambridge, MA 02138. Tel: 617/495-7888. $7.50.

E

Elsea, Janet, 155

Employee assistance programs. *See* Career Counseling, employee assistance programs

Employers. *See* Interviewing, preparation for; Research, importance of regarding prospective employer

Employment agencies, 30-31

Encyclopedia of Associations, 144

Executive search firms, 28-30

Executive Summary, use of in cover letter, 128

F

Fax machines, assessing the risks of using in the application process, 39-40

Federal hiring process. *See* U.S. Government, as employer

Federal Job Information Centers, 35, 102, 120
    See also Appendix A, 170-172

Federal Jobs Digest, 9, 11

First Impression, Best Impression, 155

G

General Accounting Office (GAO), as job information source, 19

GAO Index, 19

Government agencies
    hiring process, 117-118, 120
    sources of information on, 145
    state central personnel offices, 9
        See also Appendix B, 173-176
    state civil rights offices, 42
        See also Appendix C, 177-180
    state employment security agencies. *See Appendix D*, 181-184

Grammar, use of in resumes, 82-86
    See also Resumes, grammar

H

Handbook of Occupational Groups and Series, 120

Handbook X-118. Qualifications Standards for Positions under the General Schedule, 35, 117-118

Handicaps. *See* Discrimination, against disabled workers; Special recruitment opportunities

Hiring process, special hiring programs, 40-41

See also Government agencies, hiring process; U.S. Government, as employer

I

Information sources. *See also* Government agencies, sources of information on; Networking; Research; U.S. Government, as source of career information

Bibliography, 183-207

Congressional representatives, 18-19

for disabled persons. *See* Special Recruitment Opportunities

for government jobs, 11, 117-118

libraries, 8, 17-20, 35, 39, 118, 144-145, 152

on overseas jobs, 10-12

for temporary work, 141-142

Internal Revenue Service, 44-47
    Publication 529-Miscellaneous Deductions, 44-46
    Publication 521-Moving Expenses, 46-47

International employment, 10-12
    academic jobs, 11
    government jobs, 11
    U.S. or international organizations, 11

Interviews
    communication skills, 149-151, 155-157
    discussion of salary compensation, 151-153
    etiquette, 157-159
    failure to follow up, 160-161
    importance of first impression, 154-155
    informational, 24-26
    mistakes concerning, 143-162
    practice, 146-147
    research before. *See* Research
    thank-you notes after, 160

J

Job assistance seminars. *See* Career counseling

Job fairs, 161-162

Job hunting
    See also Information sources; Networking
    attitude toward, 1-2
    strategy for, 6-8, 17-47

Job loss
    attitude toward, 3-4
    warning signals of, 12-15

Job offers
    accepting prematurely, 164
    evaluation of, 164-166
    mistakes concerning job offers and acceptances, 163-169

letters of recommendation. *See* Letters, of recommendation
mass mailings, 15-16
older workers, 102-104
professional licenses. *See* Licenses, professional, included in resumes
proofreading of, 85-86
publications by applicant, 108
references, 108-113
samples of, 55, 58, 61, 66, 76, 80
style and format, 51, 65, 67, 72-74
"20-Second Rule," 50, 72, 74
use of preparation service, 63-64
use of word processor, 64
volunteer activities, 99

S

Salary
  negotiations, 151-153, 164-65, 167-168
  premature discussion of, 150
Skills
  See also Accomplishments
  communication, 140-141, 155-157
  educational retraining, 7
  transferrable, 31-33
Special application forms, mistakes concerning, 115-120
  See also Application for Federal Employment, SF-171
Special recruitment opportunities, 40-42
Standard and Poor's, as information source, 20

T

Taylor and Whitehouse, 112
Tax deductions. *See* Internal Revenue Service
Temporary work. *See* Alternative work patterns; Information sources, for temporary work
Thank-you notes. *See* Interviews
Trade associations. *See* Associations, trade
Turabian, Kate L., 108

U

U.S. Equal Employment Opportunity Commission, 42
U.S. Government, as employer
  application procedures, 117-118
  employment abroad, 11
  hiring freezes, 13-14

public versus private sector employment 20-22, 116-120
U.S. Government, as source of career information, 17-19
  See also Federal Job Information Centers
U.S. Government Manual, 18, 145
U.S. Industrial Outlook, 17

V

Vacancy announcement bulletins. *See* Advertisements, vacancy announcement bulletins
Value Line, as information source, 20
Volunteer activities, while job hunting, 7
  See also Resumes, volunteer activities

W

Wall Street Journal, 19, 144
Washington Post, 19
The Write Word III, 108
Word processors. *See* Resumes, use of word processors